Human Rights for the 21st Century

Stanford Studies in Human Rights

Human Rights
for the 21st Century

Sovereignty, Civil Society, Culture

Helen M. Stacy

Stanford University Press
Stanford, California

Stanford University Press

Stanford, California

©2009 by the Board of Trustees of the Leland Stanford Junior University.
All rights reserved.

Printed in the United States of America on acid-free, archival-quality paper

Library of Congress Cataloging-in-Publication Data

Stacy, Helen.
 Human rights for the 21st century : sovereignty, civil society, culture / Helen M. Stacy.
 p. cm.--(Stanford studies in human rights)
 Includes bibliographical references and index.
 ISBN 978-0-8047-4539-0 (cloth : alk. paper)--ISBN 978-0-8047-6095-9 (pbk. : alk. paper)
 1. Human rights. 2. Sovereignty. 3. Civil society. 4. Culture and law. I. Title. II. Series: Stanford studies in human rights.
 K3240.S7185 2009
 341.4'8--dc22
 2008047520

Typeset by Bruce Lundquist in 10/15 Minion Pro

Contents

Acknowledgments

THE RESEARCH FOR THIS BOOK could not have been completed without the generous support provided by Stanford Law School and the Freeman Spogli Institute for International Studies. I am also indebted to my colleagues and my students for their intellectual encouragement.

Over the past years, I have had opportunities to present my work and receive invaluable feedback from participants at workshops and symposia where I have presented aspects of my research. At my own institution, I wish to thank colleagues at faculty workshops at Stanford Law School, the Center on Democracy Development and the Rule of Law at the Freeman Spogli Institute for International Studies of Stanford University, and the Law and History Workshop at Stanford Humanities Center; the Global Justice Workshop at Stanford Humanities Center, November 2005; and Stanford Department of Africa Studies. Beyond Stanford I have benefited from the opportunity to present my ideas at the Australian Society for Legal Philosophy, Australian National University, Canberra, Australia, 2007; the Global Constitutionalism Conference, Stanford Law School, February 2007; the International Law Weekend—West, Santa Clara University, February 2007; the American Philosophical Association, San Francisco, 2007; the Brisbane Ideas Festival, Australia, March 2006; the American Society of International Law, Washington, D.C., 2005; the International Society for Social and Legal Philosophy, Granada, 2005; the University of California at Irvine, December 2005; the American Bar Association, Atlanta, 2004; and the American Section of the International Association for Philosophy of Law and Social Philosophy, Palo Alto, Calif., 2004 and Saint Louis, Mo., 2006.

Excellent research assistance and editing was provided by Adi Aron Gilat, Rachel Lee, Rajat Rana, and Cecilia Naddeo. The manuscript was prepared with superlative skill and unceasing patience by Judy Dearing, to whom I owe a special debt of appreciation.

My heartfelt gratitude goes to the anonymous reviewers of the manuscript for their thoughtful comments; to Kathleen Sullivan for invaluable encouragement; to Laura Donohue and Karoly Nikolich for careful reading of draft chapters; to Eleanor and Izabella Endre-Stacy for providing incentive; and to Netty Stacy for more sustenance than I can every repay.

Abbreviations

AFRC	Armed Forces Revolutionary Council (Sierra Leone)
AHRC	Asian Human Rights Centre (of the Asian Legal Resource Centre)
ALRC	Asian Legal Resource Centre (Hong Kong)
ARF	ASEAN Regional Forum
ASEAN	Association of South East Asian Nations
ASIL	American Society of International Law (Washington, D.C.)
CAT	Committee Against Torture (United Nations)
CDF	Civil Defence Force (Sierra Leone)
CEDAW	Committee on the Elimination of Discrimination against Women (United Nations)
CELS	Centro de Estudios Legales y Sociales (Buenos Aires)
CERD	Committee on the Elimination of Racial Discrimination (United Nations)
CMW	Committee on the Protection of the Rights of All Migrant Workers and Members of Their Families (United Nations)
COHRE	Center for Organizational and Human Resource Effectiveness (Middle Tennessee State University)
CRC	Committee on the Rights of the Child (United Nations)
CSJN	Corte Suprema de Justicia de la Nación (Argentina)
ECHR	European Convention on Human Rights; European Court of Human Rights (Council of Europe)
ECOSOC	Economic and Social Council (United Nations)
ERRC	European Roma Rights Center

FAO	Food and Agriculture Organization (United Nations)
GATT	General Agreement on Tariffs and Trade
IACHR	Inter-American Commission on Human Rights (Organization of American States)
IAEA	International Atomic Energy Agency (United Nations)
IBRD	International Bank for Reconstruction and Development (World Bank)
ICAO	International Civil Aviation Organization (United Nations)
ICCPR	International Covenant on Civil and Political Rights (United Nations)
ICERD	International Convention on the Elimination of All Forms of Racial Discrimination (United Nations)
ICESCR	International Covenant on Economic, Social and Cultural Rights (United Nations)
ICJ	International Court of Justice (United Nations)
ICTR	International Criminal Tribunal for Rwanda (United Nations)
ICTY	International Criminal Tribunal for Yugoslavia (United Nations)
IDA	International Development Association (United Nations)
IFAD	International Fund for Agricultural Development (United Nations)
IFC	International Finance Corporation (United Nations)
ILC	International Law Commission (United Nations)
ILO	International Labour Organization (United Nations)
IMF	International Monetary Fund
IMO	International Maritime Organization (United Nations)
IPEC	International Programme on the Elimination of Child Labour (International Labour Organization)
ITU	International Telecommunications Union (United Nations)
LRA	Lord's Resistance Army (Uganda)
NAFTA	North American Free Trade Agreement
NGO	nongovernmental organization
NPFL	National Patriotic Front of Liberia
OAS	Organization of American States

OAU	Organization of African Unity
OHCHR	Office of the High Commissioner for Human Rights (United Nations)
RUF	Revolutionary United Front (Sierra Leone)
SPCL	Sharia Penal Code Law (Nigeria)
SPSC	Special Panels for Serious Crimes (Ad-Hoc Court for East Timor)
UN	United Nations
UNCESCR	United Nations Committee on Economic, Social, and Cultural Rights
UNCHR	United Nations Commission on Human Rights
UNESCO	United Nations Educational, Scientific and Cultural Organization
UNIDO	United Nations Industrial Development Organization
WCC	War Crimes Chamber in Bosnia-Herzegovina
WHO	World Health Organization (United Nations)
WIPO	World Intellectual Property Organization (United Nations)
WMO	World Meteorological Organization (United Nations)
WTO	World Trade Organization

Human Rights for the 21st Century

Chapter 1

The Human Rights Problem

Introduction

When Pakistani politician Benazir Bhutto was killed in a suicide attack on December 27, 2007, she had been seeking a third term as prime minister after eight years in exile. Her election promise was that her Pakistan People's Party would implement the international standards of judicial independence that the president, Gen. Pervez Musharraf, was persistently flouting. Even before Bhutto's assassination, public anger against President Musharraf had been running high, fueled by his crackdown on the judiciary after his reelection in October 2007. He had suspended the Constitution and dismissed dissenting members of the Supreme Court, including Chief Justice Iftikhar Chaudhry, just three days before the court was expected to overturn his reelection. The legal profession's indignation with Musharraf's flagrant violation of the independence of the judiciary erupted time and again into angry demonstrations, and when a second general election was held in February 2008, some six weeks after Bhutto's assassination, Musharraf's political allies were trounced. Pakistan's new leaders—Bhutto's party and that of another former prime minister, Nawaz Sharif—vowed to restore the independence of the Supreme Court, called for the immediate restoration of the judges, and urged Musharraf to convene Parliament quickly so that the parties could begin the "gigantic task" of restoring the country's much-amended constitution. In the subsequent political turmoil, which included the resignation of President Sharif and the appointment of Asif Ali Zardari, Bhutto's widower, as the new president, the sacked judges were still not restored to their posts.

Pakistan's most serious political crisis since Musharraf had seized power in a coup in 1999 had in fact been brewing for quite a while. In March 2007, in a confrontation between modern Western-derived legal principles of judicial objectivity and unfettered military power, Musharraf had removed Chief Justice Chaudhry from his judicial post over allegations of misconduct.[1] Yet instead of meekly resigning, the flamboyant judge had embarked on a nationwide campaign, traveling from city to city accompanied by a large and noisy group of thousands of supporters, including many black-suited lawyers, all shouting in unison for human rights and judicial independence. They claimed that the chief justice's sacking was motivated by Musharraf's wish to avoid legal scrutiny of his bid for a new presidential term. The independent-minded chief justice had also been raising awkward questions about "disappearances"— Pakistanis who were presumed to have been detained indefinitely by the intelligence service without access to either their families or lawyers.

There was violence: video footage showed round after round of gas shells being lobbed at the Supreme Court's white façade while lawyers scurry to avoid harm. At yet another demonstration government forces opened fire and killed more than forty people. A senior Supreme Court official who refused to bring evidence against the chief justice was shot dead at his home. Then, when Bhutto arrived in Pakistan in October 2007, her triumphant return was overshadowed by nearly two hundred deaths caused by a suicide bomber as her cavalcade traveled through the streets of Karachi. Bhutto was unharmed in this first round of deadly violence, only to die herself two months later.

A key plank in Bhutto's reelection campaign had been hard-hitting criticism of Musharraf's treatment of judges. Yet despite Musharraf's iron military rule over Pakistan, the Supreme Court had allowed Chief Justice Chaudhry to represent himself in his dismissal proceedings before the court in 2007. Shockingly for Musharraf, the Supreme Court reinstated Chadhury and he was given a platform to speak out about human rights: "If there is one lesson we could draw from our past history of sixty years, it is to adhere to the norms and principles of the constitution. It is to enforce the Constitution in its true spirit and letter [that] guarantees fundamental rights and freedoms to citizens. . . . These fundamental rights and freedoms are sacrosanct. They are sublime. Their violation or abridgment is a serious matter. These rights . . . are fundamental issues and civilized societies take a stand on fundamental issues." According to Chief Justice Chaudhry, the job of the Pakistan courts is "to create and sustain an environment in which there is supremacy of the Constitution and rule of law. . . . The poor and the down-trodden sections of society must be given a stake and treated as equal citizens of the nation. This is how nations are formed and this is how societies move on to develop and progress."

A speech that might sound familiar in the democratic West was, in the eyes of Pakistan's military ruler, seen as something akin to treason. For much of its postindependence history, Pakistan's judiciary had been an apologist for military coups, interventions, and military interference. How is it then that in 2007 it was the Pakistani lawyers who galvanized the people into mass pro-tests using the language of human rights and freedom and at the same time polarized the judiciary and radicalized large parts of political society?

Some of the answers to this question lie in Pakistan's colonial past and its confrontation with globalization and human rights. During all of Pakistan's turbulent sixty-year postindependence history, remnants of the British Raj have continuously reappeared in its political and legal systems. Since parti-tion and independence in the 1940s, Victorian colonialism has continued as a ghostly default reference point for Pakistan's law, order, and probity. In the 1950s, almost without exception, lawyer-politicians making decisions perpet-uated the courts and legal institutions they had inherited from the British, at least as far as the formal structure of the institutions is concerned. Even when the Islamist movement forced Pakistan's politicians to face the issue of Islamic identity—a question that had produced the 1962 Constitution that established sharia as Pakistan's basic law—the fundamental anglophone structure of the courts continued.

With each successive constitutional amendment, Pakistan's colonial past has cast a shadow, though increasingly refashioned over each decade as the international principle of the "rule of law." Each successive military govern-ment, including the present one, has then countered these principles, devis-ing legalistic loopholes, keeping the judiciary weak, and eliminating potential judicial challenges to military rule. In 2007 and 2008, however, a previously docile judiciary felt so alienated that it sparked a lawyers' movement calling for true judicial independence in the name of the rule of law. These ideas are rallying Pakistan's judges, lawyers, and thousands of ordinary people march-ing in demonstrations. The Supreme Court's appeal to notions of international human rights as a check on domestic sovereignty has been both catalyst and fuel to this brushfire. As the example of Pakistan demonstrates, international human rights as part of the rule of law are today claimed around the world by people of many cultures and traditions. Ideas of human equality and fair, transparent government have been a force driving the creation of legal and political institutions to serve those principles. Even as human rights are invoked in a call for better treatment from oppressive government and harmful social practices, however, the expansion of international human rights has been criticized by both scholars and grassroots organizations. It has been argued that even as international law codifies civil, political, social, cultural, and economic rights that can be invoked on behalf of marginal groups and the poor, governments often thumb their noses at their international obligations. Other critics claim that international human rights have perverse effects, such as legitimizing the appropriation of indigenous property rights for the benefit of multinational corporations or through rationalizing interventions by powerful states in weaker ones. Others even suggest that what masquerades as human rights "progress" is really a subtle form of global subjugation that becomes even more pernicious when harnessed to new global patterns of capital and labor.

Some analysts point out that the human rights offered in international treaties that are grounded upon European philosophical and political writings reflect the individualism of Western legal and political thought and make little sense in cultures that do not share these intellectual roots. Still others criticize the concepts of international law as so inextricably entwined with Europe's harmful history of colonialism that the rights anchored in modern constitutions may simply repeat the sins of the past. U.S.-based African scholar Makau Mutua makes this argument sharply when he analogizes the human rights movement to earlier religious crusades, suggesting "the globalization of human rights fits a historical pattern in which all high morality comes from the West as a civilizing agent against lower forms of civilization in the rest of the world."[2]

International human rights, its critics allege, keep bad company: first, with Europe's colonial appropriation of the New World, then with twentieth-century aggressive nationalism that led to two world wars and countless smaller conflicts, and finally with the aggressive economic expansionism that overwhelms local systems. In an eerie reprise of international law's earliest days, during the Spanish and Portuguese evangelization of South American "Indians," today's international culture wars are fought in the name of secularism versus religion, East versus West, and universalism versus particularism.

A question has been put squarely on the table for those who promote international human rights: can Europe's Enlightenment philosophy of individual rights survive present-day culture wars and contrive to provide legitimacy for international human rights institutions and courts? Or has the justification for a universal system of rights been extinguished because Enlightenment ideals of respect for culture, religion, and political organization simply cannot engage with systems that are not built upon the same foundations?

This book is a response to these critiques of international human rights. While each has some force, I argue that these critiques are incomplete. More important, they divert attention from the need to craft institutional responses to these tensions—responses that can make the international human rights system a workable means to promote human rights across cultures and systems.

Human Rights Aspirations and Reality Today

Human Rights Aspirations

The number of international human rights treaties, declarations, and statements has never been higher. Since 1946, when the Nuremberg trials exposed the horrifying dimensions of the Holocaust and punished individuals for their role in it, international law has held out the tantalizing possibility that there may be collective-action solutions to the world's problems. The architects of the United Nations system believed that human rights, already expressed piecemeal in a handful of state constitutions around the world and slowly expanded over two centuries, could be internationalized and universalized through their expression in a collective document. These post–World War II visionaries identified core human rights and gave the various governments the obligation to provide those rights for their citizens. Since the United Nations Declaration of Human Rights was adopted, international human rights treaties created under the UN system have grown at an exponential rate, which has resulted in the propagation of international standards of human rights across an ever-expanding spectrum: from prisoners' rights to women's rights, from religious rights to children's rights, from voting rights to disability rights.

On December 10, 1948, at the Palais de Chaillot in Paris, all fifty-eight member states of the United Nations General Assembly adopted the Universal Declaration of Human Rights. The declaration recognizes that freedom, justice, and peace in the world are linked to the recognition of fundamental human rights. Eighteen years later, in 1966, the United Nations (then comprising 122 states) adopted the Covenant on Civil and Political Rights, which elaborated the rights to life, liberty, and security of person as well as the rights to freedom of opinion and expression, thought, conscience, and religion. In 1976 the Covenant on Economic, Social, and Cultural Rights declared that human rights also included an adequate standard of living, health, education, and housing as well as the right to give expression to one's own cultural identity. Many of these social, economic, and cultural rights are described as "non-absolute," unlike many of the "absolute" civil and political rights, such as the human right to freedom from torture.

In an astonishingly short period the international system has generated a human rights thrust. Today the United Nations has 192 states at its table. There are fourteen core international human rights treaties covering everything from racial discrimination to violence against women to children's human rights as well as hundreds of related international agreements. Under these treaties and agreements governments of signatory states undertake to see to it that human rights are included in their national legislation, enforced in national courts, and enacted into government domestic policy. As international phenomena go, the coupling of human rights values to legal forms is an extraordinary historical development.

Human Rights Reality

Despite the impressive structure of human rights agencies and notwithstanding the energy and action driving the creation of the international human rights system, the world remains full of human rights atrocities. While the language and the law of human rights create higher and higher expectations of good behavior, governments fail in their human rights responsibilities every day. International human rights reality still routinely lags behind human rights aspirations.

For example, even though all 192 member states of the UN have committed themselves to the peaceful resolution of internal conflicts, in the last half-century 127 civil wars occurred in 73 states, killing more than 16 million people. Right now in The Sudan, government-supported forces are massacring civilians, raping women, destroying villages and food stocks, and driving tens of thousands of people into camps and settlements where they live on the very edge of survival, hostage to abuses of the Janjaweed militia groups. Other contradictory examples abound. For instance the United States is a signatory to the UN Convention Against Torture, yet since it seeks to finesse its international obligations towards prisoners by placing them in the jurisdictional no-man's-land of Guantánamo Bay, Cuba.[3] Mexico is likewise a signatory to the UN Convention Against Torture, yet torture is reported to be widespread in the military, and corruption can be found at all levels of Mexico's federal, state, and municipal systems of administration. Virtually every postcolonial government of Australia, a signatory to the International Covenant on Civil and Political Rights, has a bad human rights record in regard to its indigenous population.

Governments also fail in their human rights obligations through simple neglect or even complete lack of interest in the human rights of certain groups in their society. These are the everyday human rights problems that lack the shock value of wartime atrocities. For instance Jordan, one of the few Arab countries where women vote and hold seats in parliament, signed the Convention on the Elimination of Discrimination Against Women (CEDAW) in the early 1990s but has not managed to pass national legislation to prevent hundreds, possibly thousands, of "honor killings." Even women who are the victims of rape are considered to have compromised their families' honor; fathers, brothers, and sons then see it as their duty to avenge their honor, not by pursuing the perpetrators but by murdering their daughters, sisters, and mothers.

Thirty years after CEDAW was adopted by the UN General Assembly, mothers in some African countries still hold their young daughters down for the ritual of female genital cutting even though national criminal legislation in some African countries prohibits the practice. China is one of 138 countries that have signed the UN Convention on the Rights of the Child (CRC), but in Yunnan province alone 7,000 children have been trafficked as prostitutes, beggars, domestics, and workers in garment factories. It seems astounding that these human rights violations occur in countries that have reasonably functional governments, administrative structures, fiscal policies, and trade relations with other countries. When the atrocities of war are added into this picture of everyday human rights neglect, the international human rights problem looks overwhelming.

What do these failures of human rights implementation and enforcement tell us about the world-scale phenomenon of human rights? If there is a disconnect between global human rights values and local human rights implementation, what is the cause? What might be its solution? Have international human rights advocates stalled in their march to civilize governments and liberalize cultures? Why can't international society have more influence on individual governments, and why can't international human rights have more influence on the actions of individuals?

Three Critiques of the International Human Rights System

The great universalist aspirations of the United Nations are today criticized from across the political spectrum. Critiques of international human rights fall into three categories. First, the "sovereignty critique" argues that the problems of international human rights lie in the international system itself. "Sovereigntists" view any attempt to supplant the role of governments as doomed to failure. They would simply leave law in the hands of the state to be decided along lines of national interest. The second main critique of international human rights arises out of the role of civil society under globalization. "Civil societists" argue that the real human rights action in these days of globalization does not spring from formal international and governmental institutions but rather from newer informal sources such as nongovernmental advocacy groups. Third, "multiculturalists" argue that *any* attempt to institutionalize international standards in a multicultural world is philosophically flawed and culturally divisive.

Sovereignty

In the American legal academy there has been spirited, even acrimonious, debate about the relevance of international law. Some scholars point to the evidence of ongoing human rights abuses in countries that have signed international human rights treaties as evidence against a worldwide human rights trend. They argue that international human rights are nothing more than political rhetoric and that words and ideas lack the power to prevent mass atrocity, influence the behavior of authoritarian governments, or alter sexist or racist beliefs. For all their moral appeal, these skeptics say, international human rights are nothing more than an empty promise that is ignored by national governments at will: human rights are merely notes in the margins of legal and political debate, supported with zeal by few and ignored by many.[4]

Such criticism of human rights has a long history. Nineteenth-century French political theorist Pierre Proudhon described international law as "a scaffolding of fictions."[5] Likewise, in nineteenth-century Great Britain, when the legal reforms of legislative positivism sought to replace ideas of "natural law" with the transparency of written laws, international law as an explanation of shared human values was ridiculed. Instead, law was portrayed as a product of people's habitual obedience to their sovereign's command. There was no room for a normative order in Jeremy Bentham's well-known scoff in the 1860s that "Natural rights is simple nonsense: natural and imprescriptible rights, rhetorical nonsense—nonsense upon stilts."[6] Rights, he said, are the product of laws created by sovereigns and legislatures: "Right . . . is the child of law: from real laws come real rights; but from imaginary laws, from laws of nature, fancied and invented by poets, rhetoricians, and dealers in moral and intellectual poisons, come imaginary rights, a bastard brood of monsters."[7]

Like Bentham critiquing natural rights, today's sovereigntists argue that there is no *intrinsic* moral valence to international human rights standards.[8] This critique points to the voluntary nature of international human rights treaties and the lack of international enforcement powers when human rights are violated. This analysis points out that states enter into treaties and other international legal commitments only when it serves their particular national interests. When a government does translate international human rights standards into its own domestic legislation, it simply demonstrates the state's internal political agreements and not a deeply shared belief in the principles of international human brotherhood. Any cooperation among states on human rights problems is the serendipitous byproduct of rational acts of national self-preservation.

Weaker states, under this analysis, simply express international human rights commitment because it looks good to the rest of the world. Such states may have little else with which to negotiate with more powerful states: poor countries "trade" state sovereignty in obeisant necessity for economic advantages from richer ones. Sovereigntists say that the very idea of an international system of government is normatively flawed and empirically wrong.[9] International human rights law is merely feel-good rhetoric, an instrumental exercise in international public relations.

This is an especially strong argument for the United States, which has often declared its independence from the international legal system—especially since the terrorist attacks in 2001. The U.S. sometimes chooses to remain aloof from the international human rights system rather than "surrender" state sovereignty to international agencies. It has signed neither CEDAW nor CRC. In 2002 the U.S. was a prominent human rights outlier when it refused to join the treaty establishing the International Criminal Court (ICC). At other times, however, Washington supports international human rights institutions, as when the U.S., in its role in the UN Security Council, agreed in 2005 to refer human rights atrocities in the Darfur region of The Sudan to the ICC. For sovereigntists, however, there is no *moral* necessity for states to participate in the international human rights system. Rather, a government's obligation is to its own people, which may or may not dictate cooperating with broader international standards.

At issue here is the meaning of state sovereignty: the assertion that governments are the supreme legal authority within their own borders, not subject to international rules or institutions beyond them. Of course, the more a country can use economic and military means to achieve its objectives directly, the less it needs to participate in international human rights institutions. The more powerful a state, the more it can play the sovereignty trump card.

"Civil Society"

While the sovereignty critique challenges human rights optimists' belief in the force of international standards, a second critique questions whether law is the best tool for advancing human rights improvements. Traditionally, enthusiasts of the international system had assumed that the gradual expansion of the international human rights treaty system would inexorably spread better human rights through the agency of legal institutions. Evidence that international legal standards and human rights declarations cause governments to change their behavior is hotly disputed, however.[10] Indeed, there is empirical support for the *lack* of practical efficacy of international law generally and international human rights law in particular.[11] Moreover it seems that countries with the worst human rights records ratify human rights treaties as often as those with the best human rights practices.

The "law" question is especially relevant in conditions of globalization: just how important can law be in a world where corporations seem more powerful than governments, where nongovernmental organizations seem to be more effective agents of change than parliament or congress, and where mass media seem to have supplanted the role of formal institutions? On some accounts civil society in a globalized world has dislodged law—both international and national—as an ordering device. Scholars who emphasize the role of civil society when markets are globalized talk instead about global networks—governmental, nongovernmental, and corporate—that perform the regulatory functions that used to be the role of formal politics and law.[12]

Some argue that globalization has reduced, or possibly even removed, the salience of sovereignty, instead placing social change in the hands of civil society. Global networks have displaced the state, it is claimed, overlaying it with multiple decentralized networks that transcend national borders.[13] These scholars point to the multiple layers of relationships between states through multilateral and bilateral obligations and regional and international institutions, arguing that international human rights norms are spread through persuasion and acculturation rather than through top-down legal coercion.[14] Civil society, not law, is seen as the engine of change and the implementer of social preferences, so much so that it is sometimes simply assumed that human rights are natural components of a reasonable society rather than distinctive norms.[15] As with the evidence about the efficacy of human rights treaties, however, empirical support for the replacement of law by global civil society networks is deeply controversial. While civil society and mass media have added new layers of complexity to political and economic structures, it has yet to be established that these new dynamics have overtaken or replaced formal legal mechanisms.

"Multiculturalism"

If the "sovereignty critique" from the political right questions the force of international law unless it serendipitously coincides with national self-interest, one might expect that the political left would automatically be *for* international law. On the left, however, social theorists of pluralism and cultural identity can be equally suspicious of the universal principles of international human rights. Postmodernists criticize international human rights as naively papering over deep cleavages in cultural identity and making false assertions of universal norms. Multiculturalists would have the state protect rather than erase conflicting visions of human rights norms. Indeed, the "nationalist" left would elevate group rights as defenses against universal norms built on individual rights. From this perspective international human rights must be treated with suspicion—there can be no one-size-fits-all approach to the content of human rights. In the eyes of some, the absence of non-Europeans in the history of human rights philosophy has discredited the very idea of human rights as a universal norm that could underwrite legal rights. Human rights are seen as irretrievably part of Western triumphalism that reached its apogee in colonial ideology.

The historical account of modern human rights is also a story of human inequality, shadowed by the colonialist mission of civilizing "benighted" peoples. From the sixteenth to the twentieth-century international law legitimized the acquisition of huge swathes of the Americas, Africa, and the Asia-Pacific region in a style of imperial fundamentalism that was supported by the science of the day. Anthropologists made clear distinctions between "savage," "barbarian," and "civilized" peoples. In 1877 lawyer-anthropologist Lewis Henry Morgan wrote in the opening pages of his book *Ancient Society*, "It can now be asserted upon convincing evidence that savagery preceded barbarism in all tribes of mankind, as barbarism is known to have preceded civilization . . . [and these] three distinct conditions are connected with each other in a natural as well as necessary sequence of progress. . . . Democracy in government, brotherhood in society, equality in rights and privileges, and universal education, foreshadow the next higher plane of society to which experience, intelligence and knowledge are steadily tending."[16]

While the colonizing West brought the constitutive aspects of the human rights tradition—sovereignty, constitutionalism, and ideas of freedom and equality—their beliefs about anthropology effectively excluded non-European peoples from human rights benefits.[17] Instead, the West's anthropological assumptions justified the legalization of unequal treaties between European and non-European peoples, with the consequence that it was completely "legal" to acquire sovereignty over non-European societies by conquest.[18]

The more recent rejection of international human rights by some postcolonial countries has led to suggestions that non-Western systems with different cultural underpinnings have an entirely different set of human rights priorities. The skeptics of international human rights argue that much of the human rights scholarship and activism seems driven by moral absolutism, that aspirations for greater human dignity can only end in clashes between competing visions of the truth like the religious disputes of past ages. International human rights are criticized for being a politics of identity that "allows inclusion only by assimilation or conversion."[19] As Canadian philosopher Charles Taylor has pointed out, "we can't assume straight off, without further examination, that a future unforced world consensus could be formulated to the satisfaction of everyone in the language of rights."[20]

There could be no better example of this than the "Asian values" debate. The first prime minister of Singapore, Lee Kwan Yew, attacked the underlying philosophy of human rights in the West for according primacy to the individual. Yew argued for a different interpretation of human rights, understood through Confucianism. Asian values, he asserted, put the social and economic rights of the community before the rights of the individual.[21] The Association of Southeast Asian Nations (ASEAN) countries of Brunei Darussalam, Cambodia, Indonesia, Laos, Malaysia, Myanmar, Philippines, Singapore, Thailand, and Vietnam conspicuously overlook each other's human rights abuses, refusing for example to sanction the rulers of Myanmar for their brutal crackdown on the Buddhist monks who took to the streets in September 2007 to demonstrate for political freedom or for their prolonged detention of opposition leader Aung San Suu Kyi.

Answering the Critiques:
A More Complex Human Rights History

These are long-standing problems in the Western tradition of law, rights, and international society. Each of these critiques points out valid and serious flaws in the current operation of international human rights. The very international institutions that were created to pursue human rights appear undermined by some of the core values and features that were part of their creation. Each of these critiques, when seen more precisely in its historical context, however, reveals that it is missing crucial elements of the genealogy of human rights. Key pieces of the human rights system as it has evolved remain relevant today. The development of international law over the past 500 years is unquestionably a blemished history, but the human rights ideals within that history are not fatally flawed. Human rights as a shared project across dissimilar cultures remains a viable vision.

Each of the three critiques overlooks a crucial piece of the international human rights jigsaw. Although the sovereignty critique is a legitimate account of the effects of national power on international matters, other long-standing features of the development of the international legal system also show a sensibility that can only be described as a moral obligation towards people of other states. The civil society critique properly notes the influence of nonlegal pressures on governments, but it is also clear that the proliferation of nongovernmental forms of activity has gone hand in hand with the creation of legal frameworks. The cultural critique of human rights is a devastatingly accurate account of misused Western power in the colonies, but the history of the Western rights tradition is also one of the desire to accommodate cultural difference within overarching principles and institutions.

The drawback of each of these critiques is that none of them on its own offers a full account that encompasses law, society, and politics in philosophical history. I argue that once these developments are disentangled from their history and their ideology, key elements of the international human rights system are more visible. A more careful analysis of the development of human rights philosophy demonstrates that important values can be disaggregated from a flawed history.

Despite many failures in their implementation, these ideas have been offered in the Western philosophical tradition as far better alternatives to singular national interests, inflexible legal institutions, and fixed ideas of human identity. Ideas about self-determination, humanitarian intervention, cultural and ethnic difference, and religious diversity were all part of the interactions between the Old World and the New World that began in the fifteenth century.[22] They have been part of the philosophical scaffolding of empire from its earliest days and need to be reemphasized in the contemporary human rights story.

Recovering a Lost Philosophical Tradition

The conventional legal story about human rights starts with the end of World War II, the Nuremberg trials, and the Universal Declaration of Human Rights. Traditional accounts of the philosophy of human rights have focused on the political history of Europe and the United States. This perspective emphasizes international law as a development contiguous with the Enlightenment, the rise of sovereignty in the Peace of Westphalia of 1648, and the rise of individual rights in modern government. The history of individual rights is therefore seen to stretch from the contributions of Thomas Hobbes and John Locke to the English tradition of individual freedom as the "birthright of the English people," to Jean-Jacques Rousseau's articulation of individual French liberty and the writings of Charles de Montesquieu and James Madison that framed the tradition of individual freedoms in the U.S. Constitution.[23]

The law and the philosophy of human rights have a far longer and more complex lineage, however, one that goes back to ancient Greece and Rome but that in Enlightenment times was deeply connected to Europe's discovery of the New World and to Europe's own religious wars. Its early principles were constructed in the shadow of the Roman Catholic Church's designs upon the souls of the heathens in distant lands, then came a steady drumbeat of laws and policies that pursued two often conflicting goals: reducing the influence of Rome on Europe's commercial activities in the New World and increasing the claims of European individuals for religious freedom at home. Europe's rapid commercial expansion required new rules to regulate the "rights" of trade and navigation, establishing the earliest principles of the "open seas," unfettered by claims of sovereignty of other countries plying the oceans. It also needed principles by which Europe's land grabs in the Americas, Africa, and Asia could maximize profits and minimize demarcation conflicts with other European neighbors in the colonies. When it became clear that colonization was bringing disease and depredation, as well as enslavement and outright massacre, to the far-flung satellites, rules were needed to constrain colonialism's worst excesses. International human rights began as two parts greed and one part compassion.

Cultural Differences   While European evangelism, voracious trade, and predatory slave activities still reverberate in contemporary postcolonial societies, these activities were criticized by some in Europe as early as the sixteenth century.[24] Of course it had always been known that other lands had different cultures, and traders had been dealing with this fact for as long as goods had moved along the Silk Road. After the discovery of the Americas, however, Portuguese and Spanish explorers and conquerors wanted to stake their claims to the new hemisphere's resources in ways that their competitors in Europe would acknowledge and respect. The Roman Catholic Church saw non-Christians as having no souls, which meant they could not be said to own their lands and so could be enslaved with impunity. When news reached Europe of hideous violence in what is now Latin America, however, it became clear that the subjugation of distant lands and peoples was producing serious political, social, and legal problems. Spanish Catholic cleric Francisco de Vitoria mounted an eloquent defense of Indian rights in his 1532 *De Indis* lecture, arguing against enslavement of the natives whom most Europeans believed were "slaves, sinners, heathens, barbarians, minors, lunatics and animals."[25] Going against the status quo, Vitoria discerned humanity in the indigenous population: "they are not of unsound mind, but have, according to their kind, the use of reason. . . . They have polities which are orderly arranged and they have definite marriages and magistrates, overlords, laws and workshops, and a system of exchange, all of which call for the use of reason; they also have a kind of religion."[26]

In the end, however, Vitoria's protests did nothing to slow Spain's—or Portugal's and other countries'—colonization of Latin America. In a sad twist to the only compassionate aspect of what was otherwise a rationalization for conquest, the ascribing of European-like rationality to the natives was instrumental in destroying their culture. While Vitoria argued for the right of the Indians to retain their own religion and to own their land, his attribution of reason to the indigenes was a double-edged sword. As soon as they either converted to Christianity or used force to keep Spanish traders from exercising Spain's "natural" right to roam freely over the land for the purposes of trade, the local populations incurred either the "protection" or the wrath of the Spanish crown. The argument for universal humanity brought the indigenous peoples up from their subhuman status but also justified the Spanish empire through legal arguments that delivered the "natives" into the jurisdiction of their colonizers.[27]

Religious Tolerance   Religion in Europe also played a central role in the development of human rights. When Alberico Gentili, a sixteenth-century writer fled Italy because of his Protestantism, he went to England where Protestantism was taking hold. Ultimately, he became a professor of law at the University of Oxford and advised Queen Elizabeth I on the principles that ought to apply to military engagement with the Spanish Armada. The brilliance of Gentili's works, which became classics of international law, is that he wrote of the world as a community comprised of a single human race—not Christians and "others," who held alternative religious beliefs. He argued for more compassion in times of war. In a time when war was only fought to secure territory or spread religion, he was one of the first to argue for war in the name of humanitarian intervention, or, as he put it, "to right human wrongs."[28] Gentili's thinking prefigured military interventions in the name of human rights in the latter half of the twentieth century by insisting that a sovereign should neither rule by fear nor have absolute discretion over citizens.[29]

Gentili's flight to Protestant England from Catholic Italy in 1580 was the impetus for the trenchant critiques of religious intolerance that he delivered as a professor of civil law at Oxford. This sentiment took root in England over the next century as freedom of conscience. The struggle between Catholics and Protestants in England led ultimately to the establishment of parliamentary supremacy over monarchical rule after the Glorious Revolution in 1688, which removed the part of the English monarchy's power that had been based on its "divine right" to rule.

Death and destruction through warfare and conquest was the problem of their time, and Vitoria and Gentili were among the first European philosophers to lambaste the human rights violators who acted in the name of religion and territorial expansion. The slow separation of church and state had begun but with the paradox that a more secular universal law of rights sharply differentiated between European "civilized" peoples and non-European peoples.

As civil war in Europe and violent conquest overseas continued, scholars crafted rules that would tie the hands of kings and princes and limit the extent of civilian suffering. First Gentili then Dutch separatist Hugo Grotius developed ideas about the legal conduct of war. Grotius lived at the time of the Eighty Years' War between Spain and The Netherlands and the Thirty

Years' War between Catholic and Protestant European countries. He witnessed slaughter, disease, and destruction that wiped out 15–20 percent of the total population of what is now Germany. The work of Grotius signaled a fundamental shift from earlier writings on international law that has shaped its contours ever since. Although both Gentili and Vitoria had claimed that their writings for the most part merely systematized the growing number of customs, usages, and state practices that had developed over the previous centuries, Grotius made the distinction between the natural law, jus naturale (the justification for his rules) and jus gentium (the customary law of nations). Jus naturale rests upon basic metaphysical principles of religion and divine authority, but customary law is quite different. It simply justifies international law through describing the practice of states and the conduct of international relations, as evidenced either by informal customs or forced treaties. While assuming universal humankind, Grotius also prefigured positivism, the new political theory that would explain the steady rise of the nation-state and its increasingly absolute claims to legal and political supremacy from the latter part of the eighteenth century to the early part of the twentieth.

Selective Compassion   All three of these early scholars of international law—Vitoria, Gentili, and Grotius—seem to have been genuinely motivated by humanitarian concerns. They were grasping for a wider view of human values beyond either blind obedience to the church or fearful self-defense of territory, towards a view that included protecting the weak from those more powerful according to higher principles.[30] This became the theme over the next century, and law was increasingly seen as the leavening influence between chaos and order. Against Thomas Hobbes's idea of the all-important sovereign—his "Leviathan"—German philosopher Samuel von Pufendorf also argued that "Any man must, inasmuch as he can cultivate and maintain toward others a peaceable sociality that is consistent with the native character and end of humankind in general."[31] Law was the key to maintaining sociability: "What would men's life have been like without a law to compose them?" "[A] pack of wolves, lions, or dogs fighting to the finish," he concluded.[32] It was a view that spread through Europe and then to the American founders Hamilton, Madison, and Jefferson as their formulation of the role of rights in the new republic.[33]

Nonetheless, these compassionate arguments applied to just a tiny percentage of any population. Privilege rather than any fundamental moral equality recognized by law was the doorway to political life. Although social conditions and the human rights agenda improved during the Enlightenment, in fact many people did not qualify to receive the freedoms guaranteed by the European and American declarations of rights. Property ownership and private wealth were both formal and informal prerequisites to political participation. Despite the advances made in fundamental rights such as the right to life and freedom of opinion, civil inequality remained prevalent.[34] "Freedom" and "liberty" were written about in neutral terms, but these principles only applied to those eligible to vote—initially, propertied white men.[35] The position of women in society still remained unequal to that of men, even in England, where women had more human rights than in any other part of Europe. Granting minority rights and freeing all repressed nationalities throughout Europe was theoretically part of the French revolutionary agenda, but although Napoleon did much to spread these ideals during his conquests, real conditions lagged far behind.[36]

Human rights in the Western tradition were crafted to suit a particular set of historical conditions: Europe's new emergence at the center of global military and economic power abroad and religious schisms at home. The European particularity can seem shocking to those familiar with the rich history of earlier systems of belief outside Europe, yet little or nothing of non-European moral philosophy was deemed relevant by the men of the Enlightenment.[37]

Abolition of Slavery   There was one development in this early period that demonstrated the potential of human rights to be a truly global movement. When the French civil code was translated into English by an anonymous barrister in the Inns of Court in London in 1804, its advancement of the legal status of homosexuals, slaves, and Jews struck a chord with the British Quakers, who had for years been advocating for an end to the slave trade. European expansionism had massively stoked the trade because the colonial powers relied upon slave labor both at home and in the colonies, and also trafficked in slaves as part of their commercial enterprise with one another. By the middle of the eighteenth century, British ships were carrying about 50,000 slaves a year and the trade was bringing in huge profits.

Philosophical opposition to slavery had been rising since Vitoria's day. From France, Montesquieu's *L'esprit des lois* (The Spirit of the Laws) had a powerful influence over the early U.S. slave abolitionist movement.[38] In Great Britain philosophers such as Adam Smith opposed slavery on both economic and moral grounds. In the *Wealth of Nations* Smith wrote: "From the experience of all ages and nations, I believe, that the work done by free men comes cheaper in the end than the work performed by slaves. Whatever work he does, beyond what is sufficient to purchase his own maintenance, can be squeezed out of him by violence only, and not by any interest of his own."[39] In his *Theory of Moral Sentiments*, he wrote: "[It is cruel] . . . to reduce them [captured indigenous people] into the vilest of all states, that of domestic slavery, and to sell them, man, woman, and child, like so many herds of cattle, to the highest bidder in the market."[40]

Yet the slave trade continued until years of wars made inroads on the economic underpinnings of slavery, especially on the business interests of particular British members of Parliament. Finally, twenty-five years of advocacy by the Quakers and the English Evangelicals was recognized in 1807 when Parliament outlawed the slave trade within the British Empire, authorizing the navy to collect fines for any slaves found on British ships. With ships active in every ocean, the British Navy became a de facto international police agency charged with monitoring and enforcing the first international human rights campaign.

As a global campaign it had extraordinary success. In 1833 Parliament passed the Abolition of Slavery Act and provided £20 million in compensation to the slaveholders. France abolished slavery in its colonies after the 1848 revolution, and Tsar Alexander II emancipated Russia's fifty million serfs in 1861. Despite these international successes, it took a bloody civil war finally to abolish slavery in the U.S. Until the U.S. Civil War the majority of bills concerning slavery were more concerned with the economy than the rights of the slaves. A proposal in 1839 by Congressman John Quincy Adams to end slavery failed. It was not until 1863, two years into the Civil War, that Pres. Abraham Lincoln issued the Emancipation Proclamation. Like the abolition of slavery in the U.K., the U.S. abolition of slavery resulted from a combination of economic factors and moral sentiment. The Thirteenth Amendment to the United States Constitution was finally passed in 1865 to guarantee the permanent abolition of slavery and the rights of newly freed slaves. It was followed by the Fourteenth Amendment to protect the civil rights of former slaves and the Fifteenth Amendment, which banned racial restrictions on voting.[41]

Of course these momentous events did not eradicate "state-sanctioned" slavery. Indeed, the trade had created new economies: some African nations had prospered so much through the slave trade that they sent tribal leaders from the Gambia, Congo, and Dahomey in delegations to London and Paris to protest its abolition in its very earliest days.[42] The Dutch system of coerced labor in its East Indian (Indonesian) colonies continued until the 1880s, and slavery similarly persisted in parts of France's African colonies until the 1940s.

Children's Rights   Concern about children's human rights began in the same way as the movement for the abolition of slavery. Indignation over the plight of child labor in factories and coal mines was a rallying point for progressive forces throughout Europe, leading ultimately in the mid-1800s to British, French, and American legislation for the protection of children.[43] As the industrial revolution progressed, many European countries passed legislation to make elementary education universal and compulsory.[44]

In the global context these were modest successes,[45] yet they demonstrated two things. First, an international publicity campaign telling the public about human rights harms could result in legal change. Most people in Europe had known nothing of slaves' conditions on the ships and the plantations or the plight of seven-year-old children in the mines. Once they knew, political movements for reform developed momentum that blossomed into new national legal standards. Second, a growing consensus in Europe about core human values of individual freedom and agency was paying off in increased international legal cooperation. Transnational activism about slavery sparked international organizations such as the Eight Power Declaration of the Congress of Vienna, the French Société des Amis des Noirs, and the British and Foreign Anti-Slavery Society.[46] Human rights ideas within states were influencing ideas across their borders.

Early Principles of Humanitarian Intervention   Notions of humanitarian intervention began with ideas of "mutual aid" in the eighteenth century, the same time the first suggestions of regional and international confederations of states were advanced.[47] German philosopher Christian Wolff wrote in *The Law of Nations* in 1749 that all the countries of the world together make up a "supreme state" that ought to have its own right to promulgate laws for the universal good. Wolff's idea was that just as people are free and equal before the law, so individual countries ought to be free and equal parts of the supreme state of the world.[48] Writing in the mid-eighteenth century, Swiss jurist Emerich de Vattel popularized Wolff in his own work, also called *The Law of Nations*.[49] It became especially influential in the United States because of its parallels with the Declaration of Independence. Like Wolff, Vattel asserted the equality and sovereign independence of states. Just as individuals aim to perfect themselves, Vattel wrote, states are obligated to mutual assistance in perfecting themselves.

Although rejecting Wolff's conception of a regulatory world state, Vattel argued that sovereigns ought to increase human happiness through mitigating wars and promoting "mutual aid" among countries. Vattel prefigured the UN structure by writing about confederations of sovereign states that could maintain a balance of power and together preserve the liberties of each nation. He even went so far as to say that states could join together to put down a violator of international law. States' obligations to each other included assisting a weaker state against a powerful enemy that threatens to oppress it, giving aid during a famine, and ensuring that it did not monopolize trade. Within national borders, the sovereign had a duty to render justice regardless of nationality, to citizens and noncitizens alike. This was an important step in recognizing the absolutely central role of governments in caring for the well-being of the citizens as well as the role of international alliances in promoting peaceful relations among states.

An International Institutional Theory to Match International Principles

The Law of Nations   For all their powerful morality and logic, these international human rights were ideals without an international home. The principles only took life when each sovereign ruler or parliament passed laws for its own people—there was no corresponding theory of international institutions to apply the same laws across all states. Previously there had been some writing about states comprising a collective value system rather than a hierarchy of "civilized" versus colonized societies, but such work had failed to capture the imaginations of enough reformers to make much impact.

A League of Nations   A comprehensive theory of international philosophy finally emerged from Western Europe in the late 1700s, centuries after the Islamic world's intricate and advanced international legal philosophy had flourished during the Ottoman empire. Much modern thinking in international law and human rights depends upon Immanuel Kant's ideas of individual rights within international society because he was able to put together both values of individual rights and global community.[50] A German philosophy professor who lived his entire life in the Prussian city of Königsberg, Kant proposed a global organization of nation-states, a voluntary "league of nations" that would ensure worldwide peace and "does not tend to any dominion over the power of the state but only to the maintenance and security of the freedom of the state itself and of other states in league with it."[51]

Kant's vision of international organization was premised upon his idea of "cosmopolitanism"[52]—a world of rational individuals who are members of a universal moral community and who share freedom, equality, and independence.[53] Such people choose to give themselves the law. "Practical" law, made by sovereign governments and ostensibly agreed upon by citizens, ought to be grounded in people's equal capacity to reason, to subject themselves and their world to rational analysis—"[man should have] the courage to use his own intelligence."[54] Kant's individual citizens, their sovereign state, and the international community each are constitutive parts of a common morality. He argued for a universal morality, arrived at through the use of reason—the attribute of all the human species. Kant's global vision was a world where morality was rooted in human freedom and each individual acted autonomously within a constitutional republic.[55]

Unlike those writing before him, Kant saw war as both morally and legally baseless. He was scathing about earlier justifications for war and aggression: "Up to the present, Hugo Grotius, Pufendorf, Vattel, and many other irritating comforters have been cited in justification of war, though their code, philosophically or diplomatically formulated, has not and cannot have the least legal force, because states as such do not stand under a common external power."[56] Instead, Kant proposed that states be founded on representative government, and this would preclude external aggression towards other states. Similarly he was critical of Europe's expansions into the New World, labeling them as

> inhospitable actions of the civilized and especially of the commercial states of our part of the world. The injustice which they show to lands and peoples they visit (which is equivalent to conquering them) is carried by them to terrifying lengths. America, the lands inhabited by the Negro, the Spice Islands, the Cape, etc., were at the time of their discovery considered by these civilized intruders as lands without owners, for they counted the inhabitants as nothing. In East India (Hindustan), under the pretense of establishing economic undertakings, they brought in foreign soldiers and used them to oppress the natives, excited widespread wars among the various states, spread famine, rebellion, perfidy, and the whole litany of evils which afflict mankind.[57]

Kant understood that law is central to guaranteeing human rights. He wrote that "our social and political relations should be governed and our public conflicts settled in a universal manner. This requires the existence of law."[58] Kant's insight, which influences moral philosophy to this day, was that true freedom could only exist when the rule of law prevails within nation-states and also in international relations.

Early International Institutions Fail   Kant was ahead of his time. His ideas lay fallow for nearly a century and were only revived when a new critique of Europe's appetite for colonial imperialism emerged at the end of the nineteenth century. The impetus came from a group of European lawyers opposed to the type of European nationalism that was being used to justify colonial brutalities across Asia, Africa, and the Pacific.[59] As Finnish legal historian Marti Koskenniemi recounts, the *Institut de Droit International* (Institute of International Law) was founded in Ghent in 1873 by two Belgians, Gustave Moynier and Gustave Rolin-Jaequemyns, and nine other lawyers from continental Europe, England, Scotland, the U.S., and Argentina. Koskenniemi writes, "They strove to become the legal conscience . . . of the civilized world . . . linked with liberal-humanitarian ideals and theories of the natural evolution of European societies."[60]

Alas, the institute was a failure, highlighted just a decade later when newly imperial Germany convened the Berlin Conference to apportion Africa among the great powers: arrangements that were agreed in Europe between the European powers that were then enacted with arrogance and terrible violence in Africa. It was clear that any early impact of the Ghent institute on European governments was negligible, and it certainly did not prevent the "scramble for Africa."[61] The institute also lacked a progressive agenda: "If they welcomed the increasing interdependence of civilized nations, this was not only to make a point about the basis of the law's binding force but also to see international law as part of the progress of modernity that was leading societies into increasingly rational and humanitarian avenues."[62]

The idea of institutionalizing human rights in international treaties and organizations was stalled everywhere until 1945. Even the League of Nations that was established by the Treaty of Versailles following World War I did not make a decisive break with the past. It had established the Permanent Court of International Justice, but the court proved virtually impotent. The U.S. never signed or ratified its charter, and other League of Nations members paid little attention to its decisions. The single shining international human rights achievement during this period was the series of conventions that came out of the First and Second Peace Conferences at The Hague in 1899 and 1907.

The Hague Conventions addressed the humane treatment of people and prohibited of the use of certain types of weapons in warfare. Yet even this partial realization of Kant's vision of a "government of governments" was unable to prevent the onset of World War II and the terrible human rights atrocities during this period. Kant's writings anticipated the evolution of international law as a discipline separate from philosophy and diplomatic relations that took place in the late nineteenth century, but his vision was too abstract for the world of nationalist realpolitik.

Flawed Ideas or Flawed Institutions?

Prefiguring today's debates about national security, Kant's message of institutionalized cosmopolitanism was overwhelmed by the urgent nationalism of the nineteenth and early twentieth century. Europe was industrializing rapidly in these years, and states jealously fought over their colonial boundaries in the New World, eager to ensure a steady supply of raw materials for their factories in the Old World. Kant's international architecture was ignored in favor of statism.[63] International society as Kant had sketched it could not compete with the nationalist visions of Germany, Japan, and the U.S as the newly rich great powers. The Spanish and Ottoman empires began to crumble, the Holy Roman and Mughal empires simply ceased to exist, and Russia and China began to fall back as world powers, leaving the British Empire as the world's superpower.[64]

Where did these developments leave the philosophical and legal project of human rights? Human rights as an international movement stalled after the abolition of slavery. At the same time, human rights, especially political and civil rights, deepened as national movements within countries. Curiously enough, although the new rights emerging in national constitutions and legislation throughout Europe and North America were couched as universal rights, these rights were mostly not extended to the colonies, at least in any meaningful or practical way. Vitoria's early attempts to persuade European states to credit indigenous Americans with a political economy of their own could not compete with the claims that Westerners were making against their own governments for human rights at home. "Uncivilized" nations had to wait for their human rights because they needed first to be taught how to take proper advantage of such rights.

The empire-builders of Europe and the U.S. increased the stakes of seeing some nations as "free" and "civilized," and others as "backward" and "uncivilized." Montesquieu, the architect of the separation of government powers and also a key influence upon Madison's work on the U.S. Constitution, wrote in the late eighteenth century that: "The difference between savage peoples and barbarian peoples is that the former are small scattered nations which, for certain particular reasons, cannot unite, whereas barbarians are ordinarily small nations that can unite together."[65] European empires viewed their colonized peoples as childlike and incapable of rational thought. Indigenes were viewed by the West as barbaric, putting them beyond the realm of moral and legal argument. This test of civilization dictated whether an indigenous population was entitled to full recognition as a legal personality that could undertake binding commitments under international law. In some places, such as Australia, the indigenes were even considered to be *pre*-legal. Although the first governors of the settlement in New South Wales were told to "treat the natives well," the international law applied to Australia's settlement was that of *terra nullius* or "empty land."[66] Unlike the situation in New Zealand, Canada, or the United States, no treaties of land ownership or transfer were struck with Australian Aboriginals. Lacking obvious townships or cultivation agriculture, they were considered too nomadic to be property owners, with the consequence that the British Crown deemed the land empty and simply took possession of Australia by default.

From the moment international law became a distinctive disciplinary practice in the West—that is, as it became part of the legal rules applied by governments in their activities beyond their own borders—Europe positioned itself as the apotheosis of civilization. International law was simply European law. Koskenniemi points out that "As a constructive theory, it was hopelessly manqué: an eclectic, fragile façade over what must often have seemed as the banal prejudices of a cultured but declining bourgeoisie."[67]

Wittingly or unwittingly this approach rationalized colonial paternalism with Darwinian arguments that portrayed the colonizers as intellectually superior precisely because they dominated the indigenous populations. The sentiments of political equality and individual human rights that were energizing Europe were not transmitted to the colonial satellites. In an uncanny reproduction of Vattel's humanitarianism that in the sixteenth century had delivered the Indians into Spanish hands through arguments about human equality, the end result of nineteenth-century paternalism simply increased colonial control over people and land in the colonies. Whereas Kantian universal humanity might have granted full equality to indigenous peoples, instead it justified the replacement of indigenous institutions with

European-style institutions because they were regarded as the universal best standard. Because colonial societies were seen as immature nations, full individual human rights were withheld from their inhabitants because they too were seen as insufficiently advanced. This was a Western habit of mind that continued until the decolonization movement of the 1970s.

Sadly the results of colonial interventions to prevent so-called native barbarism and backwardness are still felt today. In Australia and Canada, for example, authorities removed indigenous children from their families, institutionalizing them until the 1980s so that they could receive religion, social graces, and a Protestant work ethic.[68]

Australia's Aboriginal population suffers today from high rates of domestic abuse, child abuse, and deaths in custody as the consequence of prior colonial policies of familial disruption and dispossession of tribal lands.[69] It is a familiar story. Although formal decolonization ended in the 1970s when Portugal withdrew from Africa and East Timor and the French from Indochina, the consequences of colonial policies continue. In former empires the world over, including the old Russian and Chinese territories, the outrages inflicted on the colonies and satellites still reverberate today.[70] Many of today's poorest countries blame their weak institutions and poor economies on their experience of colonization and understandably cling to their postcolonial national sovereignty like a talisman.

The Language of Request

The paradox of this history of imperial expansion, disregard for indigenous cultures, and failed institutions is that the human rights *ideas*, which comprise a constitutive part of that history, have continued to spread as a global movement. Equal human rights are now a ubiquitous feature of international political language, the moral music of governments invoked in many key international relations developments in the post–World War II period. When European states handed back their empires to the indigenous peoples of Africa and the Asia-Pacific region in the decolonization movement of the 1950s and '60s, new postcolonial constitutions were laced with international human rights language, as were many of the constitutions of Latin America's post-military regime states from the 1980s. When the United States, Canada, the Soviet Union, and most of the countries of Europe acceded to the Helsinki Accords in 1975, international human rights were buried beneath issues of security, sovereignty, and war in Europe. Few people expected the Soviet Bloc countries to honor the provisions of the Helsinki Accords. No one, not even the most confident, could have predicted that the vaguely worded section about respect for human rights and fundamental freedoms that were buried midway in the voluminous Accord documents would help frame the political pronouncements that accompanied the unraveling of communism in the late 1980s.[71]

Internationally, human rights are held up as bargaining chips in the global economy. Human rights form part of the international regulation of trade under conditions set by the World Trade Organization and the International Labour Organization. International human rights are the signifier of new or transitioning governments that seek international legitimacy and want greater participation in international decision making. Countries receiving economic aid promise their financial benefactors better human rights as a quid pro quo, as when states seeking acceptance into the European Union promise they will improve their treatment of national minorities in return for money to redesign their legal and political institutions or when struggling African states promise to improve conditions in their jails as a condition for receiving unilateral assistance packages from richer countries. Virtually every formal relationship or negotiation between states in the developed and developing world now makes reference to human rights. Thousands of organizations mobilize each day—on the Internet, via direct mail, at conferences, and in meetings— and invoke international human rights to push, cajole, and persuade governments, corporations, religious authorities, schools, and families toward better human rights behavior.

In the name of international human rights the United Nations convenes international courts to force Rwandan and Yugoslavian perpetrators of genocide to appear before judges and face accusations of their atrocities. In the name of international human rights, national legal systems become hybrid combinations of domestic law and domestic judges augmented by international law and international judges, as in the instances of the Special Court for Sierra Leone and the courts trying human rights violators in East Timor and Kosovo. International human rights standards are cited in truth commissions, where government officials are called upon to confess their violations and apologize to their victims, as was the case in South Africa's Truth and Reconciliation Commission and the scores of other truth and reconciliation bodies that have been established in other post-conflict countries.

International human rights are also invoked for much more than ex post standards of judgment after civil conflict. The slew of new constitutions from the 1990s—from Eastern Europe to South Africa—carry long lists of human rights that draw upon the language of international human rights treaties. Human rights as constitutional guarantees establish prospective standards for government behavior and frame the expectations of civil society. Beyond the political cloakrooms and corridors of courthouses, the language of human rights is invoked as a language of protest and a language of claim. Governments and nongovernmental organizations around the world go into communities, both rich and poor, and talk about human rights. Schoolbooks teach about the rights of children, and labor unions talk about rights of employees. Doctors talk about the human rights of mothers, and community leaders talk about the human rights of detainees. The topic may be different but the framing exercise is the same: people claim as their due something they do not have, but possibly something that citizens of other countries do have. Human rights put this claim at the feet of governments. International human rights have become the lingua franca of global visions of equality and human dignity.

The idea behind the international human rights movement is that the international community has an interest in ensuring that governments deliver on their moral and legal promises to their citizens. For believers in the international system of law, human rights are the ultimate litmus test of a government's performance; they are the language that voices international judgment and expectation. Internationalists argue that the international community has an interest in monitoring human rights performance on the country level, which has in turn led to the creation of new international institutions that track local human rights behavior and even punish violators as criminals. The language of international human rights is carefully deployed so that human rights failures will capture international attention. The everyday language of international human rights advocates has been adopted as the cry of the everyday work of activists and community leaders, and nongovernmental organizations spread news of domestic human rights violators instantaneously via electronic media. "Ethnic cleansing" and "genocide" are more likely to attract a journalist's interest than simple "murder." "Children's rights" and "sweatshops" are the terms headlined in international campaigns about ten-year-olds chained to looms for twelve-hour work days because the sterile language of labor law simply cannot capture public imagination with the same intensity as the heated language of international human rights journalism. However, like colonization that carried the agenda of civilizing conquered societies, today's international human rights movement runs the risk of assuming that there is only one truly civilized way to live. The charge against the international human rights movement is that, just like colonialism, it invokes a rationale of benevolent transformation to European humanism as the inevitable goal of humankind. The habit of seeing the job of international law as encouraging the "uncivilized" to embrace civilization dies hard. Even John Rawls evoked nascent memories of Morgan's "standard of civilization" in *The Law of Peoples*, his only work on international justice. Rawls proposed a hierarchy of five distinct groups within two subsets, the "well-ordered peoples" who are "worthy of membership" in a "Society of Peoples" on one hand, and the "not well-ordered"[72] states on the other. While Rawls made no explicit reference to "civilization," his typology of societies is redolent of old colonial classifications.[73]

Still others point out that the entire edifice of international economic aid rests upon classifications of relative need, leading some Western human rights scholars to concede that human rights are today fraught with unhappy ghosts of the past because states are judged by whether they meet progressive ideals of international legitimacy.[74] Philosophically and empirically, international human rights as a uniform and universal goal appear to be on shaky ground.

Three Responses to Three Critiques

To summarize so far, there are three central dilemmas in human rights today. First is the concern that international human rights is either powerless rhetoric in the face of national interests or perhaps an excuse for colonial or imperial projects that jeopardize the integrity and autonomy of individual nation-states. These are the realist and anticolonial faces of the sovereignty critique. Second is the notion that nongovernmental actors—whether nonprofit advocacy groups or corporations—are better placed, more effective, and more relevant to addressing human rights issues than are laws or legal institutions. This is the civil society critique. Third is the idea that what are called universal human rights are insensitive to cultural variety or are imperialist or oppressive. This is the multicultural critique.

A historical analysis shows that even though human rights are often borne of and even viewed as justifying aggression and imperialism there is also much evidence to the contrary. Human rights have catalyzed global social movements and altered the mind-set of politicians, creating an ideology to which even the powerful pay homage. The argument of this book is that historical, normative, and practical analysis of the three main lines of critique about human rights, together with evidence of developments in contemporary international relations, suggest an institutional response.

Sovereignty as Relational and Humanitarian

The feature that emerges most clearly from an examination of the history of sovereignty is that state governments have a special responsibility for human rights. Part of the argument of this book is that sovereignty should be reconceived as a conditional entitlement of government—that a government is exempted from international interference so long as it cares adequately for the human rights of its citizens. Sovereignty has traditionally been seen as a matter of defining and defending national borders, but today it does much more than demarcate the line between one nation-state and another. Today sovereignty includes relationships of international interdependency and coexistence. The defense of sovereignty rests on normative ideas about the sovereign caring about the human rights of the citizens. Taken together, the old and the new ideas of sovereignty are creating new standards of international governance and human rights compliance that I describe in Chapter 3 as "relational sovereignty."

The ever-growing expectation in world society is that national governments treat their citizenry with a baseline of human rights decency.[75] Citizens also ought to expect their governments to take a principled position towards how other governments treat their citizens. This is already the case in many affluent Western countries, where governments find themselves under greater pressure to spread the benefits of democracy and human rights. While the effects of globalization are profound and measurable, however, it is a patchwork development with different effects in different parts of the world. The conception of sovereignty also varies within a state depending on the subject of government regulation; for example, states will assert strong sovereignty over issues such as state security and immigration but a more negotiated version of sovereignty on economic issues.

My argument about sovereignty and globalization is that the functions of states have been altered under the influence of contemporary conditions such as the combined force of global economic expansion and rapid electronic communication about human rights in other parts of the world. Relational sovereignty does not stem from an inherent notion of state or territory but instead reflects a practice that binds global players together in a process of recognition and self-declaration. That practice does, and should, set conditions.

Citizens continue to have deep connections with their own governments and they also have relationships that transcend state borders. Increasingly, citizens are entitled to expect more from their governments than simply keeping order at home and managing threats beyond the border.

Legal Frameworks for Globalized Civil Society

In Chapter 4 I argue that the civil society critique of formal legal institutions does not strike a fatal blow to the international human rights system. Rather, legal institutions are needed more than ever to formalize social politics into legal rules. It is true that globalization is reconfiguring the role of government by increasing the influence of non-state actors—corporations, civil society, even local warlords—within states, and also across borders, but these developments have not displaced law as an instrument of social change. Instead law has never been more important as one of the ways in which planning and predictability occur and as a component of custom and habit and a mechanism of enabling cooperative behavior, sometimes through enforcement, at other times through suggestion, and at still other times through the sheer force of moral argument. Legal institutions can mediate disputes in ways that neither social nor political institutions are able to do. Law can, however, provide a structure for disagreement, claims, and judgments that can in the future be overturned or superseded in light of newer disagreements. This has particular advantages when applied to human rights conflicts, both massive human rights disasters such as genocide and everyday human rights violations that take place below the international radar screen.

Law and courts have a continuing role in working out which rights ought to apply within a national system. The notion of "right" serves to define certain legal powers held by an individual against a government and also provides the master image for a philosophy of human nature, individuals, and their societies. It operates as a legal norm for everyday events and as an underlying justification of society. Haltingly international human rights are normalizing the *ideal* of such norms in a national legal system. Indeed the driving assumption behind massive international, regional, and national programs that promote the rule of law has been that formal legal order will reduce violence and increase political responsiveness. While reliable methods of measuring rule of law are yet to be fully developed, functioning courts are usually accepted as an indicator of political responsiveness of governments towards their people than where courts are either corrupt or otherwise dysfunctional.

Regional Human Rights Courts for Culture

While the history of international human rights has often been a contradiction of its own principles of human equality, the underlying values of rights have continued as catalysts for legal change. After the Cold War ended in 1989, in the heady early days of new constitutions and bills of rights in the 1990s, great things were expected from international law. Some expectations were probably unrealistic. It is fanciful, for example, to expect the criminal prosecution of a single *genocidaire* to heal instantaneously deep rifts between neighbors caused by civil conflict. Trials may be an important symbolic step in the recovery of trust, but law cannot be expected to perform the work that can only come through everyday iterations of cordial relations. Societies are comprised of subsets of people who hold many values. The multicultural critique accurately points out how cultural difference poses challenges to universal standards of human rights.

To point out the limitations of the international human rights system, however, only increases the urgency to urge refinements to legal principles and legal institutions. My response to the multicultural critique is, as I show in Chapter 5, that the human rights vision of regional human rights courts can be a credible part of legal internationalism because courts are uniquely equipped to broker different cultural values through principles and process.

Regional institutions are particularly well placed to offer reflective equilibrium between general international norms and particular cultures. Regional human rights courts can participate in defining how the standards of human rights ought to be applied by stepping in to interpret the tension between local practices and international treaty standards.[76] Whereas international human rights documents declare universal principles, regional documents are often more specific, adding new rights or refining others and taking into account special differences within the particular region and between one region and another. International principles can be cashed out in regional standards. Allowing regional variation through principled legal concepts can have value, especially for controversial issues that have previously been resistant to UN prompting.

Today's Language of International Human Rights

All the contemporary talk about globalization and civil society has not yet resolved *which* human rights, among the ever-enlarging list that is the stuff of international treaties, are the most essential part of each government's obligation

to its citizens. The Declaration of Human Rights was the result of intense negotiations among people representing different cultural and religious traditions as
well as "new" and "old" democracies. As a compromise document, it contains

> the first-generation political and civil rights found in the British, French, and
> American revolutionary declarations of the seventeenth and eighteenth centu-
> ries: protections of life, liberty, and property; and freedoms of speech, religion,
> and assembly. It also included the second-generation economic and social rights
> found in late nineteenth and early twentieth century constitutions such as those
> of Sweden, Norway, the Soviet Union, and several Latin American countries:
> rights to work, education, and basic subsistence.[77]

The peculiarity of the development of rights in the West was that a prohibition on the exercise of power (freedom *from* torture) became something
belonging to individuals as part of their inherent status as citizens (right *to*
bodily integrity). Crucial to the Western democratic tradition and political
theory of the last three centuries, but not necessarily to other non-Western
societies, is a philosophical view that emphasizes the right of individuals to
consent to the arrangements under which they live. These two levels connect
when they are steadily promoted in a legal system, and they are increasingly
being formalized in charters of rights in many post–Cold War constitutions.

International human rights advocates articulate norms of dignity, fairness,
and decency broken down into categories of "negative"—civil and political—
and "positive"—social, economic, and cultural—rights. Negative rights—
ensuring nondiscrimination in public institutions, for example—assume a
smaller role for governments and a larger role for private action groups. Positive rights, on the other hand, expect the government to play a larger role.
Whereas civil and political rights are the priority of Western governments,
governments and advocates in Africa and parts of Latin America and Asia try
to make social and economic rights more central.

Social rights have often been represented as incompatible with the rule
of law, especially in the U.S. The notion that welfare structures impair the
rule of law goes back to its earliest expression, when in the U.K. Albert Venn
Dicey discredited the very notion of an administrative state apparatus.[78] In the
United States the term "rule of law" emerged in general usage in the late 1930s
at the time of the construction of the New Deal welfare apparatus. It soon became shorthand to distinguish liberal democracies from communist regimes,
the latter being the supposed champions of social and economic rights. Still

later, critical legal scholars expressed outright hostility to a notional rule of law instead of real social justice.

Through the mid-twentieth-century welfare services expanded greatly in many industrial countries, coexisting uneasily with expansive human rights concerns. For many political conservatives, social rights fall outside the ordinary orbit of human rights, not necessarily as a matter of theory but as a matter of political history. In a debate that has been polarized from the outset, both sides have seen civil and political rights as consistent with private protections from government while viewing it as distinct from the discretionary or interventionist state action needed to ensure the availability of social rights. The great majority of human rights activists either focused exclusively on civil and political rights or invoked social and economic rights primarily through the lens of prior discriminatory access.[79] Especially in the U.S., but also among those who are regarded as legal scholars in the classical analytical tradition, civil and political rights are viewed as inviolable, while social and economic rights are considered negotiable. When, for example, the International Court of Justice defined the rule of law to embrace "the establishment of the social, economic, educational, and cultural conditions which are essential to the full development" of the human person, British analytical legal philosopher Joseph Raz criticized the court for its "promiscuous" usage of the rule of law.[80]

Today, even with rule of law ideas resurgent in the two decades since the collapse of communism in Eastern Europe, human rights are still rarely included in the same sentence as social and economic rights or welfare. The relative silence on social rights in rule-of-law literature is especially striking given the otherwise systematic nurturing of "rights awareness."[81] In its transnational context a tacit consensus encourages key actors to avoid this vocabulary altogether in favor of "poverty reduction" and "governance."[82] Despite this almost allergic reaction to the terminology of social and economic rights, there is ample evidence that today's governments and citizens alike have assumptions about their respective roles that are different from those of earlier generations. Citizens in even moderately functioning states now expect their governments to provide vaccinations for children (the right to health) and some basic public education services that depend upon the central allocation of government resources and distribution among the population (the right to education).

The distinction between civil and political rights on the one hand, and social and economic rights on the other, is controversial and has different impacts in different countries. For example, Nobel Prize–winning economist

Amartya Sen argues that poverty is not simply low income but also the deprivation of freedom and equality.[83] For Sen, being able to exercise fully or to realize these human capabilities and capacities is crucial to improving the quality of people's lives, the goal of development. Quality of life can be assessed and measured by universal norms, such as human dignity, bodily integrity, and basic political rights, liberties, and economic opportunities. This approach to human rights stresses that human beings need the full panoply of social, political, and economic rights in order to exercise optimally their central human functions and capabilities.

A second level of debate involves who the holder of a human right ought to be, an individual or a group? The mainstream view sees rights as a relation between the individual and the state, where the former is a bearer of rights guaranteed by, or held against, the latter. In this view there are no grounds for arguing that liberal societies should subsidize minority rights, because group boundaries may become individual barriers that protect a group's culture from insiders' questioning by suppressing the choices of an individual and limiting the choices of future generations for the benefit of their elders.[84] Others find group rights to be philosophically justified on the basis that human identity derives from one's ethnic or cultural group. Proponents of group rights prioritize legal protection of markers of group of identity, such as government funding for teaching a minority language in schools.[85] Hierarchies within the group pose a problem for negotiating group rights within a dominant society, often since the members doing the negotiating are an elite who may not represent the interests of other members.[86]

In the chapters that follow, I will develop arguments that law has a critical role to play in these debates and that the philosophical premises of the international human rights system have continued validity. The correct response to the critiques of international human rights is to retain the values embodied in the international human rights system while adapting legal institutions and methodologies to meet contemporary challenges. In the Western tradition human rights do two things: first, they express norms of conduct and, second and equally important, they articulate the underlying justification for those norms. The evolution of Western rights is a legal tradition, legitimating certain kinds of legal moves and empowering certain kinds of people to make them, but equally important it is a moral tradition that stretches from classical Greek and Roman writings about political organization through the European secular and scientific revolutions that still inform modern constitutions.

In this opening chapter I have set out the paradox of human rights today, a fast-developing topic of political thought with particular roots in European history that encounters three contemporary critiques. Sovereignty, civil society, and multiculturalism each pose a challenge to crafting a workable legal apparatus for human rights.

Twentieth-century confidence in universal human rights, even in a pluralistic world, has led to the creation of an international legal system that seeks to promote and sometimes even enforce human rights. Chapter 2 looks at the advantages and disadvantages of this system and concludes that a new institutional feature, the hybrid court, can instruct institutional development of human rights under today's conditions of pluralism.

Chapters 3, 4, and 5 set out a three-part agenda for refinement of the international human rights notions, methods, and institutions. Chapter 3 takes up the sovereignty critique and addresses the consequences of globalization on sovereignty. I argue that the legal and political story about the development of the modern state has overlooked key aspects that are vital for contemporary conditions. Sovereignty today should be understood as relational rather than autonomous. Humanitarian intervention and promotion of democracy ought not be seen as interchangeable, either philosophically or pragmatically.

Chapter 4 takes up the civil society critique and examines the claim that law has been displaced by civil society and economic activity. I argue that a rapidly changing world order, one with dynamic economic relations and occasional catastrophic collective security problems, more than ever needs a stronger human rights structure, one that can wrestle with both the sovereignty and the cultural identity issues. I offer "margin of appreciation" as an adjudicative approach that can assist human rights courts to weigh claims of autonomous sovereignty and cultural identity.

Chapter 5 takes up the multicultural critique and argues for the enhancement and development of the regional system of human rights courts. Regionalism is already a force that has adjusted to the era of global trade relations and regional security. Adapting the insight of hybrid courts to include the articulation and administration of human rights is best rooted in principled human rights variation. I argue that properly designed regional human rights courts are uniquely suited to adjudicate human rights claims for cultural exceptionalism.

Chapter 6 draws these themes together and suggests how a multipronged approach might be applied to some controversial international human rights issues.

Chapter 2

Institutionalizing
International Human Rights

Introduction

The political career of Charles Ghankay Taylor, former president of Liberia and a man with a $2 million U.S. government bounty on his head, ended in 2006 on a windswept tarmac in Monrovia, Liberia. UN officials manacled him, charged him with war crimes and crimes against humanity, and conveyed him to the holding cells of the Special Court for Sierra Leone in Freetown. From 1989 to 1997 Taylor had led the National Patriotic Front of Liberia (NPFL), a rebel group that sought to unseat Liberia's president, Samuel Doe. In 1997 Taylor was chosen president in an election in which one of his campaign slogans ran, "He killed my Ma, he killed my Pa, but I will vote for him."[1]

During his seven-year presidency, Taylor allegedly oversaw the death and mutilation of tens of thousands of people, embezzled a personal fortune from illicit trade in diamonds, and even committed cannibalism. His presidency was marked by the forcible recruitment of child soldiers—girls and boys as young as nine years—into Liberian government armed forces.[2] Young boys who put up resistance were flogged and sent to the front. Young women and girls were raped and forced to become "wives" to the soldiers and male child combatants. Children attempting to flee with their parents towards the border with Sierra Leone were stopped at checkpoints and taken away from parents to a military base, where their heads were shaved and they were brutalized. Those children whose parents could not afford to buy their freedom were immediately sent to the front. Under Taylor's command these children were part of military forces that conducted cross-border raids and human rights abuses in neighboring countries, including operations for the Revolutionary United Front (RUF), a Sierra Leonean rebel group.[3] Taylor gave the RUF guns and other military equipment in exchange for diamonds, helping to fuel the RUF's activities that included mass rapes, cutting off the limbs of its civilian victims, and "Operation Pay Yourself," which encouraged troops to loot anything they could find.

These human rights atrocities occurred despite the fact that Liberia had signed or ratified the core United Nations human rights conventions and treaties, including the Convention on the Rights of the Child (CRC), which prohibits recruitment and deployment in the armed forces of children under fifteen. The Liberian government during Taylor's presidency even filed human rights reports with the UN committee of the CRC describing how the government was taking steps to comply with its international human rights obligations. Not surprisingly, these reports failed to include accounts of Taylor's forced conscription of children or his knowledge that his own forces were assaulting and raping young girls and boys.[4]

In 2003 Taylor finally gave in to mounting international pressure and went into exile in the Nigerian tourist city of Calabar. Although the Nigerian authorities agreed in 2006 to return him to Liberia at the request of that country's new president, Ellen Johnson-Sirleaf, Taylor instead "disappeared" from his luxury home in exile. He was eventually captured near the Nigeria-Cameroon border, trying to flee the country with sacks of U.S. dollars and euros in a car bearing diplomatic license plates. Taylor was arrested and clapped into handcuffs. He soon found himself in a cell in Freetown under jurisdiction of the Special Court for Sierra Leone.[5]

The Special Court for Sierra Leone is an ad hoc body that comprises both international and national features and is referred to as a "hybrid" or "mixed" international tribunal. It was established in 2002 through an agreement between the United Nations and the government of Sierra Leone. As a "hybrid" the special court differs from other international tribunals such as the international criminal tribunals for the former Yugoslavia and Rwanda. A key difference is that the bench is composed of both Sierra Leonean and international judges, as well as by local and international staff. The court, based in Freetown, also has a vigorous outreach program to spread news of its activities beyond the capital to rural areas where most of the population lives. The court's mandate is to "prosecute persons who bear the greatest responsibility for serious violations of international humanitarian law" committed in Sierra Leone and also to adjudicate violations of Sierra Leonean domestic law, including crimes against humanity and war crimes, and to address other serious violations of international humanitarian law, such as sexual violence, abductions, forced labor, recruitment of child soldiers, and looting.[6]

The Sierra Leone court began trials in 2004. Taylor is its highest-profile defendant and the first African head of state to be indicted for serious crimes under international law by an internationalized criminal court. He is charged with eleven counts of war crimes, crimes against humanity, and other serious violations of international humanitarian law committed by Liberian forces in neighboring Sierra Leone.[7] The alleged crimes cover murdering and mutilating civilians, including cutting off their limbs, using women and girls as sex slaves, and abducting adults and children and forcing them to perform forced labor or become fighters during Sierra Leone's uprisings. Nine other defendants are on trial, all like Taylor charged with crimes committed during Sierra Leone's brutal 1989–2002 civil wars. Like Slobodan Milošević and Saddam Hussein before him, Taylor claims that no court, especially a foreign court, has the power to place him on trial. When initial proceedings began in June 2007, Taylor declared in a letter that his lawyer read to the court that he was boycotting the proceedings because he alleged they would not be fair and impartial. Despite such tactics Taylor's trial started in June 2007. Because of fears of fresh instability in Sierra Leone and Liberia, the trial has been transferred to The Hague, and the Sierra Leone court is implementing procedures to ensure that Sierra Leoneans, both urban and rural, are updated daily on the progress of the trial. It is expected the trial will cost around $62 million.[8]

Unlike the Milošević and Saddam Hussein trials, however, the Taylor proceedings have attracted little criticism for being an instrument of "victors' justice." The president of the Appeals Chamber is a Sierra Leonean lawyer, and of the nine other justices, one is Sierra Leonean, one is Nigerian, and another is from Cameroon. Three other judges are from postcolonial countries (Sri Lanka, Samoa, and Senegal).[9] Unlike the Milošević trial held at the International Criminal Tribunal for the Former Yugoslavia (also in The Hague), the distant location of the Taylor trial is less problematic to the Sierra Leone population because criminal trials against other human rights perpetrators are being conducted in Freetown.[10] Unlike the trial of Saddam Hussein, which was heard before a single Iraqi judge in Baghdad, the Freetown court has attracted little criticism for parochialism or political bias.[11]

The Special Court for Sierra Leone exemplifies a new phenomenon in promoting international human rights. First, it is part of the broader revival of international criminal law over the past decade and a half. The Nuremberg and Tokyo trials after World War II represented the initial phase of using criminal prosecutions as a tool of international human rights, but that sort of legal mechanism stopped through the Cold War years. The use of international criminal law for human rights ends was revived in 1994 with the creation of the International Criminal Tribunal for the Former Yugoslavia (ICTY) and the International Criminal Tribunal for Rwanda (ICTR) and further advanced in 2002 with the formation of the International Criminal Court, now the top international criminal body. The Sierra Leone court and several others like it exemplify an even more recent refinement, however—the hybrid court. This development merges international and national legal institutions in new ways.

In the 1980s, before these new legal developments, the "soft" law of international treaties had been the main plank of the international human rights system. From the 1950s to early 1990s the UN human rights treaty system developed in the hope that national governments would incorporate international standards into their own domestic legal systems. Human rights activists argued that accession to an international human rights treaty demonstrated a principled commitment to international human rights values on the part of a national government. There is some evidence of a causal link between international law and a government's promotion of human rights within a domestic legal system, and it was claimed that this link demonstrates the influence of international law in changing values within states.[12]

With the appearance on the scene of new institutions of international criminal law, however, today's international human rights system has both "hard" and "soft" law—criminal courts and human rights treaties. Each has achieved some good human rights results, but each has limitations. In this chapter, I clarify the advantages and disadvantages of both in the current international system of human rights, identifying features that ought to be retained and suggesting where change and reform are needed. The international human rights treaty system of "soft" standards is ambitious but often lacks bite. On the other hand the international criminal system of "hard" legal standards attacks the most egregious mass human rights violations but cannot address the everyday failures of governments to protect their citizens' rights.

As I will show, these drawbacks have been intensified by today's global conditions and philosophical debates about these new conditions. Hybrid courts, as a more recent legal innovation that uniquely fuses international law within a national legal system, offer a subtle modification to the dual system of treaties and criminal law. I examine hybrid courts as an ingenious way of resolving some of the problems in the human rights system, a structural approach that can go beyond its current criminal usage to more accessible civil and administrative contexts.

Difficulties of Instituting International Human Rights

The history of the Universal Declaration of Human Rights in the late 1940s provides a vivid account of an international agreement as a maelstrom of dissent, criticism, optimism, and hope.[13] The 1945 United Nations Charter, unlike that of the League of Nations before it, was signed by every state in the world (which at the time numbered only 56, compared to 192 today). International law was progressively institutionalized in United Nations documents and instruments, and the massive expansion of international bureaucracy and specialized agencies since 1945 marks the transition of international law from a bare-bones system of formal rules to a dense system of coordinated programs.

There was much controversy over *which* rights were truly international. Some countries considered social and economic rights the top priority. Others advocated a balance between traditional political and civil rights on the one hand and newer social and economic rights on the other.[14] For the first time, however, and notwithstanding these differences, international human rights documents progressively took on legal language in the decades following World War II. International human rights agreements now cover a vast range of government activities. Most countries are members of the principal UN human rights treaties bodies that monitor national governments' implementation of political and economic rights, nondiscrimination against women, children's rights, the prohibition of torture, and migrants' rights.[15] For all the flaws that its critics then and now are justified in pointing out, this development is vitally significant because of the legal framework it instituted. Its accomplishments are profound.

The UN Declaration of Human Rights is not a legally binding document, however. Many people at the time the declaration was made saw the lack of enforceability as a fundamental flaw.[16] Despite the public commitment that states make when they sign international human rights treaties and covenants, governments routinely fall well below their international human rights promises. These shortcomings fall into three main categories.

Domestic Implementation Problems

If the number of new laws about human rights were the test of national commitment to international human rights principles, then it could be said that the international human rights dream has been achieved. After the fall of communism the democracy movement of the 1990s led to a flurry of human rights laws in national systems. Between 1990 and 2005 more than fifty new constitutions were written in Europe, Latin America, and Africa (Africa alone accounting for thirty-six), each containing extensive references to fundamental human rights.[17] Besides new legal and political institutions, many nations with authoritarian pasts set up institutions to reveal previous human rights abuses; by 2005, for example, twenty-four truth and reconciliation commissions had been established to look into the violations of former governments or military juntas.[18]

Nation-states are both the strongest and the weakest link in the implementation of international human rights. While virtually every state in the world has signed the UN Charter and the UN Declaration of Human Rights and has committed its governments to putting those principles into legal effect, international human rights treaties have no *direct* legislative effect within most national legal systems.[19] National governments, not the international community, administer everyday human rights standards within their countries. The head of government as the representative of a government's executive branch signs international agreements through a ratification process, but democratic divisions in at least some constitutional structures mean that the country's parliament or legislature may not be willing to endorse that ratification. Functional and cooperative national systems—the political systems that write the laws and legal systems that enforce them—form the essential baseline for human rights protection that impacts people's everyday lives.

The paradox of contemporary human rights is that despite the astonishing spread of human rights discourse, particularized enforcement is still highly imperfect. The legal implementation of international human rights is extremely problematic. The human rights record of national governments varies immensely. Differences in levels of national political commitment to human rights, national economic capacity to introduce human rights reforms, and degrees of national judicial enforcement create a colossal human rights implementation predicament. The one-size-fits-all approach to universal human rights standards does not capture the disparate willingness and capacity of states to implement those rights. It is a problem that the UN human rights system struggles with and can only partially resolve.

Some countries are reluctant to incorporate international human rights standards in their domestic laws because they see them as a challenge to their sovereignty. States frequently use the shield of sovereignty to minimize their international human rights responsibilities, as when the governments of The Sudan and Colombia arbitrarily arrest and detain opponents on the grounds of government necessity.[20] In other cases a country might refuse to accept international assistance for human rights action, even though its domestic legal system is struggling. Chile, for example, has systematically rejected requests by several European states to extradite some of the worst criminals from the military regime of Augusto Pinochet, claiming sovereign authority to punish crimes committed on its own territory. Chile's domestic criminal process is slow and the victims and witnesses of the Pinochet era are getting older, yet national interests under the banner of sovereignty prevents external involvement. Argentina on the other hand has overturned the amnesty laws of its military junta. The Argentine congress repealed the laws in 2003 and the supreme court confirmed the action in a decision in 2005. In its decision the supreme court referred to the jurisprudence of the Inter-American Court in stating that the junta's amnesty laws constituted a national obstacle to the duty of state parties to the American Convention to prosecute and punish "grave breaches to the international human rights law."[21]

Even countries with high-functioning legal systems vary tremendously in their legal deference to the international human rights system. The United States, for example, with its independent judiciary, constitutional protections for human rights, and long tradition of liberalism, is often considered the flag-bearer for political rights. The justices of the U.S. Supreme Court, however, have been sharply divided on the relevance of international human rights law to U.S. constitutional interpretation, and, in comparison with many other countries, neither U.S. federal nor state courts take much account of international standards in deciding cases that come before them.[22] In other countries where national human rights laws are far more rudimentary than those in the U.S., judges can do little to enforce international treaty standards of human rights without the necessary legal tools. Autocratic or authoritarian governments may prevent their courts from enforcing those domestic human rights laws that do exist. A functioning legal enforcement framework is crucial to better human rights, but according to the international good-government watchdog group Transparency International, at least one-fifth of judiciaries around the world are either not fully independent of their national government or are downright corrupt.[23]

Sometimes participation in the international human rights treaty system is merely a fig leaf for national governments that wish to appear as if they are serious about implementing change. For example, in the early 1990s numerous human rights commissions were established across Africa by governments making the transition to democracy after repressive or authoritarian single-party rule. These commissions had very mixed results. In Cameroon for example the credibility and autonomy of the human rights commission was tremendously hindered by strong presidential control over its operation and the appointment of commissioners. The Tunisian commission was regarded as nothing more than a mouthpiece for the defense of government abuses. While legislation established commissions in Ethiopia, Mali, Niger, and the Central African Republic, little care was taken to set them up in ways that could inform legal reform.[24] The African cases demonstrate that in order for international human rights treaty commitments to mean something on the ground two preconditions are necessary: a functional legal system *and* a national government genuinely driven to attain international human rights standards.

Still other countries are simply too poor or overstretched to incur the costs of administering human rights. For example, when some states ratified the Convention on the Elimination of Discrimination against Women (CEDAW), they tempered their treaty commitments with "reservations" because they could not afford to implement them. India supports the requirement of Article 16(2) to establish a marriage registry, but achieving compliance with a registry is not feasible given the many variations in customs, religions, and literacy levels that exist across India's vast population.[25] Similarly Mexico's reservation to CEDAW makes it clear that the state will only grant "material benefits" under the convention as its economic resources permit.[26]

Nonetheless, human rights are urgent, and new problems are emerging because of new global economic conditions. Globalization has brought new wealth but it also brings new human rights issues. For example there has been a decline in the membership of trade unions over the past fifteen years owing to the spread of privatization and globalized production, reducing the leverage of unions to battle with employers for workers' rights. The relative impotence of unions has affected many of the world's poor, and this has led to a reversal of human rights in countries of the global South such as India, where forced labor is becoming the new form of indentured servitude.[27] The loosening of the ban on citizens' travel to the West following the collapse of the Soviet Bloc has created massive new prostitution and other human trafficking opportunities, leading in some places to a significant decline in the human rights of women and children.[28] In the post–Cold War period, the surge of ethnic conflicts around the world has vastly increased the numbers of children recruited into armed conflicts.[29] Each of these problems shares the feature of a national government unwilling, or simply unable, to enforce its international human rights treaty obligations.

International Bureaucracy Problems

The principal UN human rights mechanism of "soft" human rights treaties is supplemented by several other methods of legal or institutional reinforcement. They are not coordinated approaches and they produce uneven results.

United Nations Human Rights Committees   With jurisdiction over all the countries in the world, it is hardly surprising that the UN human rights treaty system is cumbersome and slow. Seven different committees track the human rights performance of 192 countries. National governments are obligated to submit regular reports of their human rights progress to these committees. The committees also receive reports from local nongovernmental organizations and will sometimes travel to a country to conduct an inspection. If a government is lagging on its international human rights promises, a committee will report this in its public recommendations. Beyond "naming and shaming" a government for its poor human rights performance, however, UN human rights committees can do little more to prod national governments to keep their treaty promises.

CEDAW again provides an illustration of the relative impotence of UN human rights committees. Like the other main treaty bodies, CEDAW reviews each country's reports on women's rights, which are due from the government at specified times under the terms of the convention. The committee has a massive backlog of reports; its resources are so thinly stretched that, for example, a report due from Libya in 1990 and finally submitted in 1999 has been assigned for review in 2009.[30] Attempts have been made to expand CEDAW's capacity: its session times have been extended in recent years,[31] and a pre-session working group has been created that prepares lists of questions to which submitting states can respond in advance.[32] These efforts have not solved the problem, however.[33] Were it not for the failure of many state parties to submit their reports on time, or at all, the committee's workload would be even more crippling.

Countries Reporting on Each Other   "Naming and shaming" as a tactic is not necessarily more effective when it is done by powerful individual countries virtually replicating the UN human rights committee's reporting processes.[34] The U.S. Department of State submits "country reports" to Congress each year, not only about countries that receive U.S. foreign assistance but *all* countries that are UN members.[35] For example, for more than a decade before his resignation in 2008, Zimbabwe's Pres. Robert Mugabe had been a target of both UN and U.S. criticism. When thousands of makeshift houses in several townships were bulldozed by the Zimbabwe government in 2005, both the UN and the U.S. State Department published critical reports.[36] The Mugabe government in Harare promptly responded by terminating a U.S.-funded program to develop the committee system in the country's parliament, accusing the U.S. of intending "regime change" and the forced removal of President Mugabe.[37] The 2005 UN report suffered the same fate after it was labeled by Mugabe as an example of Western imperialist control in the guise of universal human rights.[38] Mugabe repeated his criticism as recently as July 2007, accusing Western governments of using human rights as part of a plot to destabilize his twenty-eight-year rule.[39] Similarly, British Prime Minister Gordon Brown's trenchant criticism of Mugabe's refusal to hand over political power to his opponents who won the popular vote in Zimbabwe's general election in early February 2008 produced furious claims from Mugabe of "British imperialism."

Using Another Country's National Court System for Mass Atrocities   Another fallback strategy when the UN human rights system fails is the use of national courts in one country to pursue individual human rights abusers in another. This is a new and still evolving approach to human rights advocacy, one that inevitably raises thorny interpretative problems of sovereignty and multiculturalism. It is a practice that began in the U.S. in the 1980s with a decision handed down by a U.S. court of appeals in *Filártiga v. Peña-Irala*.[40] Relatives of a Paraguayan national who was kidnapped, tortured, and murdered in Paraguay brought a civil suit in the U.S under the U.S. Alien Torts Claim Act. It was claimed that a U.S. court could adjudicate the case because the murderer, a Paraguayan police official, now lived in the U.S. The U.S. court decided it would honor the international prohibition against torture, regardless of the place of the violation or the nationalities of the victim and the perpetrator, ordering Peña to pay $10.4 million to the victim's family. Since the *Filártiga* decision, about 100 similar suits relating to human rights violations in other countries have been filed in the U.S., using the massive monetary civil judgments of U.S. courts as a way of pursuing foreign human rights violations.

More recently, in 1999, the law lords of the British House of Lords (Britain's highest court of appeal until 2009) upheld the arrest in England of former Chilean president Augusto Pinochet on charges brought by a Spanish court of torture and conspiracy in violation of international human rights treaty law.[41] Although Britain returned Pinochet to Chile rather than Spain because of his age and ill health, the law lords' ruling established the precedent that former heads of state cannot shelter in Britain if they are facing legal proceedings elsewhere for egregious human rights violations.

While both the *Filártiga* and the *Pinochet* decisions have been hailed as signals that some national courts may be willing to act on the basis of international law, it is unlikely that national courts will open the floodgates to cases originating with another country's human rights problems. There may be exceptions for a cause célèbre or in a case where a human rights violator is alleged to have committed torture or mass murder, but the vast majority of individual human rights violations are not spectacular international incidents, leaving them with neither a national nor an international legal forum.

Everyday Cultural Behaviors Neglected   Human rights violations justified as "culture" are the most resistant to UN pressures of "naming and shaming" because governments can discount the UN as culturally out of touch, or even imperialistic. Criticisms from rich Western countries such as the U.S. meet the same fate. Both types of pressure have little effect on governments that isolate their countries from the international community.

Governments are particularly resistant to attempts of others to intervene in its cultural practices, and international bureaucracies are the least likely to influence such a government's behavior. For example, "honor killings"— women murdered by brothers and fathers for having sex outside marriage or refusing an arranged marriage—are not uncommon in traditional, male-dominated Arab societies as well as in predominantly Muslim communities. They are now on the rise in Europe's Middle Eastern and Asian immigrant communities living in places such as Albania, Brazil, Uganda, and Turkey. Fadime Şahindal, a twenty-six-year-old Kurdish Muslim university student with a Swedish boyfriend, was murdered by her father in Sweden in 2002. He insisted that she marry a man from Turkey, their home country. A year later, in Britain, Abdalla Yones, a Kurdish Muslim, stabbed his sixteen-year-old daughter, Heshu, and slit her throat after she started a relationship with a

Christian boyfriend. Over a four-month period in 2005, six Muslim women living in Berlin were murdered by family members for bringing dishonor on their families. Yones was sentenced by a British court to jail for life, but each year in the Middle East the murder of hundreds of women and girls by male family members goes unpunished.[42] The execution of a female family member for perceived misuse of her sexuality is a difficult social and political issue. Legitimacy for such murders stems from a complex code of honor ingrained in the consciousness of some sectors of those societies, and local activists campaigning for equality find it difficult to stop them.[43]

UN institutions can be out of step with contemporary international conditions, as even the UN acknowledges. When for example the UN secretary-general's 2004 High Level Panel on Threats, Challenges and Change emphasized the interconnectedness of terrorism, civil wars, and extreme poverty, then-UN Secretary-General Kofi Annan enthused about the "opportunity to refashion and renew our institutions."[44] In the meantime, while this reform process takes place, the gap between international human rights treaty promises and national human rights realities continues under a UN system that is slow and sometimes perceived as irrelevant. With memories of empire so recent in large parts of Africa, Asia, and Latin America, it seems unlikely that the UN human rights system on its own can do the job of galvanizing governments. Problems with the UN treaty system that result from the sheer size of the organization, together with national implementation problems owing to different levels of political will, economic capacity, and legal enforcement, indicate the need for approaches besides the UN committees. The best chance to exert positive influence comes from other countries in that region, other postcolonial neighbors that are immune from the charges of imperialism that are leveled at the UN, the U.S., or Europe.

Credibility Problems: The Cultural Critique

The cultural critique has it that universal standards of human rights lack credibility because cultural differences are expected to give way to universal international human rights standards. Of the three problems dogging the UN human rights system the cultural one is the thorniest. Cultural critics argue that universal international human rights standards overemphasize the existence of shared human identity and underemphasize deep cultural cleavages in human identity. International human rights are then criticized for naively papering over important cultural differences and making false assertions about universal norms.[45]

Putting multiculturalism into the system of states with international law becomes even more complex than an individual raising cultural issues in a national court. In the international setting multiculturalism requires administering a human rights system premised upon a universal framework as well as requiring respect for cultural diversity. Women's rights demonstrate the intricacy of multiculturalism on the international stage. Some women's rights activists in the developing world reject Western feminism because it derives from the Western philosophical tradition of individual autonomy. In a replication of the "culture wars" in the West, these philosophical differences are used by interest groups on both sides of the political fence as part of strategic jockeying. For example when a non-Western government enters a reservation to the CEDAW treaty on the grounds that the treaty goes against its culture, the government's position may not be representative of the opinion of women in that country. Instead, that government may simply be leveraging the philosophical uncertainty to provide a convenient excuse for avoiding any challenge to the status quo.

In an important normative sense the cultural critique goes to the very heart of the UN's credibility as an international organization representing all of the world's cultures. In international human rights the right to freedom of cultural expression can directly conflict with basic human rights of bodily integrity, gender nondiscrimination, and individual autonomy. The UN's goal of "equality among all people"—the central tenet of Article 1 of the UN Declaration of Human Rights—coexists with Article 22, "the right to culture." These two goals—uniform human rights standards on one hand and a nuanced approach to cultural difference on the other—are conceptually in tension and even more difficult to administer in practice.

At its core the cultural critique of human rights takes philosophical issue with the a priori assumption that a one-size-fits-all approach to human rights can apply to the world's many different cultures. It is a position taken by some postcolonial scholars in the global South and some left-wing political figures in the global North. The cultural critique of human rights claims that *any* universal attempts to fix standards about the good life are an imposition of political will from the outside. Rather, international human rights are a sham, simply Western imperialism cloaked in high-sounding rhetoric about shared brotherhood and belief in universal standards.

This position implies that there can be no genuinely universal human rights, none that can justifiably be ascribed to all human beings irrespective of their membership in this or that political community, nation, religion, or ethnic group. It also implicates the international institutions designed to secure compliance with international human rights treaties. At its strongest, it is a root-and-branch denial of international human rights, akin to saying that the UN is an emperor without clothes, with no culturally neutral foundations upon which to declare human rights.

Multiculturalism as "cultural accommodation" is often suggested as the way out of this philosophical thicket, a better alternative to universal standards of human rights.[46] Multiculturalism is cited, for example, when an immigrant or minority defendant raises a cultural defense in a Western court, claiming that he was unaware of the illegality of his actions because of his cultural background—asserting, for instance, that physically assaulting his wife to chastise her would be acceptable in his country of origin.[47] By using this defense, a defendant hopes to have criminal charges against him under national laws dropped or at least to have his punishment significantly reduced.

Because of the principle of universalism that underwrites the UN's existence, the UN human rights system cannot easily provide a forum for these debates. Debate is desperately needed, however, because the fact is that the cultural critique, like the sovereignty critique, makes some simple errors when it rationalizes disregard for international human rights treaties. Whereas the sovereignty critique overlooks the effects of globalization, the cultural critique overlooks the influence of the international human rights movement—a political and social movement that motivates domestic populations. The lack of a UN forum to debate such subtleties simply encourages less compliance with international standards, which in turn erodes the entire system's claim to legitimacy. In the meantime human rights abuses continue.

Achieving Human Rights Through International Treaties

The UN Human Rights Committee System

International treaties are the core of the human rights system, a major institutional achievement that until the 1990s was also the only formal international mechanism that examined the progress of human rights within states. The language of human rights has become so ubiquitous today that it is hard to imagine that the first UN human rights treaty bodies were not really active until the 1960s, almost twenty years after the UN Declaration of Human Rights.[48] Although Cold War tensions made it difficult to achieve broad consensus about the meaning of universal human rights, in 1966 the UN adopted three new covenants on human rights: the International Convention on the Elimination of All Forms of Racial Discrimination (ICERD),[49] the International Covenant on Economic, Social and Cultural Rights (ICESCR),[50] and the International Covenant on Civil and Political Rights (ICCPR).[51] By this time the nascent regional human rights systems of the European Coal and Steel Community (forerunner of the European Union and then comprising only six countries—Belgium, France, Italy, Luxembourg, The Netherlands, and West Germany) and the Organization of American States (of North, Central, and South America) had formed and were crafting their earliest regional human rights documents.

UN institutions were established to monitor the main UN treaties and covenants. The veteran was the UN Commission on Human Rights (UNCHR), formed under the Universal Declaration of Human Rights in 1947, and comprising (then) all fifty-three countries in the world. As the UN's principal mechanism and international forum that was concerned with the promotion and protection of human rights, the UNCHR was singularly unsuccessful.[52] Governments that violated human rights had equal status with those that did not, so the commission had little credibility. It was replaced in 2006 with the UN Human Rights Council, which has already been similarly criticized for being overly political. Even so, the council's status as a lead UN institution carries influence. For example, one of Raúl Castro's first official international acts upon stepping into office as Cuba's president in February 2008 was to sign onto both the ICCPR and the ICESCR and agree to open Cuba to the scrutiny of the council. Previously Cuba had determinedly resisted scrutiny by the human rights apparatus, accusing it of pro-U.S. bias. Cuba's actions in joining the top UN human rights treaty bodies are unlikely to make overnight changes to human rights practices on the island, but they demonstrate the isomorphic effect of international human rights as a movement that influences national governments over time.

There are seven major international human rights covenants, and each has its own committee responsible for monitoring and reporting on the performance of individual nation-states.[53] In addition to the committees for the International Covenant on Civil and Political Rights (ICCPR) and the International Covenant on Economic, Social, and Cultural Rights (ICESCR), the UN has established the United Nations Committee on the Elimination of Racial Discrimination (CERD); the United Nations Committee on the Elimination of Discrimination against Women (CEDAW); the Committee on the

Protection of the Rights of All Migrant Workers and Members of Their Families (CMW); the United Nations Committee against Torture (CAT); and the Committee on the Rights of the Child (CRC).

These committees use their mandates from the UN to collect data, monitor, and report back to other international organs as a monitoring and reviewing forum for the fulfillment of the states' obligations under each human rights treaty. All states that ratify a UN human rights treaty are required to submit a report as well as periodic brief updates to the treaty committee. These reports come before the committee for examination, and the committee in turn reports to the UN General Assembly with a summary, offering suggestions and recommendations.[54] Some of the committees can hear complaints by one government against another,[55] and some have procedures for an individual or a group of persons to file a complaint against their state.[56]

The work of the various UN human rights committees over the past years has unquestionably brought improvements in many countries. These improvements include amendments to national constitutions, changes in existing laws and regulations, and completely new laws to make domestic human rights violations a punishable offense in a national legal system. Procedures of dialogue developed by the committees have also been valuable because they allow for exchange of views among governments and a clearer analysis of human rights policies. For example at its 1989 session the CEDAW committee discussed the high incidence of violence against women, requesting information on this problem from all countries. In 1992 the committee adopted a requirement that national reports to the committee include statistical data on the incidence of violence against women. The extent of violence in women's private lives across cultures and countries has begun to be exposed through this simple measure.

Problems with Human Rights Treaties

The UN committee system has distinctive limitations, however. It is not clear that joining an international human rights treaty *necessarily* implies a national government's commitment to its principles. The UN bureaucratic processes are far from seamless, and governments can breach the procedures with relative impunity.

Joining an International Human Rights Treaty   While some empirical data support the idea that governments sign an international human rights treaty because they believe in its principles, there are other, less high-minded factors at work, both with respect to entry into the treaty system and to compliance with the treaty requirements. It seems that non-Western states are no less likely to ratify international treaties than Western states, though disagreements about human rights principles of culture and religion are just as likely today as were ideological conflicts during the Cold War. It also seems that the content of a treaty does not much affect the inclination of states to ratify it. Before the end of the Cold War, communist countries were no more likely to ratify the International Covenant on Economic, Social, and Cultural Rights, or less likely to ratify the International Covenant on Civil and Political Rights, than were noncommunist countries.[57]

Some have suggested that international conferences leading up to treaty signings are venues where states can be encouraged to sign on to human rights concerns and be coaxed to change fundamental preferences.[58] There is no solid empirical evidence to support this claim. On the contrary, such conferences may simply provide an opportunity for countries to dramatize their rhetorical, often superficial, commitment to international principles.[59] The type of government considering the treaty and the costs associated with treaty compliance seem to be the most reliable predictors for participation in the human rights treaty system. Countries with better human rights practices are more likely to ratify the two main human rights covenants (the ICCPR and the ICESCR) because they have nothing to lose by internationalizing their current practices. For example during the Cold War democratic countries were more likely to ratify the human rights covenants than countries with autocratic regimes because they were already doing what the covenants required. Today, postcommunist countries are likely to accede to both covenants, even though their political commitment to human rights now seems just as questionable as in the Cold War period.

The "costs" to governments of implementing the various treaties differ. The International Covenant on Economic, Social, and Cultural Rights, for example, has few monitoring and enforcement mechanisms, making the "cost" of treaty accession low. The International Covenant on Civil and Political Rights, on the other hand, has more stringent implementation and enforcement mechanisms. Autocratic governments are therefore unlikely to sign on to the ICCPR and more likely to sign on the ICESCR. States that have appalling human rights practices often seem to have joined to as many human rights treaties as some of the countries with the best human rights practices.[60] The only conclusion is that when treaty enforcement mechanisms are weak, a country may choose to enter into the treaty system for symbolic reasons. Treaty ratification may be nothing more than the desire to earn credentials as a good human rights member of the international community and the hope that other rewards, such as foreign trade and investment, might follow.

Effects Over Time of Joining International Human Rights Treaties   The longer-term effects of treaties on the human rights record of governments seem equally unclear. While some research has found that states that have joined the treaty system have better human rights records than those that have not, these data, not surprisingly, track along lines of democratic versus non-democratic countries. Paradoxically, other research seems to suggest that sometimes human rights have become worse after a government signed an international human rights treaty. In the same vein, research on the impact that ratification of the International Labor Organization's first child labor convention had upon child labor rates suggests that the formal treaty process had no significant effects.[61] This means that a causal connection between human rights treaties and human rights improvement on the ground may be tenuous at best and nonexistent at worst.[62] At best signing a treaty may confirm a government's preexisting commitment to human rights. At worst it may lead a government to believe that, having apparently satisfied its international audience, it can now do what it likes at home.

Failure to Report to UN Human Rights Committees   States routinely fail to submit their country reports to UN treaty committees on time or even at all. For example, the reports of Antigua and Barbuda to the UN Committee on the Elimination of Racial Discrimination for the period from 1989 through 2005 were submitted to the committee only in March 2007.[63] The committee's suggestions and recommendations do not carry legally binding status, which means that beyond showing bad faith towards their treaty-based obligations, defaulting state parties suffer no adverse consequences. According to Amnesty International, the UN Committee Against Torture gave Egypt nineteen recommendations in 2002, most of which have not been followed.[64] Such minimal enforcement mechanisms make international human rights treaties different from most other international arrangements. Unlike other subjects of international treaties such as trade, finance, or the law of the sea, the observation of international human rights standards within a state do not require the cooperation or approval of other states.[65]

These problems demonstrate that *all* the potential methods for inducing human rights improvements in a state need to be better understood. Some argue that the international human rights system should be updated with a better understanding of the processes whereby governments "acculturate" to newer beliefs about how countries should behave in the contemporary international system.[66] Acculturation begins when an institution such as a government identifies a norm that precipitates a conscious change on its practices, usually because the "bad" behavior is sanctioned and the "good" behavior is rewarded. Extended to human rights, this model suggests that human rights improvement will result from broad membership rules for treaty regimes with "[i]nstitutions . . . [that] advance the social processes by which states adopt norms identified with being a 'modern state.'"[67] At the very least the debates about accession to the human rights treaty system and subsequent enforcement treaty mechanisms point to gaps in the international human rights system that need to be narrowed.

Achieving Human Rights Through International Courts and Tribunals

International Courts as a Tool for Better Human Rights

When Charles Taylor stands before the Special Court for Sierra Leone to answer to charges of crimes against humanity, the international community watches a process that was forged in the aftermath of the Holocaust. Large-scale human rights violations were first criminalized in 1946, at the Nuremberg trials. The crimes of the Holocaust were considered so terrible that the legal principle was enunciated that the entire international community had a moral stake in bringing the criminals to justice.

The UN Convention on the Prevention and Punishment of the Crime of Genocide (1948) and the UN Convention against Torture and Other Cruel, Inhuman or Degrading Treatment or Punishment (1984) declare absolute bans—international "peremptory norms"—against genocide and torture as human rights violations that "outrage the conscience of mankind."[68] Although most governments agree that mass killing, especially when intended to wipe out a race, ethnic group, or religion, is unjustified under *any* moral paradigm or *any* test of practical necessity, the genocide convention and the torture convention proved virtually meaningless in their earliest days because the UN had no enforcement procedures with any bite. A 1950 recommendation by the International Law Commission (the ILC is a UN body formed in 1948 to gradually codify international law) to create an international criminal court languished under Cold War constraints.

All this changed in 1989 with the end of the Cold War. The number of UN peacekeeping operations dramatically increased—from seven in 1988 to sixteen in 2004—and other UN post-conflict peace-building activities surged.[69] This activity revitalized the ILC's recommendation and reintroduced the use of criminal law to enforce international human rights standards.

The International Court of Justice

Especially during the Cold War years the International Court of Justice (ICJ) was regarded as the standard-bearer of the post–World War II internationalist vision because all the members of the UN are ipso facto parties to the court. As the principal judicial organ of the United Nations and the only one with universal membership, the ICJ is based upon the principle of equal national sovereignty.[70] Until recently though, the International Court of Justice has had little role in promoting human rights, and even today its human rights role is marginal. Its importance lies in its very existence as a specifically *legal* international structure with global jurisdiction.

Under the court's founding statute, international law is both "positive"— the law of international treaties and charters—and comprises the norms and standards of international customs as well as scholarly writing by international lawyers.[71] Because the ICJ's function is to settle legal disputes between states, however, there are significant limitations on its role in enforcing international human rights. First, it has no jurisdiction over how a state observes human rights within its own borders.[72] Second, the principle of national sovereignty means that a state can ignore or sidestep ICJ decisions by picking and choosing which specific parts of the court's jurisdictions to acknowledge and implement. Australia did this as recently as 2002, when it withdrew from the jurisdiction of the maritime division of the ICJ because of a dispute with East Timor.[73] Finally, the major drawback to the ICJ's international relevance is that it has no jurisdiction over allegations of egregious human rights violations that concern only one government even when they occur abroad, as when abuses occurred in the U.S. detention facilities at Abu Ghraib in Iraq and Guantánamo Bay in Cuba.

Despite these lacunae the ICJ remains a key international judicial forum, referred to at different times as the "international constitutional court" or "ultimate appellate jurisdiction."[74] Notwithstanding the ICJ's jurisdictional limitations, its role is changing, albeit slowly. During the Cold War years the court averaged about one judgment a year, and it now has about twenty-five cases on its docket. Most cases still involve boundary disputes between states or commercial disputes between foreign governments,[75] but the court has more recently been asked to rule on the merits of human rights.[76] For example in 2003 and again in 2005 the ICJ ordered the U.S. not to execute Mexican nationals on death row until the ICJ had finished hearing their cases.[77] It has ruled that a Belgian court's arrest warrant for a former foreign minister of the Democratic Republic of Congo, based on universal jurisdiction over war crimes and crimes against humanity, violated his official immunity from prosecution in foreign courts.[78]

Since the early 1990s the ICJ has presided over claims accusing states of launching illegal wars and sponsoring war crimes and crimes against humanity. Most significant, in February 2007 the ICJ ruled that Serbia and Montenegro breached its obligations under the Convention on the Prevention and Punishment of the Crime of Genocide, 1948, by failing either to prevent the Srebrenica Genocide in Bosnia in 1995 or to cooperate with the International Criminal Tribunal for the former Yugoslavia (ICTY) in the prosecution of those responsible for the genocide.[79]

This ruling marks the first time that the ICJ has found a country in violation of the genocide convention.[80] It also ruled that Serbia and Montenegro's failure to transfer Ratko Mladić, one of the most wanted fugitives from the events in Bosnia and Herzegovina, to the ICTY amounted to an ongoing violation of Serbia and Montenegro's obligations under the UN genocide convention.[81] At the same time, this decision underscores the structural and normative limitations of the ICJ as an enforcer of international human rights. Unfortunately the court declined to find that genocide had been committed in the many other instances of mass killings and rapes across Bosnia and Herzegovina, that the government in Belgrade had been directly complicit in any acts of genocide, or that Serbia and Montenegro had financial liability for its failure to prevent the Srebrenica atrocities.

The ICJ has been criticized for failing to keep pace with new actors on the international human rights stage.[82] For example nongovernmental organizations that were such important players in the drafting of the Treaty of Rome, which ultimately led to the establishment of the International Criminal Court in 2002, have had a very small role in the ICJ. While third parties to a dispute are permitted, at least in theory, to intervene in ICJ proceedings, in practice the court has taken a restrictive approach.[83] Procedures allow for "friendly" amicus curiae interventions, but the court has only done so once, in 1950, following South Africa's refusal to allow South West Africa (now Namibia) to begin the transition to independence.[84] Twenty years later the court refused to let the same organization—the International League for Human Rights—submit information in another case before the court.[85] More recently, in 1996, the court refused a request by International Physicians for the Prevention of Nuclear War to submit information.[86]

International Criminal Law

Post-Cold War Developments   In 1993 the ILC submitted to the UN General Assembly a new draft statute for an International Criminal Court. Over the next few years national governments, largely spearheaded by the U.S., codified the international humanitarian law that had been developed in the preceding century and which the Nuremberg and Tokyo tribunals had crystallized. A smorgasbord of legal institutions was created. International intervention in Rwanda resulted in the International Criminal Tribunal for Rwanda; international intervention in Yugoslavia and Kosovo led to the creation of the International Criminal Tribunal for the Former Yugoslavia; international action underwriting the Lomé Peace Accord produced the Special Court for Sierra Leone, and intervention in East Timor produced the Ad-Hoc Human Rights Court on East Timor. Fifty years after the Nuremberg trials new international courts and tribunals have consolidated the use of criminal law as part of a universal human rights scheme.[87]

Many of those promoting these new "hard" law institutions had unrealistically high expectations for them. In addition to punishing individual violators and furthering the symbolism of international standards of justice, other touted benefits included deterrence of future human rights violations and contributions to peace-building and social trust in post-conflict societies. In fact, there is little empirical evidence to prove or dispute that courts can produce such outcomes. It is still too early to discern the broader social consequences of the new generation of international courts because they are so hard to test empirically. In other words no clear evidence yet exists that shows that criminal punishment of a human rights violator somehow contributes to post-conflict peace in a shattered society. Nor is there any clear proof that punishment of last year's human rights monster will deter next year's tyrant.

On balance, however, international criminal law prosecutions are important for their symbolism and their emphasis on individual responsibility. The symbolism of individualized punishment is too important to discount, and criminal law is unquestionably helping to set new standards of international procedure as well as creating a body of legal principles that individual states look to as precedent. International criminal law courts and tribunals have several functions. They attribute individual blame through respectable legal processes with transparent legal standards and seek to capture the attention of those who most need to be persuaded that violence and tyranny are over. Holding individuals legally responsible for human rights atrocities puts human agency at the heart of international human rights, starting with the normative assumption that because it is individuals that do harm it is individuals who ought to be held culpable.

While international criminal law comprises a relatively small component of the panoply of international human rights because of its focus on the very worst violations, some of its institutional innovations that I describe later in this chapter also hold out promise for more everyday human rights. At the same time, just as the international system of human right treaties has been criticized for its entrenchment of Western values on one hand and its bureaucratic and unenforceable practices on the other, international criminal courts and tribunals have encountered problems in their relatively short lifetime.

The ICTR and the ICTY   When the UN launched post-genocide nation-building activities in Rwanda and the former Yugoslavia in the mid-1990s, it made criminal justice for human rights violators a priority, establishing the International Criminal Tribunal for Rwanda (ICTR) and the International Criminal Tribunal for the Former Yugoslavia (ICTY). Both tribunals are important landmarks for the expansion of international humanitarian law. They were created under Chapter VII of the UN Charter—the provisions that give the UN authority to intervene with military force when a state conflict endangers international peace and security. The ICTY, located in The Hague, has jurisdiction over serious violations committed on the territory of the former Yugoslavia since 1991. These are crimes of international humanitarian law under the 1949 Geneva Conventions, such as violations of the laws or customs of war, offenses of genocide, and crimes against humanity. The ICTR has jurisdiction for serious violations of the humanitarian law of genocide, crimes against humanity, and violations of the Geneva Conventions committed in 1994 by Rwandans in the territory of Rwanda and neighboring states, as well as violations committed by non-Rwandan citizens in Rwanda.[88] The seat of the Rwanda tribunal is across the border in Arusha, Tanzania.

Any fair assessment of the work of these two tribunals shows mixed results. The Yugoslavia tribunal has so far concluded one hundred six proceedings, of which five have ended with acquittals, fourteen cases were referred to national jurisdiction, thirty-six persons are deceased or had their indictments withdrawn, and fifty-one persons were sentenced.[89] The Rwanda tribunal by April of 2007 had handed down twenty-seven judgments involving thirty-three accused.[90] Both tribunals have experienced setbacks. The Rwanda tribunal, for example, was initially very slow to open trials. Once they began the trials dragged on for years, not only because they are complex but also because they rely on testimony from witnesses who mostly live outside Arusha, in neighboring Rwanda. Many witnesses testify in Kinyarwanda, the language of Rwanda, not in French and English, the official languages of the court. The ICTR had to employ and train interpreters and translators before it finally switched to using simultaneous interpretation in order to speed up proceedings.

The ICTY has been more efficient than the ICTR in solving issues related to language and distance, but it has faced its own obstacles too. For example, when former Serbian president Slobodan Milošević appeared at the tribunal in The Hague in the four years before his death in 2006, it was reported that Serbs back home still loyal to Milošević took heart from daily televised expressions of his furious rejection of the Western power that the tribunal epitomized, giving ongoing impetus to preexisting ethnic tensions.[91] He died when just fifty hours of testimony remained to conclude his trial. Throughout, Milošević's support among Serbs continued because they were enraged to see their former leader standing in the dock in The Hague. In fact the tribunal probably fed into the common perception among Serbs that the world is stacked against them—a sentiment that continues to influence politics in the Balkans and was a factor contributing to Serbia's furious reaction to Kosovo's declaration of independence.

Both tribunals represent the paradox of the international human rights system. There are real advantages to pursuing human rights violators in international tribunals rather than domestic courts. To do so emphasizes that human rights are for everyone, that each person is entitled to the right to life and that the entire international community has an interest in upholding it. By putting universal human rights into a court setting where individuals are held responsible, it emphasizes the responsibility of people for the harm they have done to others, and putting a former head of state on trial emphasizes the responsibility that governments owe their citizens. Scholars generally agree that the tribunals have played a crucial role in codifying international humanitarian law and in carving out a place for international criminal law in the most serious internal conflicts.[92]

There are also real disadvantages to putting an international tribunal in charge of domestic human rights crimes. For such a court to work it needs the good will of key countries. To date the Serbian government has failed to hand over the former Bosnian Serb leader Ratko Mladić and only recently handed over Radovan Karadžić. Both have been at the top of the ICTY's most-wanted list since the transfer of Milošević to the ICTY in 2001. The delay in bringing Mladić and Karadžić to trial in The Hague seriously undermines perceptions of the tribunal's success.[93] The ICTY and the ICTR are also very expensive, and major donors like the U.S. have complained that they do not produce enough convictions to merit their costs.[94] It is also true that the tribunals have suffered from mismanagement. Not surprisingly, the U.S. government is on record saying that it prefers offering economic, technical, and logistical support to domestic legal systems rather than fostering dependence on international tribunals, which it characterizes as slow, expensive, and too removed from the victims' experiences.

The tribunals also suffer from the fact that they exist utterly outside any legal framework. Unlike national courts they have no inferior, superior, or sister courts. While they have generated a good deal of important jurisprudence that establishes international standards of humanitarian law, there is less likelihood that this will be of use in guiding the immediate, day-to-day work of domestic court systems. Most important, both The Hague and Arusha are located outside the country where the human rights violations occurred, inviting the same accusations of "victors' justice" that were directed at the Nuremberg and Tokyo tribunals. Miles away from victims and perpetrators alike, the distant locations feed perceptions of the courts as political rather than legal and give ample fodder to their critics, as the Serb support for Milošević during his trial demonstrates. The ICTR in particular has been criticized for its lack of connection to and knowledge of local history and culture and for the lack of congruity between the ICTR process and that of Rwandan national courts.[95] The outreach program at the ICTR has tried to address this critique by disseminating basic information about the court to communities, facilitating frequent discussions through seminars, town hall presentations, and training of legal professionals. Despite some progress with limited resources, however, the efforts of the outreach program to engage the Rwandan population and to make the tribunal more transparent have been largely ineffective.[96]

Not only are the results of the tribunals mixed, but their contribution to rebuilding legal, political, and social cohesion in societies torn apart by bloody civil conflict remains unclear. There is as yet little empirical evidence that these tribunals will be an aid to efforts for peace in the regions affected. Some see the tribunals as an important part of regional reconciliation because they raise the profile of human rights crimes, but at best they are a small part of the peacemaking process.[97] Others, while recognizing the value of the international courts and tribunals as precedents for international law, believe that the ICTY, and to an even greater extent the ICTR, remain distant and weak, and are generally slow at bringing justice to the traumatized regions on which they focus. Scholars from Africa argue that the ICTR can have little positive impact because it is not part of a broader effort to deal with the underlying roots of racial, gender, and religious tensions that gave rise to violence in the first place. These critics see the international tribunal, absent that effort, as merely assuaging the conscience of states that failed to prevent the atrocities of 1994.[98]

In response to this criticism and also to the grindingly slow progress of Rwanda's own domestic prosecutions of the less important defendants (many of whom have spent years in custody awaiting their trials), Rwanda's Pres. Paul Kagame has devolved criminal adjudication to a state-organized form of popular courts known as *gacaca*, a traditional community-based forum for conflict resolution. International criticism of the two tribunals has stung the UN Security Council into action, leading it to adopt resolutions requiring both the ICTY and the ICTR to complete their investigations by 2004, trials by 2008, and appeals by 2010.[99] In response to these resolutions, the ICTY endorsed a strategy intended to ensure a phased and coordinated completion of its mission by the end of 2010, concentrating its own prosecution and trial activities on the most senior leaders of the Yugoslavian conflict and referring cases involving intermediate and lower-rank defendants to national courts.[100] The Rwanda tribunal has also agreed on a completion strategy.[101]

The International Criminal Court   Carried on the optimistic wave of human rights advocacy unleashed with the end of the Cold War and the creation of new states and adoption of new constitutions, the governments of the world voted overwhelmingly in favor of the proposal by the Treaty of Rome for the creation of the International Criminal Court (ICC) in 1998. When the ICC statute entered into force in 2002 it established the first permanent international tribunal to try crimes of genocide, crimes against humanity, and war crimes, which together were seen as the most severe and atrocious crimes when executed as part of a political plan or on a widespread basis. The ICC treaty criminalizes sexual and gender violence as war crimes and provides procedural protections for female victims and witnesses, evidentiary rules that protect victims of sexual violence, and provisions for hiring staff with expertise on gender and sexual violence. Unlike the ad hoc tribunals for Rwanda and Yugoslavia, the ICC is financially independent from the UN and is funded only by the 105 states that have joined it. It sits in The Hague, but its judges represent the all the world's legal systems.[102] Its chief prosecutor is Luis Moreno-Ocampo, an Argentine national chosen for his work prosecuting military figures for human rights violations committed during the Argentine "dirty war" in the 1980s.[103]

The U.S. is not now a member of the International Criminal Court. The administration of Pres. Bill Clinton voted against the statute's final version after negotiations had failed to secure exemption from the court jurisdiction for U.S. soldiers and government officials. President Clinton ultimately capitulated, however, and signed the treaty in his very last days in office in 2001. Despite support for the ICC in most countries, the administration of Pres. George W. Bush announced in 2002 that the U.S. would withdraw its signature from the treaty, and the U.S. government negotiated separate bilateral agreements with ICC signatories for blanket immunity for U.S. nationals. It also passed the American Service–members Protection Act of 2002, giving the president the power to use all means necessary to secure the release of any American detained by the ICC. The act also limited U.S. involvement in overseas peacekeeping missions unless the UN exempted U.S. troops from ICC prosecution and restricts foreign aid to countries unless they prevent delivery of Americans to the court. Among commentators the legislation earned the title "The Hague Invasion Act" for its expansive grant of power to the president to set free any Americans detained by the ICC. In what began to look like international comedy, the Dutch parliament passed a resolution in response, protesting this affront to their sovereignty.

While U.S. opposition to the ICC may seem paradoxical given its unique role in fostering and drafting much of the Rome statute and devoting years to the negotiations, it is a paradigmatic example of the traditional position of inviolate national sovereignty that does not yield to laws created outside national borders.[104] Other countries also considered the concerns of the U.S. but decided on balance that more was to be gained by joining the ICC. For example, Australia reviewed the possible impact of the ICC statute upon the country's sovereignty, defense system, international obligations, and legal system. It ratified the ICC statute and passed Australian federal legislation implementing it, though emphasizing the primacy of Australian jurisdiction within its own borders by creating complementary jurisdiction within its own domestic legal system. While recognizing some of the criticisms that the ICC will subvert national sovereignty and national law—concerns that are epitomized by the U.S. position—the Australian government emphasized the countervailing benefits to Australian defense forces, prisoners of war, and civilians that would flow from the protection of an international court dedicated to enforcing international law. For the U.S., however, fears that the ICC might pursue a political agenda against U.S. government officials through malicious prosecutions has overwhelmed notions of international human rights solidarity.

It is still too early to assess the effect of the ICC. Chief Prosecutor Moreno-Ocampo has received huge numbers of individual complaints as well as many references from governments, but to date he has opened cases in relation to only four human rights situations (the Democratic Republic of Congo, Uganda, the Central African Republic, and the Sudanese region of Darfur) and has issued fewer than ten warrants of arrest. Hearings in The Hague have now commenced against defendants from the conflicts in Democratic Republic of Congo and Uganda. While U.S. concerns about the ICC exercising its jurisdiction over essentially domestic issues seem to have been overstated, other concerns about the single universal standard of international criminal law have more traction. Precisely what the ICC's effect will be on countries emerging from civil conflict—without an established tradition of Western human rights and liberal governance—remains to be seen.

For example the ICC's use of criminal indictments and criminal trials with Western-style criminal adjudication creates clear "winners" and "losers," thus possibly making it harder for war-torn societies to pursue nonlegal reconciliation processes. Arrest warrants issued by the ICC prosecutor in 2005 for four senior leaders of the Lord's Resistance Army (LRA) in Uganda allege decades of widespread killings, mutilations, rape, abduction, and forcible conscription of civilians. Almost one and a half million people live in squalid camps because of the LRA. One indicted senior leader, Joseph Kony, will not venture out of his bases in the bush in Uganda, Congo, and southern Sudan for fear he will be captured and sent to the ICC in The Hague. The Ugandan government has indicated it would be willing to grant "amnesty" to Kony and the other leaders named in the ICC indictment if a permanent peace deal were reached. Some commentators are now urging that the ICC remove the indictments in order to allow the Ugandan government to negotiate a peace deal with Kony, arguing:

> If peace and security are the ends, it should not matter that a murderous mad-man and four of his henchmen are allowed to go free. This may sound like an appalling suggestion but when the indictments are the only things preventing stopping further misery for 1.4 million people crowded into makeshift living conditions (and further bloodshed, almost certainly), it may be worth strong consideration. But that depends on whether or not the I.C.C.'s definition of jus-tice is what a man deserves for his past crimes or what a community deserves for their future.[105]

It is still too early in the life of the ICC to draw any general conclusions about its efficacy and effects. To generalize from the Ugandan situation that international criminal proceedings may interfere with domestic processes overlooks the symbolic authority that international processes may have in other situations—and yet the need for national peace in a conflict-torn area may justify moral trade-offs in the international arena.

"Universal Jurisdiction" in National Courts   At the opposite end of the spectrum from international criminal trials are criminal prosecutions conducted by a third-party state. These are even more controversial. For example in 1993, using the standards of the 1949 Geneva Convention and the 1977 Geneva Protocols I and II, Belgium passed a law allowing for punishment of severe violations of international human rights that occur anywhere in the world. In 1999 jurisdiction was extended to include the crime of genocide. The moral logic of universal jurisdiction is that some human rights violations are so egregious that all people and all governments are morally outraged, justifying criminal proceedings in any country's legal system as proxies for universal sentiment. Belgium's universal jurisdiction law has transformed this common moral interest into a legal right, ostensibly granting Belgium the power to hold war crimes and crimes against humanity committed by foreigners outside its own territory.

Adopting this approach, in 2001 a Belgian court heard cases against four Rwandans—two nuns, Consolata Mukangango and Julienne Mukabutera; a businessman, Alphonse Higaniro; and a university professor, Vincent Ntezimana—alleging their participation in the massacre of more than 7,600 ethnic Tutsi at the Sovu convent in Butare. After the massacre the defendants fled to Belgium, where they were ultimately arrested and charged. Following an eight-week trial, the Court of Assizes of the Administrative District of Brussels sentenced them to Belgian prisons for terms ranging from twelve to twenty years. The U.S., China, and Russia reacted strongly to these trials, especially when several highly political cases were deposed in Belgian courts against former Israeli prime minister Ariel Sharon (accused of involvement in a 1982 massacre in Lebanon); former Palestine Liberation Organization leader Yasser Arafat (accused of terrorist actions); and U.S. Pres. George W. Bush, U.S. Vice Pres. Dick Cheney, and former U.S. secretary of state Colin Powell (accused of responsibility for the 1991 Baghdad bombings).

Those opposed to universal jurisdiction argue that it is a breach of state sovereignty for Belgium to prosecute these officials and that no state has the authority to try a crime, no matter how heinous, from another state's jurisdiction if it has no sovereign interest over acts that constitute the crime.[106] Confronted with the sharp increase in deposed suits, Belgium amended its universal jurisdiction to require that the accused must either be Belgian or residing in Belgium. Despite these amendments, however, some cases that had already begun continued including the indictment in 2005 of Chad's dictator Hissène Habré for crimes against humanity, torture, and war crimes among other human rights violations.[107] Other international warrants issued by the Belgian court for Rwandans living outside Belgium are still outstanding but only for those alleged criminals whose victims were Belgian citizens.[108]

The Rwandan nuns trial also elicited mixed reactions among both victims of the Rwandan genocide and human rights advocates. The case was welcomed by some as an important first step in convincing states to fulfill their commitments under the Geneva Convention and to prosecute those in their jurisdictions who have committed atrocities. Among other Rwandans, however, the case was criticized as an unjustified attempt by Belgium (and France) to evade responsibility for the tensions and passions that they helped generate during their colonial regimes. More important, the Belgian trials display many of the disadvantages of international human rights trials with few of the advantages. The distance and isolation from the victims in the Rwandan community could not have been more pronounced—it was much greater than the distance issue that plagued the ICTR in Arusha—which meant there was absolutely no engagement with domestic Rwandan judges, court personnel, or even the Rwandan public.

The Hybrid Courts Model

An Innovation

The most promising use of criminal courts, yet the least well known, are the so-called hybrid courts. These courts address some of the problems encountered by international courts on the one hand and national courts on the other by offering a combination of each. Created in post-conflict Kosovo to apply international standards within national courts and comprised of a mixture of domestic and international judges, the hybrid criminal courts apply the jurisprudential idea of individual responsibility for human rights while acknowledging different national institutions and different cultures. Of course these new international hybrid courts do not exist in a vacuum. *Gacacas,* Rwanda's community-based alternative to their own national criminal legal system and the ICTR, and truth and reconciliation commissions (another alternative to criminal trials) are other novel examples of states using their own domestic institutions both to assign responsibility for past human rights abuses and to reestablish the credibility of their national legal systems. More generally the hybrid courts offer an intriguing model for human rights institutions.

To date five such courts have been established as a collaboration between the UN and national courts: the Kosovo War and Ethnic Crimes Court, the Ad-Hoc Court for East Timor, the Special Court for Sierra Leone, the Special Tribunal for Cambodia, and the War Crimes Chamber in Bosnia-Herzegovina. Kosovo, East Timor, and Sierra Leone each had their political and legal infrastructure badly damaged by terrible human rights violence that was marked by conflict between ethnic and cultural groups. Consequently there was little trust in domestic legal institutions for fear they had been captured by one or another of the warring factions. International oversight was sought to guarantee impartiality in criminal cases arising from the former civil conflict. Cambodia's extraordinary chamber was established in 2003 to hear cases against the Khmer Rouge from the "killing fields" more than thirty years earlier, and the chamber in Bosnia and Herzegovina was formed in 2005 to hear cases arising from the conflict in that country.

Among the set of international courts and tribunals established over the past fifteen years, the hybrid criminal courts offer particular structural advantages. Though housed in national court buildings and staffed in part with domestic judges and court personnel, these five innovative institutions apply *international* humanitarian and criminal law to criminal proceedings against former human rights violators who committed mass crimes. Each is operating in a *national* legal environment, thus introducing international human rights and criminal law standards into domestic courts.

Like most uses of international criminal law for ex post punishment and ex ante nation building, hybrid courts cannot offer a perfect solution. The five courts have had varying degrees of success, and each has flaws that require some institutional modification. Not all of the hybrid courts necessarily have all the most beneficial features, but the hybrid court model suggests a way out of some of the problems associated with the exclusively international criminal tribunals such as the ICTY, the ICTR, and the ICC. They also provide a structural principle for other, noncriminal human rights conflicts. The hybrid institutions capture some of the most valuable elements of both international *and* domestic legal institutions while avoiding some of the flaws of each.

Kosovo   The Kosovo War and Ethnic Crimes Court, created in June 1999 to relieve the ICTY of the trials of lesser offenders, deploys more than three hundred international and local judges in courts throughout Kosovo. The Kosovo hybrid court has jurisdiction over war crimes, serious violations of international humanitarian law, and serious ethnically motivated crimes.[109] Initially the court was designed so that local judges comprised a majority of the trial panels, and some trials were held in front of panels of only Kosovar Albanian judges. Later, following recurrent charges of ethnic bias, the number of international court panels was increased.[110]

The involvement of international jurists in hearing war crimes has been one small indicator of impartiality in a deficient system of domestic governance. By March 2006 there had been eighteen trials, some involving multiple defendants, that resulted in fourteen guilty verdicts.[111] The Kosovo hybrid courts are still fraught with problems, many arising from insufficient funding, and still inadequate, as ongoing political violence attests. Notwithstanding such limitations, the institutional model of a combination of international and domestic legal expertise is slowly building legal capacity in Kosovo, an experience that can only help as post-independence Kosovo now makes the transition to full functional sovereign autonomy. The most salient lesson from the Kosovo hybrid court has been the need for careful attention to the cultural and political affiliation of judges to counter the appearance of bias and avoid exacerbating ethnic schisms.

East Timor   The East Timor hybrid court provides a different institutional lesson. It was established in 2000 at the direction of the United Nations Transitional Authority for East Timor. East Timor's judicial capacity was extremely limited after the 1999 conflict because the courts had been operated mostly by Indonesian judges who had little local credibility after the conflict. The Special Panels for Serious Crimes (SPSC) is a commission that sits in Dili, the capital, and comprises two foreign judges and one East Timorese judge with jurisdiction to apply a combination of international and Indonesian law in cases of genocide, crimes against humanity, war crimes, and torture.[112] Like the hybrid court in Kosovo, the East Timor court's full potential remains untapped because it lacks adequate funding. It struggles with inexperienced personnel and vacancies in key positions. Too few judges have been hired, and the trial courts have been forced to suspend proceedings periodically due to lack of personnel.[113] By far the greatest drawback to its effectiveness has been Indonesia's ongoing refusal to surrender high-level military personnel and officers to the court.

Despite these obstacles the SPSC has completed fifty-five trials, most involving relatively low-level defendants; eighty-four individuals have been convicted and three acquitted.[114] On a dollar-for-dollar analysis, it has been far more productive than either the ICTY or the ICTR. The lesson from East Timor is that for a hybrid court to succeed post-secession, the UN or the international community needs to be willing to use its influence to force the former sovereign state—here, Indonesia—to cooperate in related domestic legal processes.

Sierra Leone   The Special Court of Sierra Leone is the most successful hybrid court to date. Its trials commenced virtually on the day it opened its doors; its proceedings and the results are explained and disseminated around Sierra Leone quickly and effectively. Established in 2002 following the Lomé Peace Accord, the special court currently comprises eleven judges, of whom six are trial judges (four appointed by the UN and two nominated by the government of Sierra Leone). The remaining five are appeals judges, three UN appointees and two Sierra Leone nominees. Five years after its establishment, the special court has indicted (and in some cases, tried and sentenced) the main leadership of the Armed Forces Revolutionary Council that spearheaded the destruction of Sierra Leone and the pillage of Freetown in January 1999. Former Liberian president Charles Taylor is on trial for war crimes and crimes against humanity, including the murder and mutilation of civilians, the use of women and girls as sex slaves, and the abduction of both adults and children to perform forced labor or become fighters. In June 2007 the trial chamber of the special court rendered guilty verdicts against other ringleaders on the first-ever successful international charges of conscripting children under the age of fifteen into armed forces.[115] The court has efficient courtroom management and an active interventionist courtroom style that protects the rights of the accused as well as the interests of vulnerable witnesses. It goes to great lengths to protect the identity of witnesses and also provides them medical assistance and psychosocial counseling. Most important, the court disseminates its work to the domestic population, "mak[ing] robust and innovative outreach and communications efforts to increase Sierra Leoneans' awareness of the court's work. The Public Affairs Unit creatively engages and trains local media, and produces audio and video summaries of the court's work. The Outreach Unit canvasses the country with information about the court through video screenings, discussion, and dissemination of written material. The court magnifies its reach by targeting particular sectors of society such as students, and conducting trainings for civil society."[116] Even Human Rights Watch, so often skeptical of human rights institutions, believes that the Sierra Leone court is creating an invaluable legacy by strengthening respect for the rule of law, building local professional capacity, and reaching out to the population of Sierra Leone to communicate its work.[117] Its drawback is less legal and institutional than political. The Sierra Leone government still drags its heels on broader reforms beyond the ambit of the special court.

Bosnia and Herzegovina   The War Crimes Chamber in Bosnia-Herzegovina (WCC) represents the latest model of an internationalized justice mechanism embedded in a domestic legal system. Established in 2005, it operates within the Criminal Division of the State Court of Bosnia and Herzegovina to try the most serious war crimes committed during the conflict. A limited number of cases are referred to it by the ICTY, but the underlying concept of the WCC is that accountability for gross violations of human rights ultimately remains the responsibility of the people of Bosnia and Herzegovina. The chamber's procedures are modeled on those of the European Court of Human Rights. If it finds a violation it may issue a cease and desist order or grant monetary relief. With the assistance of the Council of Europe it distributes the text in several languages of all decisions issued by the chamber throughout Bosnia and Herzegovina to judges, lawyers, prosecutors, international organizations, national ministries, embassies, international and national NGOs, and other interested institutions.

The chamber's body of case law fulfills an educational role concerning the rule of law by applying the European Convention on Human Rights and other international and regional instruments. Unlike the ICTY cases that involve more senior officials, the proceedings before the WCC involve mid- and low-level functionaries who are alleged to have participated directly in crimes committed during the conflict, which makes it more likely that the WCC cases will resonate with victims within Bosnia and Herzegovina. Eight of the fourteen judges (including the court president) are international members who were appointed to the chamber by the Committee of Ministers of the Council of Europe, a procedure that ensures that the WCC presently contains a significant international judicial component. The court has an aggressive transition strategy for phasing out the international judges and increasing the number of domestic judges, however. In the meantime it is essentially a domestic institution operating under national law that will encourage a strong commitment to local ownership of the human rights accountability process. Like the Kosovo and East Timor hybrid courts, the WCC operates on a relatively small budget, but now it does a better job of integrating its legal activities within the domestic legal system. The court is located in Sarajevo, which makes it accessible to the local population. Fourteen cases have been heard since the WCC's inception in 2005, a better rate than that of the ICTY. It offers tremendous potential to make an impact on rebuilding the rule of law in Bosnia and Herzegovina.

Cambodia   The case of Cambodia best illustrates the limitations of hybrid courts. After almost a decade of negotiations with the UN, Cambodia finally established an extraordinary chamber to try the aging Khmer Rouge leaders who led the bloody regime in Cambodia that killed millions in the 1970s. In 2002, after five years of difficult compromises, the UN broke off negotiations when Cambodia refused to sign a memorandum of understanding that would have prevented political interference with the trials by Cambodian officials. Finally it was agreed in 2003 that the court would be composed of a majority of Cambodian judges along with a minority of judges nominated by the UN, although under a supermajority rule no judicial decision of any consequence can be made without the consent of at least one international judge.[118] The special tribunal officially began its work in May 2006, but the struggle to have the

Cambodian government agree to international human rights standards did not cease. It is now manifested through disagreements about details of court rules and procedures. Like the East Timor hybrid court, Cambodia's special tribunal is hampered by the lack of cooperation from its own government officials, especially those who were possibly involved in Khmer Rouge atrocities.

Institutional Shape

Each of the hybrid courts operates on a slightly different model. While all employ both national and international staff, the proportions vary. In Sierra Leone the majority of the judges of the special court as well as the registrar and the prosecutor are appointed by the UN; the remainder are appointed by the government of Sierra Leone. There is no obligation for the government-appointed judges to be Sierra Leonean nationals, which theoretically means that all the judges could be international. Cambodia's special tribunal, on the other hand, has a majority of Cambodian judges, and even the UN appointed international judges must be approved by the Cambodian Supreme Council of the Magistracy. Cambodian and international members also serve as equal co-prosecutors and co-investigating judges. The Kosovo court is closer to the Cambodian model: the UN special representative, upon the request of the prosecutor, defense counsel, or accused, can designate an international prosecutor, an international investigating judge, and / or a panel of three judges with at least two internationals. In East Timor each bench must include two international judges and one East Timorese judge. The WCC is unique in its scheme for phasing out international involvement; within five years of its inception it will have only national panels.

Different combinations of substantive law also exist in the five hybrid courts. While all mix both national and international law, the SPSC of East Timor has the widest jurisdiction. Justiciable actions include murder and sexual offenses under domestic law and international crimes set out under the ICC statute. East Timor is the only hybrid to have universal jurisdiction. The tribunals of Sierra Leone and Cambodia are also mandated to apply both international and domestic laws. The hybrid panels in Kosovo and the WCC in Bosnia and Herzegovina on the other hand have jurisdiction only over crimes under domestic law, although their domestic law also incorporates international crimes.

Likewise the hybrid courts are financed through different mechanisms. The Kosovo and East Timorese courts are partly funded from the UN administration budgets and partly by the national budgets of those territories. The special tribunal in Cambodia is partly funded by the state but primarily by international donors. The Sierra Leone special court is supported entirely by voluntary international contributions.

Human Rights Advantages of Hybrid Courts

Operating at their best, hybrid courts offer significant advantages for adjudicating human rights abuses in countries where the international community has intervened. Hybrids can overcome some of the problems posed by purely international and purely local court systems in four ways. First, if hybrid courts pay careful attention to judicial appointments and exercise jurisdiction over *all* the potential defendants, they can help overcome the legitimacy problems within domestic systems in circumstances where little trust remains among ethnic groups in the aftermath of serious civil disruption. Second, hybrids can help with building or rebuilding domestic legal capacity because they are located inside national borders and employ local judges, lawyers, and court personnel. Third, when hybrids effectively disseminate their institutional work, they are likely to help replace a culture of impunity with new norms of human rights.[119] Finally, carefully established hybrid courts avoid some of the impressions of international imperialism that have been associated with the international criminal tribunals of Rwanda and the former Yugoslavia, just as the Nuremburg and Tokyo trials were criticized by some in the 1940s for applying "victors' justice."[120]

Sierra Leone's special court diffuses the victors' justice critique by appointing local as well as international judges and through consistent dissemination of the court's work to both urban and rural communities. Court proceedings, including the trial of Charles Taylor (transferred to The Hague owing to security concerns) are streamed live over the Internet to the special court in Freetown where the public is invited to attend. Court transcripts are available in print media, and several blogs provide news analysis with a particular emphasis on reaching West African audiences. The result is that "The Special Court has been far more successful in integrating Sierra Leoneans into the process, establishing a cooperative relationship with the government of Sierra Leone, and communicating the importance of its activities to the families of victims and the citizens of Sierra Leone through its outreach and public affairs programs."[121]

Most important, the special court has not delayed the trial and sentencing of important ringleaders of the violence. In July 2007, Alex Tamba Brima and Santigie Borbor Kanu were sentenced to fifty years' imprisonment, and

Brima Kamara was sentenced to forty-five years' imprisonment. They will likely serve their sentences in Europe owing to security concerns in Sierra Leone. The Sierra Leone court has not balked at recognizing different degrees of complicity in the violence by giving lesser sentences to those convicted who could demonstrate that they made efforts to restore Sierra Leone's democratically elected government.[122]

Of course the hybrid courts still have drawbacks. One concern is the distribution of power between domestic and international judges. Another is the distribution of judicial power among members of various ethnic and political parties, which may lead to an overcorrection problem, as occurred in Kosovo when large numbers of Serbs, who are a minority in the country, were initially appointed to serve, tainting the legitimacy of the bench.[123] Where underfunding problems exist, as in the case of East Timor, and ICC jurisdiction is available and viable, it may be better to transfer legal accountability to the international forum because lack of domestic resources may lead to results inconsistent with international norms.[124] Overall, though, it seems that an increased international presence on the judicial bench has more advantages than disadvantages because institutional legitimacy is strengthened.

The most appealing feature of hybrid courts is their flexible approach to the delivery of human rights in domestic systems that either cannot or will not themselves redress wrongs. It is a model that can extend beyond criminal courts to be applied to civil and administrative courts and tribunals. Because of its position between purely domestic institutions and purely international institutions, the hybrid model, appropriately adapted in ways suggested in Chapter 5, can improve both institutional capacity and institutional credibility for addressing past human rights abuses. The hybrid model creates an institutional framework for increasing local input and for interpretation of international human rights norms in situ.

Getting It Right

Taken together the three problems of the present UN human rights system—the delays of the treaty committee system, laggardly national human rights implementation, and the philosophical critique of international human rights as the new colonizing move of Western empire—pose a monumental challenge. They make the task of establishing human rights standards across different cultures philosophically troubling and pragmatically challenging. It is possible to speculate, though difficult to prove, that each of these problems undermines human rights results on the ground. Together they make a persuasive case for institutional changes to the human rights system.

There are three possible types of reform or response. One approach is to hold sovereignty as the ultimate trump card of international human rights standards, leaving powerful states to define their own standards and the other countries of the world to respond according to their relative global status. A second alternative is to cede human rights development to local, national, and international governmental and nongovernmental organizations that have proliferated in the post–Cold War era. A third alternative is to allow cultural practices within states to define differential human rights standards out of respect for multicultural identity.

Each of these three approaches has a feasible basis, either philosophically or pragmatically. As singular approaches to human rights policy, however, sovereignty, civil society, and multiculturalism are insufficient. In the following chapter I examine the claim that national sovereignty as autonomous political authority trumps the international system. I argue that the sovereignty critique of human rights is neither morally sufficient nor empirically apt in contemporary world conditions.

Chapter 3

Relational Sovereignty and Humanitarian Intervention

Introduction

Since the end of World War II, sixteen million people have died in civil wars.[1] Civil wars have broken out all over the globe, in seventy-three countries of Africa, Europe, South America, and Asia.[2] In 2005 alone more than 23.7 million people were displaced by civil conflicts in fifty countries. Like refugees, these internally displaced people were forced to flee their homes because their lives were in danger, yet unlike refugees, they have not crossed an international border. Nearly six million of these people received little significant assistance from their own governments, and in sixteen countries there was no UN humanitarian involvement. The Sudan had the largest internal displacement situation—5.4 million people—and Colombia was second, with as many as 3.7 million displaced people. In the very worst situations—Myanmar (Burma), The Sudan, Democratic Republic of Congo, Zimbabwe, Côte d'Ivoire, Colombia, Iraq, Somalia, Uganda, and Nepal—the statistics on violence, hunger, disease, and a multitude of human rights violations are staggering. In all fifty countries, 70–80 percent of displaced people are women and children.[3]

Typically the worst human rights abuses occur in countries with a colonial past that are ruled today by authoritarian governments. These internal human rights disasters, already devastating to the people living there, often spill over into surrounding countries. Refugees move across borders, and criminal networks leverage the domestic chaos to smuggle people, drugs, and arms. All this takes place despite the creation of the United Nations and a vast new body of international human rights documents; all this, when more governments today have signed on to international human rights treaties than at any time in history. States have made agreements with the international community about human rights at home but are not keeping them. Why does this problem continue? Is this a problem that the international community is obliged to solve? How should it be understood?

Sovereignty lies at the core of these questions. International law and human rights are intricately connected to the principle of state sovereignty. Sovereignty is not merely an abstract concept; it is a fundamental principle of legal thinking that has direct consequences for legal institutions. The historical concept of sovereignty is redolent with the absolute power of monarchs to do as they wish with their subjects. In the contemporary world sovereignty gives each state the international right to rule autonomously within its own borders. Sovereignty also grants each state its legal status before the United Nations, yet over the past two decades a series of international events has challenged this traditional perception of sovereignty. At the end of the Cold War an international debate started about the meaning of state sovereignty because the creation of more than twenty new sovereign states in Europe and an altered balance of power in Africa and Latin America shook old foundational beliefs.[4] Then in the past decade the forces of globalization and "securitization" have accelerated the debate even further. It is not just the nature of sovereignty but its very existence that is being examined.[5]

When Immanuel Kant wrote two centuries ago that cosmopolitan values would ensure a peaceful world, he had in mind a global compact made up of states that ruled their people by "rightful government."[6] A sovereign "in the person of the legislator who represents the united or general will of the people" would exercise "the will of reason."[7] Kant's ideal government was reasonable—neither autocratic nor majoritarian—and also comprised an independent judiciary for interpreting and enforcing the law. Reasonable governments such as these would treat their own citizens with respect and keep their promises to other states. Kant's *Perpetual Peace* urged that international law, administered by a "league of nations," should displace belligerence between nations, endowing each with a common interest in settling their disputes through negotiation rather than war.[8] For Kant violence carried completely unacceptable moral costs.[9] Even his passionate defense of the American and French revolutions and his blind eye to the crimes of the Jacobins could not persuade him that the violent overthrow of despotism was justified.[10]

Kant's arguments have been immortalized in today's international system. Sovereignty is the central tenet of the 1946 UN Charter. Article 2 states very simply, "The Organization is based on the principle of the sovereign equality of all its Members."[11] The sacredness of preserving national sovereignty is contained in the principle of noninterference with the sovereignty of other states. Article 2(3) of the charter states, "All Members shall refrain in their international relations from the threat or use of force against the territorial integrity or political independence of any state."[12] National borders are sacred under the UN Charter. International law requires the world to stay out of civil wars and internal strife no matter how bloody and destructive they are with just one exception—when internal conflict threatens to engulf other countries. Unless war is *between* states, sovereignty under international law creates a figurative wall at the border—at least, that is, under the traditional theory of sovereignty.

Traditional sovereignty as the cornerstone of international law under the United Nations Charter deems every state the equal of every other, irrespective of its relative military might, economic power, population, or land mass. The same principle of national sovereignty means that every government is sovereign over its own people—no other state or other external group has authority over any other state government. No permanent international military force exists to keep governments to their international treaties or promises. According to the traditional view of sovereignty, there is no coercive power under international law that can *force* a government to provide human rights to its domestic population. National sovereignty supersedes international law, including international human rights law, and gives absolute autonomy to governments in their own territory. The happy fiction of international law is that the doctrine of national sovereignty will not only ensure world peace, but will also honor the intrinsic rights of people within their borders to govern themselves according to their own values and preferences. Left to their own devices and free from outside interference, national governments will exercise Kantian "rightful rule and reason" on behalf of their citizens.

Reality of course is different. Governments are often the worst violators of human rights. Leaving some states to their own devices presents human rights risks to their populations, with both domestic *and* international consequences. Within a county the risks of an unstaunched internal human rights crisis may be countless more deaths and even further erosion of the country's social and economic capital. Regionally and internationally the risk is that governments that do not care about "rightful rule and reason" may send their human rights troubles abroad. Violent or careless governments may create opportunities for terrorists to train and organize across borders, and criminals may take advantage of a breakdown in order to export illegal drugs to neighboring countries or traffic women and children for prostitution. Inviolate national sovereignty seems to present no reliable guarantee of human rights at home or of world peace abroad.

Sovereignty's failings have never been so obvious to the global community. When Myanmar's monks risked their lives in September and October of 2007 by demonstrating against the military junta, cell phone images of police rounding them up and beating them were instantly accessible around the world on YouTube. When Tibet's monks demonstrated against Chinese rule in March 2008, the news went out instantaneously, despite shutdowns of Internet servers by governments across Asia. Within hours and even minutes the world knew what was taking place thousands of miles away. Furthermore, the international community has increasingly acted in the name of human rights—even taking actions backed by military force—in disregard of the traditional barrier of national sovereignty. Variously justified as humanitarian intervention, promotion of democracy, regime change, or preemptive war, ad hoc developments such as these have called into question whether the traditional conception of sovereignty can survive in the contemporary world. Newer piecemeal interpretations of sovereignty have emerged. Indeed, sovereignty seems to have become a free-for-all, a political and legal concept that is liable to be interpreted instrumentally to suit the purposes of the military or political task at hand.

Depending upon their historical experiences and their place in the geopolitical order, states differ markedly in their interpretation of their own sovereignty and the sovereignty of other states. States with a colonial past, including many in Africa and the Asia-Pacific region, typically claim strong sovereignty vis-à-vis others in order to ensure that their experiences of colonial rule are not repeated. Some new versions of national sovereignty encourage suspicion of the concept of international human rights itself, lest this be a Trojan horse for more Western colonialism. This occurred when Singapore's Lee Kuan Yew justified political restrictions on free speech in the name of "Asian values." States ruled by military juntas cling to an understanding of sovereignty as an expression of ideal domestic rule, picking and choosing among international human rights the ones that will promote their own political agenda, as when Hugo Chávez trumpets social and economic rights in his program of de-privatizing Venezuela's natural resources. Some states with more military and economic power strongly assert their sovereignty in the international community as a way of stonewalling criticism of their domestic human rights records, such as was the case when the United States defended the high incarceration rate among African Americans, China sought to thwart concerns about its large number of political prisoners, and Russia defended its actions in Chechnya. Still other countries—for example Cuba and North Korea—stand aloof, and of course some are simply too poor to debate the philosophical foundations of sovereignty at all.

Two key factors contribute to the confusion about sovereignty. First, conventional legal and political accounts of sovereignty focus on particular historical dates, making too much of the Peace of Westphalia in the seventeenth century as the genesis of the modern meaning of sovereignty, and the formation of international institutions such as the United Nations in the twentieth century, as the apogee of international cooperation while preserving national sovereignty. This approach is too simplistic. Sovereignty certainly gained definition through such events, but just as crucially the meaning and effect of sovereignty has been shaped by the internal developments on rights in the West, the West's management of its colonial empires, and the dynamic between these two factors. A better understanding of this dynamic is required. With a deeper grasp of this dynamic, some aspects of sovereignty as it is traditionally understood can be jettisoned and other aspects that continue to be relevant can be retained.

Second, conventional explanations of sovereignty tend either to overemphasize the internal aspect of sovereignty as a validation of domestic political autonomy or overemphasize the external dimension of respect for other states' borders. The former gives governments too much leeway for violence or corruption. The latter gives too little credence to the moral obligations between people of different countries. Neither explanation adequately accounts for globalization or the internal capacity of a government—economic or institutional—to implement human rights reforms. Neither explanation accounts for the trend toward humanitarian intervention of the past decade.

In this chapter I argue that sovereignty needs to be carefully rethought. A better understanding of the historical forces behind the traditional concept of sovereignty can better guide the decisions of both national governments and international institutions when they take military action abroad in the name of human rights. The solution to the sovereignty problem lies in redefining it and adding new factors. These include the unprecedented levels of international awareness of and political interest in human rights problems that emerge from instantaneous international communications, new pooled multinational arrangements, and the internal resources of each state that are available for human rights reforms. The environment today is significantly different from that of earlier periods.

The balance of these factors will change over place and time and will rarely if ever be static. A pattern of serious and wide-scale human rights abuses has become the canary in the mine, a predictor of failed domestic governance. Neighboring countries justifiably have an interest in human rights across the border. At the same time international interest in a country's human rights situation must be balanced with the knowledge that certain types of external intervention may not improve things. Indeed intervention may even worsen an internal human rights situation. I suggest here a new understanding of sovereignty that puts human rights at the very center of the definition, the referent against which governments justify their domestic policies and the international community assesses its involvement in domestic affairs. I also argue, however, that international interest rarely justifies military intervention and that armed intervention by the international community should be limited to very rare cases of mass violations of human rights and must carry stringent provisos. International interest in human rights can and ought to justify international and regional condemnation and institutional action, something to be explored further in Chapters 4, 5, and 6.

Philosophical Foundations of Sovereignty

Initially influenced by the Christian distinction between the congregation as the body of Christ (the sovereign state) and the individual soul (the citizen), sovereignty is a political and philosophical concept that developed in parallel with ideas about human rights. The conceptual starting points for sovereignty and human rights differ, however: ideas about sovereignty derive from an analysis of the power and legitimacy of governments evidenced in a government's relationship with its citizens, whereas ideas about human rights proceed from an analysis of the rights and entitlements of citizens.

Contemporary thinking about sovereignty is a product of the dynamic relationship over the past five centuries between European nation-building at home and imperialism abroad. Europe was both architect and propagator of the modern concept of sovereignty, an idea it sent around the world along with imperial rule, which was ultimately more effective in creating an intellectual framework for nation-building and imperial governance than either the Russian or Ottoman expansions that preceded it. Modern principles of sovereignty emerged from the juxtaposition of practices of states abroad (in warfare and colonial trade) and developments in European (and later, North American) domestic politics. Both principles now exist in international treaty law: that a state's behavior beyond its own borders is expressed in the four Geneva Conventions that codify in treaty form international rules of warfare; and principles about a government's behavior towards its own citizens are expressed in the Universal Declaration of Human Rights and the two principal human rights covenants accompanying it, the International Covenant on Civil and Political Rights (ICCPR) and the International Convention on the Elimination of All Forms of Racial Discrimination (ICERD).[13]

Traditional European Sovereignty

The traditional European story about sovereignty starts with its own history of nation-building as the grip of the Holy Roman Empire lessened. The Peace of Westphalia in 1648 fragmented Europe, consolidating a century of restless search for religious independence by Protestants chafing under the rule of the Catholic Church.[14] The Peace of Westphalia was a "constitutional moment" when European sovereignty became defined as a national government's rightful claim to autonomy relative to outside powers.[15]

With the emergence of national government European political philosophy began its long journey of describing the rights and responsibilities of governments towards their citizens. Key British, French, and American intellectuals provided explanations of government power that inspire thinking to this day. In his magisterial *Leviathan*, Thomas Hobbes wrote of citizens' social contract with their ruler in which they granted him unfettered sovereign power in return for peace and security.[16] The intellectual power of Hobbes's sovereignty—the provision of safety from domestic chaos and protection from threats beyond the borders—influences contemporary ideas about sovereignty at a time of heightened fears about national security. John Locke's *Second Treatise of Government* went one step further, tying the hands of the sovereign in order to ensure that citizens' rights were respected. Locke's sovereign had to work harder for his people, providing more than Hobbes's minimal state.[17] Jean-Jacques Rousseau put sovereignty squarely into the hands of citizens, giving governments the job of implementing and enforcing their will.[18]

Sovereignty and European Colonial Territories

From the fifteenth century onward events well beyond Europe increasingly shaped the way that European states viewed their own political autonomy relative to their closer neighbors. European sovereigns agreed upon the laws of war at home in order to limit the harm they would inflict upon each other as equal states on European soil. Traffic on the high seas increased however as Europe pursued the riches of the New World. The Americas, Africa, and the Asia-Pacific region seemed free for the taking, so European ideas about sovereignty had to be refashioned.

Colonization, the process that spread European law around the globe, required the ancient regime to redefine (and usually defend) the basis of its political power against reluctant native peoples as well as against European neighbors who wanted access to the same New World outposts. Europe's colonial expansion emphasized a Hobbesian understanding of sovereignty, both in Europe and abroad and accelerated the reordering of Europe into nation-states that recognized each other's political autonomy in dealing with their growing overseas empires. The inviolability of European political power was stressed as was the inviolability of the new borders of the great powers' colonial holdings. Just as sovereignty at home in Europe was an expression of exclusive territorial control, so the emerging definitions of the limits of sovereignty abroad were driven by claims to geographic possession of colonial lands and peoples. On the other hand the corridors between the West and its colonies such as the "high seas" needed a different theory of legal identity. For example, when Dutchman Hugo Grotius wrote in his treatise that the high seas were common property and should be equally open to all who wanted to sail them, he wanted to preclude the particular territorial claims of the Portuguese, who had barred Dutch traders from lucrative ports in the East Indies.

Claims of European States over Its Colonial Peoples

In writing the templates for conduct governing Europe's colonial satellites, some early philosophers attempted to coax rulers to adapt laws in the colonies to new ideas of freedom and equality. Just as domestic sovereignty had relied upon the myth of the original social contract uniting individuals within their borders, international law of the seventeenth and eighteenth centuries relied upon the myth of a European village nation. The indigenous peoples of Europe's colonies—"natives"—held limited legal status relative to their occupying colonizers (or sometimes, no legal status at all) because they were deemed unready for full, European-style citizenship.[19] Sovereignty for the people of European states increasingly implied Locke and Rousseau, and for colonized peoples it meant Hobbes's *Leviathan* ruling from Europe. Mostly the emergent European thinking about human equality and human rights stayed at home. New World resources were exploited with little respect for indigenous claims of ownership of their traditional lands, at least in any practical sense.

During the second wave of colonization, in the nineteenth century, human rights in the colonies gained little traction even as European states consolidated their colonial empires and negotiated carefully with their European neighbors over their New World borders. The differences between European and colonial sovereignty became even clearer by the end of the nineteenth century. By then Europe had added nine million square miles—almost one-fifth of the land area of the globe—to its overseas colonial possessions, including practically the entire African continent and vast holdings in Asia, the Pacific, and Latin America. The "informal" imperialism of Europe administering its colonies through military influence and economic control gave way to more direct rule of the overseas territories. When the 1884–85 Berlin Conference divided Africa among the United Kingdom, the French Third Republic, and the German Empire, Hobbesian sovereignty across the various empires, mediated by European governments, was virtually complete.[20]

One aspect of sovereignty during this period was the emphasis on the rules of competition by which European governments could lay claim to colonial territory. The ground rules of New World sovereignty were ever more clearly spelled out in order to avoid conflicts back home. No country was to stake claims in Africa without first notifying the other European powers. No territory could be formally claimed prior to being effectively occupied. Not surprisingly the issue of governance of people within the colonial states was almost completely ignored in the rush to establish external boundaries and keep other European colonizers away from rich resources.

Europe often put a human rights façade on its imperial landgrab by condemning the overseas slave trade, prohibiting the sale of alcoholic beverages and firearms in certain regions, and expressing concern for the endorsement of missionary activities.[21] Being "for" human rights meant spreading human rights abroad and was expressed as bringing the benefits of Christianity and civilization. Indeed these sentiments were part of the legitimation of empire. On the other hand infamous human rights violations like those in King Leopold's Belgian Congo demonstrated that sovereignty and human rights did not *automatically* go hand in hand.[22] Sovereignty could be as equally associated with tyranny as with freedom.

Postcolonial and New UN Sovereignty

The first iteration of Westphalian sovereignty had transformed large swathes of the world into European empires where the human rights of indigenous peoples were frequently ignored. The second iteration came after World War II, in the postcolonial period of the 1950s and '60s. In a quixotic turn, when Europe finally came to divest itself of its last empires, postcolonial countries in Asia and Africa adopted as emphatically a Hobbesian version of sovereignty as had their European progenitors. Sovereignty as a principle of inviolate national autonomy was confirmed in the UN Charter and relied heavily on the conventional Westphalian paradigm. In an ironic repetition of troubled history, conventional European sovereignty was part of the conceptual package that granted former colonies their own international legal status.

Young states breaking away from their European colonial rulers gave themselves sovereign autonomy within their own borders but did so in the language and the institutions of their former colonists. They created new constitutions but retained the old colonial court systems, albeit with more indigenous judges. Postcolonial government ministries and civil services mostly carried over the structures of previous colonial administrators.[23] They discouraged any moral obligation to those in other states, and Article 2 of the UN Charter positively excluded intervention as a matter of international law. At precisely the same moment that the UN Declaration of Human Rights and its main covenants were enshrining the contemporary system of international human rights, international sovereignty was defined as a "thin" responsibility—at heart, merely a duty or obligation that each state owed to all others to observe each others' territorial borders.[24]

One key difference, however, would have long-term effects. The new postcolonial national constitutions sought to correct many decades of colonial oppression by incorporating ideas of racial equality. These ideas had developed in the West from classical liberal rights that had gradually expanded to include minority rights. The UN Declaration of Human Rights established human equality as the benchmark of human rights, and the postcolonial states made sure that their new constitutions combined Hobbesian sovereign autonomy *and* racial equality.

Contested Meanings of Sovereignty

Kant had foreseen the potential schism between domestic and international philosophy. He had attempted to provide instead a total philosophy, one that accounted for the exercise of domestic power within a nation-state as well as relationships between nation-states. Kant rejected Hobbes's authoritarian view of sovereignty as a black box around the nation-state and criticized it as an application of mathematics and geometry to human and social affairs. People were not merely driven by Hobbes's presentiment of civil apocalypse, Kant argued, but also by the desire for truth and justice.[25] While Kant's conception of sovereignty aimed at improving the everyday life of citizens by stressing their rationality and their contribution towards their own governance, his Eurocentrism was clear: the best chance that people outside European civilization had was colonization because "these peoples—the Caribs and the Iroquois among them—ha[d] no history" before they came into contact with "civilized" society.[26]

Although Kant's vision of individual rights in international society provided the inspiration for the United Nations, realpolitik meant that each state continued to hold fast to its own national sovereignty even while participating in the new international institutions. From the very first years of the United Nations, sovereignty as inviolate Hobbesian autonomy had trenchant critics. Hersch Lauterpacht, a member of the UN International Law Commission and judge of the International Court of Justice from 1955 to 1960, roundly criticized concept of inviolate state sovereignty in the UN Charter.[27] He worried that giving states too much autonomy would leave them deciding for themselves what human rights to apply at home and that this would prevent international human rights from becoming more systematic around the world.[28] Rather than investing sovereignty with a mystical status that the international community would be bound to honor, Lauterpacht argued that governments ought to regard themselves as bodies in the service of individuals, applying the rule of law and international human rights as the integral method of government.[29]

Such skepticism about the reverence for sovereignty in international law continues to this day. Columbia University law professor Louis Henkin, an influential American scholar of human rights, makes a similar point when he argues that sovereignty in the international system ought to represent the values of the people rather than being seen as the expression of the values of a nation-state. For Henkin, sovereignty is "a mistake, . . . a mistake built upon mistakes, which has barnacled an unfortunate mythology."[30]

Modern-day debates about the concept of sovereignty are recapitulating many of the arguments that circulated in the 1880s and '90s. Then the nay-sayers of international law argued that international law could not really be "law" in the same sense as national laws.[31] Without an international equivalent of national parliaments, courts, and police forces, these nineteenth-century critics argued, international law was simply a series of contractual agreements between sovereigns and national governments that could be, and were, broken by powerful states whenever it suited them. Diametrically opposed to Kant's ideas of cosmopolitan collaboration between states, the anti-internationalists' concept of law was something exercised by sovereigns solely within the borders of their states. This argument is applied to international law to this day.[32]

The lines of division in today's international law debates—Westphalian sovereignty on the one hand, Kantian cosmopolitan cooperation on the other—were already in place when the Institut de Droit International was established in Ghent, Belgium, in the 1870s. Westphalian sovereignty had conceptualized each state as an island, regulating its internal affairs through its own laws and only occasionally interacting with other states—usually at times of war and when diplomacy was required. The alternative posed by institute members saw Europe (though not yet the entire world) as a relational system of sovereign states interacting with each other territorially through the activities of commerce and legal processes of diplomacy and treaties. The institute posed law as the product of popular conscience rather than the creation of sovereign will.[33]

More than a century later the principle of sovereignty as inviolate national autonomy has been challenged by international military interventions in civil conflicts. This is a new phenomenon that arose from global conditions in the 1990s that challenged the meaning of national sovereignty in much the same way that European colonization of the New World challenged earlier understandings. During the Cold War period, neither the UN Security Council nor individual governments dared to intervene over issues like human rights, genocide, oppression, and torture. Since the UN intervention in Haiti in 1994, however, humanitarian intervention has put the concept of inviolate national sovereignty up for renegotiation. The number of such military interventions has been relatively few, a patchwork of inconsistent justifications and too-often sluggish international responses that have had varying degrees of efficacy. International interventions have occurred in response to instances of genocide or ethnic cleansing, and occasionally and selectively in order to promote democracy.[34] Arguably such events of recent decades have reshaped understandings of sovereignty,[35] but there is a vigorous debate over how this has taken shape.[36] International sentiment about sovereignty continues to evolve even while the aftermath of the intervention in Iraq has led to a backlash in cosmopolitan hopes. These developments make it clear that some of the historical roots of sovereignty remain relevant today while others are outdated and should be reconceived.

Relational Sovereignty

Sovereignty today is more complex than was implied in both the Peace of Westphalia and the postcolonial period. The economic interdependence of states has grown with the end of the Cold War, the expansion of the European Union, and the increasing influence of the World Trade Organization and the World Bank.[37] The proliferation of regional and international organizations has subtly led to a diffusion of state influence beyond their sovereign borders, especially the economically stronger states relative to the poorer states.[38] Of course the distribution of these economic and political changes is uneven and often unjust. Even so, contemporary globalization has blurred the distinction between domestic politics and international politics and in more pronounced ways than that of the trading organizations and established religious institutions of prior centuries.[39]

The difference today is that global communications provide graphic, moment-by-moment evidence of the disparity between the rhetoric and the reality of human rights equality. The diversity of economic interests and the disparities of wealth, culture, and standards of life among countries has led in turn to new expectations of government performance. States are now widely understood to be "instruments at the service of their peoples, and not vice versa."[40] Statehood seen this way means that governments function as protectors of the freedoms articulated by the human rights tradition—a situation Kant could not have foreseen.

Sovereignty today is consequently freighted with new meaning. What would once have been seen as a parochial national issue may now have regional or international importance.[41] A country's claim to sovereignty—the sort of strong claim that under the traditional definition of sovereignty would have kept other states beyond its borders at bay—is no longer an absolute barrier during a human rights crisis.[42] For corrupt or violent governments sovereignty may be transferred to external military interveners in order to halt human rights violations. The sentiment that national sovereignty can be breached in cases of massive human rights violations has led to new attempts to establish stable domestic governance following military occupations in post-conflict zones such as Kosovo and East Timor. New thinking about sovereignty has led to alternative institutional arrangements such as trusteeships and shared sovereignty arrangements to legitimize handover arrangements while establishing good governance and protection of human rights.

Equally countries that wish to participate in global economic life must incorporate international standards as the price of their admission. Assessments by external actors—national governments and commercial interests alike—weigh human rights standards when evaluating their involvement in another county. For poorer countries wanting to join regional or international trading blocs, becoming a fully autonomous trading partner may be deferred while a poor human rights record is corrected. It may even result in external actors placing conditions upon the terms of economic aid. While sovereignty for the most economically powerful states such as the U.S. and China can more easily continue in the traditional Westphalian model, sovereignty for most countries today, especially for the poorer ones, is a qualitative status rated by external actors.

State sovereignty is increasingly defined through a country's relationships with *other* states and through the contingencies of international economic, military, and diplomatic relationships. Relational definitions of sovereignty include the interest that one country may have in the quality of human rights in another. They combine the traditional notion of sovereignty captured by Hobbes and the Westphalia treaties, that of sovereignty as an expression of popular political will in classical rule-of-law terms, and the idea that governments act as co-coordinating mechanisms between one nation-state and the rest of the world. Of course pure national self-interest in the old Hobbesian-Westphalian sense still applies when governments are in jeopardy from external military (or terrorist) threat or internal political threats, but even on issues of national security, cooperation with international neighbors is increasingly the norm.

The idea of sovereignty as relational extends beyond the Westphalia model and includes three features: the postcolonial spirit of equality of human rights, new conditions of greater knowledge about human rights harms, and increasing levels of economic transactions across state borders. It captures not only external recognition of a government's political control over territory, but also an element of judgment about the quality of that control.

International Humanitarian Intervention

The UN Charter

When Kant wrote *Perpetual Peace* more than two centuries ago, he argued that world peace would come when states gave respect to the sovereignty of every other state. He proposed a global compact of the world's nation-states, each of equal status irrespective of their military might, a confederation, or "league of states." The league would have no coercive military power because that would "violate the internal sovereignty of states."[43] Unlike Hugo Grotius and Emmerich de Vattel, who favored outside intervention to stop internal brutality that "insult[s] the conscience of civilized people,"[44] Kant advocated a total ban on intervention. Indeed had he known about them, he would probably have criticized the two earliest humanitarian military actions of the modern age— the liberation of Greece from the Ottoman invasion by Great Britain, France, and Russia in 1827 (just shortly before Kant's death);[45] and U.S. Pres. William McKinley's intervention in Cuba to "end barbarism, killings and massacres . . . and which parties in conflict were very reluctant to stop."[46]

The 1946 United Nations Charter formalized Kant's injunction against military aggression in the principle of inviolate national sovereignty. Article 2(4) of the charter prohibits the use of force or threat of force by one state against another, allowing only two exceptions: Article 51 in Chapter VII permits a state to use force in self-defense if an armed attack occurs against it or an allied country[47] and the UN Security Council is authorized to employ force to counter threats to breaches of international peace.[48] In other words there is nothing in the written text of the UN Charter that permits international military intervention to stop or prevent human rights violations, even when the violations reach extremes such as genocide or, as the international community lately witnessed, ethnic cleansing.[49]

Chapter VII taken at its face value prohibits *any* humanitarian military action across a national border by any outside force, whether a member state or an international force drawn from several member states, as a contravention of the UN's principles of inviolate national sovereignty.

Post–Cold War Justifications for Interventions

In the past decade or so the UN Security Council has authorized several Chapter VII interventions in violent civil conflicts—in Somalia, Rwanda, Haiti, and Bosnia and Herzegovina.[50] Each of these interventions has occurred with seeming disregard for the traditional doctrine of inviolate national sovereignty as international soldiers have been sent across a state border to rescue citizens from human rights violations. There have also been multilateral military interventions outside the UN Charter when a group of countries has acted of their own accord, as when NATO sent troops into Bosnia in 1995 after the massacre by the Serbs of some 7,000 Muslim men in the UN "safe haven" of Srebrenica.[51] These interventions were all humanitarian military operations intended to stop egregious human rights violations taking place within the territorial borders of a member state. More recently still, the U.S. has justified its military invasion of Iraq, which took place outside the provisions of Chapter VII of the UN Charter, on the grounds of humanitarian intervention intended to promote democracy and establish new institutions.

Debates about the Legitimacy of Intervention

These humanitarian interventions exemplify the tension between sovereignty as a concept of territorial control and human rights as a concept of individual well-being. The need for intervention in a humanitarian crisis is often time-specific; a swift response is required to save lives when a government appears unable or unwilling to defend its citizens from genocide, war crimes, or ethnic cleansing. Proponents of humanitarian intervention to stop such atrocities argue that the international community has a duty to prevent egregious violations of universal human rights, using military force if necessary and disregarding a government's claim of inviolate national sovereignty. They argue that in circumstances when the only way to prevent further loss of life is through sending in UN peacekeeping troops, a de facto exception to inviolate national sovereignty ought to be read into the understanding of Article 2(4) of the UN Charter so as to legitimize entry across a country's border by external military forces or peacekeepers.[52] Still others argue that humanitarian intervention may be justified by individual rescuer states, acting unilaterally and without the backing of the UN Security Council. This latter justification is used by those who point to the slow processes of the UN Security Council to reach a unanimous decision under Chapter VII powers.

Both arguments place international human rights above national sovereignty and rely on the universal right to life and freedom enunciated in the UN Declaration of Human Rights, repeated in all subsequent international human rights documents, and either expressed or implied in the constitutions of all states in the world today. The U.S. argument for humanitarian intervention for the promotion of democracy also relies on international human rights ideas for justification, specifically Article 21 of the UN Declaration of Human Rights, the right to free elections. Each of the justifications—the right to life arguments and the right to democracy argument—make universal human rights more important than state sovereignty.

Naturally, international intervention is controversial, especially among smaller countries that have a colonial past, and especially when promotion of democracy is invoked to justify intervention. Opponents of humanitarian intervention have argued that Article 2(4) of the UN Charter prohibits *any* military intervention in another country, irrespective of human rights violations.[53] Although usually based on the traditional definition of sovereignty as inviolate national autonomy, this position has been reiterated by Harvard philosopher John Rawls in *The Law of Peoples*, written just before his death in 1999. Rawls argued against military intervention, most certainly intervention for political reasons such as the promotion of democracy and probably also with humanitarian motives. His point was that liberal societies have an obligation to tolerate "decent" non-liberal societies and that this ought to disqualify military, economic, and diplomatic sanctions. He extended the principle of nonintervention to include a prohibition on economic inducements to countries to influence them to change their governance—precisely the sort of economic transactions that have in the last decade become commonplace in international monetary aid programs. Rawls's rejection of all types of interventions reinforces the old version of sovereignty as national inviolability, even while he endorses the principle of human rights as universal and international. Human rights of life, liberty, personal property, and formal equality, though morally due to all people, do not, in Rawls's view, give license to outsiders to intervene with armies or even money.[54]

Triggers for International Humanitarian Intervention

Returning to the face-value meaning of the UN Charter, we can state that military interventions to prevent genocide or authoritarian rule are not grounds for international military intervention under traditional international law. Nonetheless this meaning of the doctrine of state sovereignty has been overlooked in some circumstances in the past decade. The recent history of humanitarian intervention suggests that human rights violations may create an environment that seems to invite international action to protect a people from human rights harms such as torture, genocide, ethnic cleansing, and crimes against humanity. Should this new international permission to breach national sovereignty be understood more strongly so as to create a *responsibility* on the *international community* to provide humanitarian intervention in each and every case? How should the moral reasons for humanitarian rescue shape understandings of sovereignty in the international legal system?

International Interventions

Since the international community's failure to prevent the deaths of 800,000 people in the 1994 Rwandan genocide, international debate about international intervention to prevent egregious infringements of human rights has tilted in favor of intervention. For example in 1999, when Slobodan Milošević's brutal regime was systematically expelling Kosovar Albanians from their homeland, NATO forces invaded Kosovo to stop the harm. In that same year UN peacekeepers stepped in to stop the slaughter of East Timorese by Indonesian militiamen. Both Kosovo and East Timor were dire cases of protracted internal conflict where the death toll was mounting daily. Facing these circumstances, the international community bypassed national sovereignty and crossed a state border in order to prevent further human rights violations.

Given the wording of the UN Charter, these interventions seem a triumph of practical action and moral sentiment over outdated legal definitions. In the name of rescuing human rights victims UN-authorized interventions in recent years have used legal gymnastics to overcome concerns about inviolate national sovereignty. Each time, the civil war in a country was ingeniously reinterpreted by the UN Security Council as a threat to international peace so that the conflict could be brought formally under Chapter VII of the charter. Without that interpretation, the doctrine of inviolate national sovereignty in international law would have kept peacekeepers at the border. In fact in 1999, when Serbs were killing, raping, and forcibly removing Kosovars, NATO was so concerned about the UN Charter's guarantee of sovereignty that it did not even try to seek prior Security Council approval; it simply intervened without official UN sanction.

When the UN Security Council uses Chapter VII "international peace and security" justifications to intervene to rescue a population under duress, however, it forces a square peg into a round hole. These awkward interpretations are contested by smaller countries. For example the Security Council cited fears of a civil conflict threatening peace and security when it passed Resolution 940 under its Chapter VII powers to justify the international military mission to Haiti in 1994. In fact Haiti's problems were so tied to its own domestic politics and national history that it was unlikely the conflict would affect other states. The U.S-led United Nations intervention was opposed by many Latin American countries, which saw the intervention as a cloak for restoring the rule of Jean-Baptiste Aristide rather than truly motivated by the goal of saving Haitian lives.[55]

Five years later similar tensions between international law and international moral sentiment arose regarding East Timor. When rampaging Indonesian militiamen were slaughtering East Timorese by the hundreds in 1999, the murders were graphically documented in pictures circulated by the world media. As terrible as these violations were, however, there was little risk that Indonesia would allow the conflict to spill beyond the immediate region to threaten the peace or security of the region. In these circumstances a Security Council resolution based on Chapter VII of the UN Charter would have impinged directly upon Indonesia's claim of sovereignty over East Timor. The sovereignty problem in this civil conflict was ingeniously circumnavigated when UN Sec.-Gen. Kofi Annan stated that senior Indonesian officials risked prosecution for crimes against humanity if they did not consent to the deployment of a multinational force in East Timor.[56] The choices Annan laid out were for the Indonesian government either to send troops itself to stop the killing or permit international troops to land in Dili.[57] East Timor was an international bargaining chip for sovereignty and human rights standards. In the end Indonesia gave permission for international peacekeepers to land in East Timor. This device has since been called the "Annan Doctrine": the coerced waiver of the traditional prerogatives of sovereignty in the face of prosecutions for crimes against humanity.[58]

NATO's 1999 intervention in Kosovo similarly emphasized the tension between traditional and newer ideas about sovereignty when human rights are at stake. NATO acted in Kosovo because the UN could not. Russia's veto power in the Security Council had stalled UN intervention, and lives of innocents were being lost with every second of delay. The Independent International Commission on Kosovo, formed one year later, concluded that though NATO's actions may not have been strictly legal under the traditional understanding of sovereignty, the intervention was nevertheless legitimate because it had resolved a humanitarian crisis and enjoyed widespread support within the international community and civil society.[59]

In the wake of the Kosovo and East Timor affairs, sovereignty has become a more ambiguous concept, effectively downgraded from being an absolute barrier to outside states intervening in places where a government is killing its own people or failing to intervene where people are killing each other. It is unclear though just how serious a humanitarian crisis needs to be in order to trigger international intervention. This conceptual lack of clarity has affected international debate even more since the U.S.-led invasion of Iraq.[60]

Initially the United States justified the Iraq invasion as preemptive defense against weapons of mass destruction—a broad interpretation of the self-defense exception to inviolate national sovereignty under Article 2 of the UN Charter.[61] Allegations of Saddam Hussein's links to al-Qaeda completed that argument. At the time of the invasion, violations of human rights in Iraq were secondary to the main rationale of preemptive defense.[62] As the initial justifications for invasion were shown to be without merit, however, the U.S. administration increasingly emphasized human rights as its rationale. Pres. George W. Bush argued that the desire for freedom and human rights was universal and that the U.S. was dedicated to supporting peoples' claims for democracy—by force if necessary.[63] Bush's position moves the rationale for humanitarian intervention much beyond genocide, extending it to include the toppling of an undemocratic government.

Fictions Produce Problems

De Facto Triggers for Intervention   The commission of genocide as a de facto exception to inviolate national sovereignty has allowed states such as the U.S. and the U.K. to build an even more elaborate interpretation about exceptions to national sovereignty—an interpretation standing on the shoulders of another interpretation—that humanitarian intervention can extend to regime change even when there is no evidence of recent genocide. The U.S. intervention to rescue Iraq by bringing it democracy was an outgrowth of the international humanitarian interventions of the 1990s, yet a closer examination of the past decade's military interventions reveals that at a moment in history when the moral arguments for humanitarian military action have never seemed more persuasive, the practical grounds to sustain those moral arguments are doubtful. Efforts to fit humanitarian intervention into the existing international legal apparatus are elaborate artifices that create uncertainty and ersatz standards. There are dangers should international humanitarian action get ahead of international law, and not just because of lack of clarity about what are the triggers for intervention. The well-intentioned desire to improve human rights abroad may distract attention from the lessons of history about *post*-intervention human rights. History has demonstrated how difficult it is for outsiders to rebuild a conflict-torn society, and more recent interventions retell that cautionary tale. Kosovo, Iraq, and to some extent East Timor are recent and sometimes savage warnings that an international policy of intervention triggered by mass human rights violations may be unable to deliver enough post-intervention security to guarantee human rights improvements.

Kosovo   While the international rescue of Kosovo is often held up as a test case for changing the old meaning of inviolate national sovereignty, this instance also demonstrates how difficult it is for outsiders to impose sustainable human rights. Governed by the UN Interim Administration Mission in Kosovo and independent by its own declaration since February 2008, Kosovo has become an international experiment in society-building. Seven years after NATO's intervention, though, Kosovo seems as far from stability and social peace as ever. The past decade's victims have become today's victimizers. Disappearances and retaliation killings have not stopped but simply have reversed, with the non-Albanian (mainly Serb) population now being victimized by the ethnic Albanians.

In other words, it is not at all clear that the 1999 intervention has produced a lasting human rights solution. Despite frequent assurances from UN authorities that Kosovo is on a path to reconciliation and true home rule, NATO and the European Union (the key regional bodies that have recognized Kosovo's sovereignty in the face of Serbia's objection) will clearly need to maintain a long-term military presence there to guarantee that there will be no forced expulsion of the Kosovo Serb population. In other words, human rights in Kosovo continue to be in jeopardy. Instead of peace "a noxious social and political residue pervades today's Kosovo. Instead of cooling communal conflict, interethnic hatred remains as heated as ever . . . any chance of even beginning the much-needed reconciliation process must now be pushed far into the future."[64]

East Timor   East Timor presents only a marginally more optimistic post-intervention story than Kosovo. Peacekeepers stopped the violence after the landslide vote by the East Timorese in favor of independence from Indonesia, and three years later, in 2002, East Timor became the first state in the twenty-first century to join the United Nations. Notwithstanding the size of the task that faced the country after the international humanitarian intervention, the euphoria was immense among East Timorese: their liberation came after more than twenty years of Indonesian rule and 200 years as a Portuguese colony before that. There was no question that international intervention had stopped a terrible human rights crisis, and there it was clear that international help in establishing self-rule was both welcome and necessary.

At the same time, the East Timorese road to self-determination has not fully resolved its human rights issues. A very poor country with one of the lowest GDPs in the world, East Timor was faced with the task of rebuilding the 70 percent of its infrastructure that had been destroyed as the Indonesian militiamen's parting gesture. In April 2006 riots in Dili resulted in deaths, and more than twenty thousand people fled their homes. Fierce fighting between pro- and antigovernment troops broke out, with the violence following the lines of old ethnic schisms.[65] Australia, Malaysia, New Zealand, and Portugal have sent troops back into East Timor. An International Stabilization Force remains there today, even after new rounds of elections. Producing a stable post-conflict society is proving much more difficult than the initial military intervention to stop the slaughter.

Iraq   The case of Iraq provides an even starker warning about the cocktail of sovereignty, intervention, and human rights. Those who believed the Iraq invasion was good for democracy in the Middle East saw their views confirmed in the ink-stained fingers of Iraqi voters who queued up to vote in the various elections held between January and December 2005. By any estimation, however, five years after the invasion the human rights situation for Iraqis is worse than it was before, precisely because of the U.S. "rescue."

This outcome is unsurprising when seen in the context of a longer history. The invasion of Iraq is not the first time that U.S. or multilateral forces have engaged in state-building in troubled countries, ostensibly in the name of bringing the benefits of Western-style political rights. U.S. military forces underwrote U.S.-style governments in the Dominican Republic (1924), Nicaragua (1933), Cuba (1934), and Haiti (1934), all of them failing to achieve their goal. By 1939 only one democracy existed in the Latin American region—Costa Rica—where the U.S. had never intervened. Iraq is repeating an old pattern of failures, cautionary tales that underscore the complexity of trying to foster human rights through external militarily coercive means. Like the failed interventions in Latin America the "coalition of the willing" in Iraq has found that implementing human rights from the outside is difficult.

Distractions from Reality   The realities of Kosovo, East Timor, and Iraq—recent examples to which earlier ones could be added—show that extolling the virtues of new statehood at the end of a period of violence and repression may be an empty gesture when old human rights problems are replaced by new ones.[66] The best of humanitarian intentions will not necessarily herald a new chapter in human rights. Unless humanitarian interventions can guarantee the most basic rights to life and security, the antagonisms that inspired the intervention in the first place may be reinforced rather than diminished. Even if outside countries have sufficient knowledge of domestic politics and pressures to provide the most basic of human rights, hopes of quickly building a culture of Western-style human rights seem highly ambitious, even hubristic. Installing democratic, human-rights-oriented regimes by military force simply fuels suspicion that these interventions are old-style colonialism in the new guise of democracy and human rights.

These artful interpretations of Chapter VII of the UN Charter that a human rights crisis threatens international peace and security—or unilateral proxies for that fiction that put national troops instead of UN peacekeeping troops on the ground—have deflected attention from the central issue: whether it is likely that an intervening force will be able to consolidate human rights and markedly improve everyday conditions for the public. Resolving the tension between national sovereignty, human rights, and forced international action has never been more urgent.

Democracy Promotion Does Not Justify Humanitarian Intervention

The response I offer puts relational sovereignty as the central indicator against which the international community ought to measure its humanitarian interest in national affairs. My argument is that a national government's traditional inviolate sovereignty should be disregarded not only when intervention is conducted in order to prevent genocide or crimes against humanity, but also when wide-scale deaths through starvation or lack of resources can be attributed to government action or inaction. This is unquestionably an extension of the understanding of intervention that has emerged over the past decade and follows from the nature of international humanitarian interest that I describe below. It also follows from my definition that humanitarian intervention properly understood ought not to justify military intervention to put democracy in the place of autocracy, or even demagoguery.

Human Rights at Gunpoint

Intervention may stop an immediate human rights crisis, but recent evidence suggests that it may not succeed in delivering longer-term human rights.

Kosovo (still limping along in repetitions of its conflict-ridden past); East Timor (requiring ever more military help from outside to quell civil conflict); and Iraq (daily reeling from chaos) are reminders of the case for traditional sovereignty. Humanitarian interventions can misfire so badly in fact that human rights may be worse after an intervention than before.

If the idea of international human rights intervention is to have a sound justification, it is worth thinking through some of the checks and balances on the international community's use of military force in the name of human rights. It needs to be better understood that there are moral, practical, and legal dimensions to humanitarian intervention that may, or may not, point in the same direction. These dimensions need to be teased out, disaggregated, and better understood. I suggest here a threefold test: moral, practical, and procedural.

Widespread Egregious Human Rights Harms

Humanitarian crises in Rwanda, Kosovo, and to a lesser extent, The Sudan, have established that the international community has a moral interest in preventing genocide. The test of widespread harm has already emerged for international intervention in genocide.[67] For example after the Rwanda and Kosovo crises, then-UN secretary-general Kofi Annan stated that if all diplomatic efforts had failed, military intervention might be triggered if a human rights crisis reached levels of genocide or ethnic cleansing.

The threshold for international humanitarian intervention ought to be the determination of a government's direct culpability in causing, or failing to prevent, the widespread death of innocents. Annan's test should be interpreted to mean that military intervention might also be justified in cases of widespread starvation caused by a regime's persistently negligent or intentional failure to distribute minimally necessary goods and essential sustenance. Situations of widespread death through malnutrition or preventable disease should render an uncaring government equally as *morally* culpable as would genocide. The rationale for international intervention should apply to both overt violence *and* death and disease. The method of causing those deaths is less relevant than the intent and involvement of governments and the number of people killed.

There is no *moral* difference between deaths caused by a government's brutality to its people and those caused by a corrupt government's failure to distribute social and economic goods among all its population when those resources are available. Terrible malnutrition, starvation, and disease, when directly caused by a government's culpable inaction, are not categorically different from a gruesome death at the hands of militiamen. Total numbers of deaths may be the same or greater where governments leave their populations to starve, and likewise, the pain and anguish experienced by victims will be no less intense. Such behavior ought therefore to have the same moral status as genocide or ethnic cleansing. In either case a sovereign government has failed in its role to protect its people.

A murderous, corrupt, or neglectful government's failure to prevent the death or injury of its citizens breaches the social contract in its most essential Hobbesian form. It certainly breaches the social contract under contemporary international conditions of swift transmission of knowledge about human rights crises and swift offers of international aid for victims. While death by government violence or civil war may seem to represent the more shocking abrogation of a government's duty to care for its people, such a comparison overlooks some of the most fundamental responsibilities of governments—their obligation to distribute at least minimal social and economic goods to those in the grip of a human rights crisis that is causing massive deaths. When a despotic or corrupt government refuses to help its citizens and also refuses to allow the international community to provide uncoerced assistance, the moral conditions for military humanitarian intervention have been met.

It is worth remembering that the rationale underlying humanitarian intervention is the international community's interest in protecting a suffering population. This justification for intervention ought to apply equally to death delivered by governments by degrees over weeks and months. The critical moral assessment is whether a government caused harm when it could have prevented it. This means of course that governments that are so weak or ineffective that they have virtually no capacity for meaningful humanitarian action—commonly referred to as "failed states"—do not arrive at the threshold moral standard that would justify military intervention because such governments do not intentionally cause conditions causing death. They are incompetent rather than culpable. The crucial element for the moral triggering of military humanitarian intervention is a government's capacity to help its citizens coupled with its intentional withholding of government resources.

Properly understood under contemporary conditions, sovereignty includes the duty to prevent malnutrition and disease through better distribution of scarce social goods. The moral threshold of military humanitarian intervention should be extreme and widespread harm, whether this comes from deadly civil mayhem or malnutrition and disease. Intervention should be morally permissible under these circumstances, because intentional or negligent failure of a state to distribute public goods is a failure of national sovereignty.

Moral sanction to intervene simply gets across the first threshold, however. A moral trigger on its own cannot create a legal obligation nor address the practical likelihood that intervention will subsequently produce human rights benefits. Kosovo, Iraq, and the string of U.S.-led interventions in Latin America in the first half of the twentieth century have all demonstrated that intervention needs both a moral *and* a practical assessment. The next requirement is to establish that intervention is likely to result in human rights improvements.

Improving Human Rights

For states to act as good samaritans it needs to be clear that the circumstances of international intervention are likely to provide a remedy to suffering populations. The practical justification for humanitarian intervention ought to be that the interveners are likely to stop the dying *and then be able to make durable improvements in the human rights situation.*

This is a very tall order. Kosovo illustrates the difficulty of overcoming the religious and ethnic schisms that led to human rights problems in the first place, and even now that Kosovo has claimed its own sovereignty, the danger remains that ethnic tensions will flare again into mass violence. Iraq demonstrates the huge burden borne by interveners when domestic groups are not only killing each other but also attacking the interveners. East Timor reveals the frustrating slowness of human rights changes when social and political infrastructure has been devastated. U.S. interventions in Latin America show that lasting change imposed from the outside may simply be impossible. Taken together these examples attest to the immense practical difficulty of bringing about human rights through external military force.

Setting the bar so high for practical humanitarian intervention presupposes several things. First, people are unlikely to accept human rights at the point of a gun. Yale Law School scholar W. Michael Reisman's formulation of sovereignty as something that rests with citizens and not with governments puts it well because it places sovereign power where it really belongs.

Interveners are at best merely acting as proxies for people who have not had the domestic means to give expression to their political preferences.[68] Put differently, humanitarian intervention is a substitute for citizens' self-help. For intervention to have credibility there needs to be substantial, reliable evidence of a groundswell of popular opposition to a government that is heedlessly abusing human rights.

The sobering and unpalatable truth is that even when internal conditions might indicate support for intervention it is possible and even likely that intervention will not bring substantial longer-term human rights improvements. East Timor for example seemed to provide incontrovertible evidence that external human rights assistance would be welcome, because the 1999 referendum results showed significant popular support for independence from Indonesia. The vote came after decades of pro-independence activity. It seemed beyond doubt that the East Timorese wanted self-rule, needed help when the violence broke out, and welcomed external intervention. Despite these auspicious beginnings, establishing a human rights order in East Timor has been fraught with difficulty.

In addition to the need for local support the rescue of human rights victims must be—*and must be seen by victims to be*—the single motive for intervention. The ethical principle of the good samaritan has been interpreted by Western courts over the years as requiring rescuers to have pure intent—that is, to have in mind only the interests of a victim whom they seek to rescue, without any other ulterior motive. Neither the initial justification by the U.S. of its invasion of Iraq—preemptive defense—nor its ex post justification of bringing democracy to the people has persuaded enough of Iraq's population to believe in the legitimacy of U.S. occupation. As a result human rights conditions in the country continue to be terrible. In contrast East Timor's struggles to establish democracy since the 1999 intervention are attributed by East Timorese and the international community alike to its colonial past—its rule by both Portugal and Indonesia—as well as to the failings of East Timorese politicians. East Timor's difficulties are not laid at the feet of the interveners but are blamed on economic and social conditions derived from centuries of past colonization and the scorched-earth policy of the departing militiamen. Secure in the widespread desire of the East Timorese for independence from Indonesia, Australian peacekeepers enjoy high credibility among the local population because there is no doubt that their presence is motivated by humanitarian concerns, nothing more.

Multilateralism

The best indicator that genuine humanitarian intent lies at the heart of military intervention is that it is instigated by a broadly-based international or multi-national coalition. The success in East Timor relative to the situation in Iraq can be attributed in part to the fact that external help arrived under the aus-pices of the United Nations. Military intervention was a multilateral response to wide-scale hideous human rights abuses that were in progress—killings, rapes, razing of property, and the like. Oil reserves beneath the Timor Sea were not perceived as the motivation behind the UN's intervention.

U.S. credibility in Iraq on the other hand suffers as a result of its leadership in the military intervention, unsanctioned by the UN. The invasion of Iraq did not take place for the sake of stopping a civil conflict (as it did in Kosovo and East Timor) nor in the name of restoring a democratically elected official (as in Haiti). The U.S. leadership of the Iraq invasion is an unfortunate re-versal of the tendency towards multilateralism in the post–Cold War period. Multilateralism works better than unilateralism because it dilutes impressions of national hubris. A process-driven multilateral intervention led by an in-ternational body such as the UN or a regional organization such as NATO is better able to defend its actions from charges of self-interest.

Democracy and Human Rights

Democracy under the UN System

Participatory political rights are part of the international human rights regime. Article 21 of the UN Universal Declaration of Human Rights says there is a universal right "to take part in [a] government" and also that the "will of the people shall . . . be expressed in periodic and genuine elections which shall be . . . held by secret vote or by equivalent free voting procedures."[69] Until the slow tragedy of the occupation of Iraq, democracy as the modus vivendi for delivering liberty and human rights was unquestioned. Nobel Prize–winner and philosopher Amartya Sen described democracy in the twentieth century as "the 'normal' form of government to which any nation is entitled—whether in Europe, America, Asia, or Africa."[70] In *The Law of Peoples* Rawls wrote of democracy as the best feature of a liberal society, a feature that ought to grant full membership in international society.[71] "Decent hierarchical societies" also should be members of international society, but not the rest—"outlaw states," "societies burdened by unfavorable conditions," and "benevolent absolutisms."

Kant certainly believed that more and more "republics"—what today translates as democracies—would form as the ineluctable consequence of sensible reasoning. Republican forms of government would lead a trend toward world peace, Kant wrote, as "[in a Republic] . . . the consent of the citizens is required in order to decide that war should be declared . . . nothing is more natural than that they would be very cautious in commencing such a poor game, decreeing for themselves all the calamities of war."[72]

Today some construe Kant as implying moral connections between democracy, peace, and human rights and argue that "compliance with the norms prohibiting war-making [are] inextricably linked to observance of human rights and the democratic entitlement."[73]

Democracy as a Human Right

During the 1990s some international lawyers argued that Article 21 of the Universal Declaration of Human Rights establishes a right to democratic governance, a right that had evolved since 1948 and particularly since the end of European communism.[74] Proponents of a universal human right to democracy point to the world's new states, from southern Africa to Eastern Europe to Latin America, which have made human rights and democracy the centerpiece of their constitutions, thus creating "democracy [as] an . . . entitlement in international law."[75] For example American legal scholar Thomas Franck argued that states increasingly needed to demonstrate "fair access to political power and participation in societal decisions" to secure full membership in international society.[76]

In fact the intrinsic good of democracy today seems to be so taken for granted that any alternative type of regime is viewed as second best. For some the belief in democracy as the best system possible is unassailable, a view promoted in a tone that is "millenist (sic), triumphalist, upbeat. The examples being set by liberal nations' treaties and their transgovernmental networks in the wake of the victory over communism mark the beginnings of a global 'new deal' or a 'new liberal democratic order.'" International law is often a part of this mood, with liberal international law promising to replicate the liberal welfare state.[77]

For some this has led to the suggestion that military invasion ought to enforce the entitlement to democracy. It sees the use of external force to breach the national sovereignty of a undemocratic country as potentially justified because of hoped-for gains in building up its *internal* sovereignty and its domestic liberal governance structures. The hope is that healthier state systems will eventually permit the restoration of external sovereignty, leading to legal recognition of a newly legitimate national government that other states see as credible. W. Michael Reisman for example has argued that clear violations of a country's popular political preferences ought to allow outsiders to intervene where they intend to restore power to a government that has a rightful claim. Reisman has suggested that in the right circumstances, intervention could be exercised both by UN and unilateral forces.[78] By this calculation UN intervention in East Timor would have been lawful *whether or not* the Indonesian government had finally allowed UN peacekeepers to land. Intervention may even have been permissible much earlier, as early as 1975, when Indonesia took over East Timor by force after the Portuguese colonial administration pulled out and the East Timorese first asserted their wish for self-rule.[79]

The policy implications of this worldview are profound. Applying the moral philosophy of Sen and Rawls to international policy assumes a direct and causal connection between democracy, better human rights, and economic wealth. When Kant in his political writings stated that the greatest problem, "the most difficult and the last to be solved by the human race, is attaining universal justice,"[80] he was making a philosophical point: "a philosophical attempt to work out a universal history of the world."[81] Moral hopes are only a starting point for international policy that require careful checks and balances when put into action.

Following the terrorist tragedies in Bali, Beslan, London, Madrid, Moscow, Mumbai, New York, Philippines, and Washington D.C., the pro-democracy argument has taken a new twist, that the purpose of building up weak states is not just to improve human rights abroad. Rather it is seen as a good investment in global safety and stability.[82] Aimed at reversing the trend of growing terrorism, regional instability, conflict, and humanitarian crises, this strategy starts with the assumption that more democratic institutions will build better international neighbors.[83] The rationale for humanitarian intervention based upon international concern for wide-scale human rights violations in another country is getting lost in a debate about international security. My aim here is to urge a return to an understanding of humanitarianism that places human rights at the core of its definition.

Humanitarian Intervention from Here

International humanitarian intervention to stop mass deaths, by murder or by neglect, has great moral urgency. Looking at some of the past decade's humanitarian interventions, it is still too soon to say whether the institutions established will be more able to deliver human rights than previous regimes could do.

Military interventions with ambiguous intentions can have disastrous results. Even interventions perceived as truly humanitarian have not produced quick human rights results. Efforts to improve human rights from the outside can risk making human rights worse, or conflict may simply be pushed underground only to reemerge later. Failed human rights interventions may be more dangerous than no intervention at all, because the international stage amplifies grievances and provides combatants access to resources from outside the region.[84]

International expectations of domestic governments include respect for basic human rights, such as the right to life and to bodily integrity. In the past decade these expectations have been directly affected by military interventions. It is important, therefore, to have clear principles to guide humanitarian interventions, whether these be authorized by the UN or undertaken multilaterally by groups of states. The risks of humanitarian intervention are so high that only the most serious cases of mass murder ought to be considered legitimate, and even then only after hard-headed assessments have demonstrated that an international presence will likely fulfill its humanitarian task.

Humanitarianism as democracy-promotion goes too far, and ought not to provide a rationale for military intervention. History suggests that successful transplantation of democratic institutions requires the level of baseline political and civil organization that existed in pre–World War II Germany and Japan. Unlike an internal civil war or military coup that has the goal of establishing democracy, externally imposed democracy seems contradictory: it is the use of force to claim that a particular vision of life is universal, when the very heart of freedom and liberty is the freedom to determine one's own particular vision. For better or worse, critics of the U.S. and other Western countries are likely to connect messianic self-assurance about Western democracy with human rights promotion abroad per se. Liberalism is a philosophy of consent, and promotion of democracy as it has been done in Iraq threatens the very foundations of liberalism.

The promotion of human rights should be accomplished by persuasion not aggression. To the extent that human rights can be an international program it should be one of multilateral cooperation and not unilateral conviction. Despite its fits-and-starts nature and its frustrations, the work of the international system of human rights as one of persuasion and emulation through gradual change implemented from within by local populations and aided from outside by incentives and rewards has the best long-term chance of success. This method puts states back in control, with all of the drawbacks this necessarily implies about governments that do not fully implement the Western vision of human rights. This vector intersects with the concept of sovereignty and fully engages economic globalization, electronic technology, and international sentiments about human rights that have shaped our understanding of sovereignty. Sovereignty today is best seen as a relationship between governments and citizens in which the international community unilaterally, bilaterally, and multilaterally exercises an interest. I call this relational sovereignty.

The argument I have made here revives the moral foundations of both sovereignty and humanitarianism. Death at the hands of one's own government evokes a moral outcry elsewhere in the world. Yet international rescue should be reserved for the very worst cases of a government killing its people and not invoked in service of liberal idealism or national self-protection that wishes to install democracy abroad. Once intervention is seen as a moral response that imposes a high evidentiary burden on the intervener, international attention will be forced back to the slow, incremental, and multilateral process of making the case for the liberal human rights vision.

I have emphasized three key criteria for international military intervention in the name of human rights—moral, practical, and procedural. An expanded moral justification for intervention should go hand in hand with much more realistic evaluations of the practical limitations of interventions. The moral justification for intervention I suggest is that governments risk losing the shield of sovereignty by killing their citizens, whether through acts of genocide and widespread killing or through callous denial of available social goods such as food and medicine. The practical and procedural thresholds are the likelihood that intervention will produce better human rights, and that better decisions about intervention come from multilateral processes. The latter thresholds are high because the deck is stacked against interveners. Interveners, especially those with superior military strength, are unlikely to bring lasting human rights improvements.

The ongoing humanitarian crisis in Darfur has shown that there is a difference between gaining acceptance for a working theory of humanitarian intervention and making the theory work. When in 2005 the UN General Assembly approved a rule they called "the responsibility to protect" that gives international forces the right to step in militarily if governments are committing genocide, it was thought that more favorable international reactions would simply follow from international statements of intent. The phrasing of the resolution sought to break an impasse between sovereigntists and internationalists, though the question came up only after a national government had shown itself unwilling to act to prevent genocide or mass slaughter. As the spokesperson for the Enough Project, a Washington, D.C.–based group dedicated to preventing genocide, notes, "In the daily slugfest of international policy making, [Responsibility to Protect] hasn't survived the first test: Darfur."[85] Instead, even though the UN has tried to take the lead, member states have failed to fulfill promises of money and troops, and the Sudanese government has allowed UN peacekeepers into Darfur only on the condition that it be part of a joint mission with the African Union. The 7,000 African Union peacekeepers and 19,000 UN troops proved inadequate in reducing the violence in Darfur, however.

Whether moral triggers such as Darfur ought to be acted upon with military intervention depends upon the practical likelihood that an international intervener will be able to improve human rights. The practical limitations on interventions flow less from respect for international borders and more from a hard-nosed assessment of what an international intervener will be able to do in the months and years after intervention. While governments that inflict harm on their people ought to lose the traditional protections of traditional international law, the international community ought not to intervene unless a genuine human rights rescue can be implemented.

In this chapter I have sought to refocus the connection between international law, military force, humanitarian ideals, and human rights improvements. The emphasis has therefore been on the actions taken by governments, either on behalf of their own people or the population of another state. Some argue however that focusing on government action misses the point in today's globalized world: the failures of the international system are an inevitable product of a system that overstates the actions of national governments and understates the role of "civil society." In the next chapter I respond to the "civil society" critique of international human rights law and legal institutions.

Chapter 4

Reciprocal Judging

Introduction

In 2006 in the U.S. state of Georgia a Muslim gas-station clerk from Ethiopia named Khalid Adem was sentenced to ten years in prison for aggravated battery and cruelty to his two-year-old daughter. He had removed her clitoris with a pair of scissors in his suburban kitchen. The case fuelled a passionate debate in the U.S. and across the African continent. At the time Adem was charged, many U.S. states—including Georgia—had no laws prohibiting female genital cutting. Georgia responded by introducing legislation. Response in Adem's homeland was mixed: a senior official in the Ministry of Women's Affairs praised the punishment "because what he did is a violation of child rights." Ethiopian Prime Minister Meles Zenawi on the other hand said that, while it was his government's policy to discourage the practice, it was still common and "[i]f a whole community is involved in this practice, you cannot jail an entire community. You have to change the mindset, and that takes time."

Each year in Africa some three million girls and women are "cut" under a custom viewed by many traditional cultures as a necessary rite of passage. The procedure originated in Africa and remains today a mainly African cultural practice, though it also takes place in immigrant communities in the West. It predates Islam and is widely practiced even in countries such as Ethiopia and Kenya, where the predominant religion is Christianity. The consequences can be dire: they include prolonged bleeding, infection, infertility, and death. For those who suffer infibulation—the severest form of female genital cutting, in which all external sexual organs are cut away—cutting is repeated with each new birth to allow passage of the baby. About 130 million women in the world, principally in Africa, have undergone some form of cutting.

More and more laws are being passed to prohibit the practice. Roughly half of the African countries where the practice occurs have passed criminal laws prohibiting it. In 1994 Australia and Norway joined Sweden and the United Kingdom in passing laws against female genital cutting. France, Germany, Italy, and several U.S. states have laws that criminalize it, yet across Africa and in those Western countries that have attempted to use criminal law, courts have dismissed most cases for lack of evidence, often despite strong evidence from the victims and even confessions from their parents or the practitioners. Data from those African countries suggest that the criminal laws have not worked. Instead the average age of victims is simply decreasing. In Tanzania for example in order to avoid detection cutting is now carried out on some newborn babies, which leads to even more deaths than in the past. In Kenya, where the criminal penalty for practicing female genital cutting on females under eighteen is up to fifteen years' imprisonment, cutting is now performed on infants when they are already sick with a childhood illness so that if there are any problems there will not be suspicion among neighbors and relatives. In some parts of Burkina Faso, villagers reportedly have given local leaders large sums of money so they may have their daughters circumcised without fear of arrest or prosecution. The views of the girls themselves are rarely sought by local prosecution agencies, and in the event that they are, they are reluctant to testify against family members.

The impulse to use national criminal laws to change community cultural practices repeats a method that seems to have worked in the past. For example by the beginning of the twentieth-century dueling was almost universally prohibited by law as a criminal offense after a long history of national bans. King Henry IV of France outlawed dueling in 1602, making participation in a duel punishable by death. English legislation during the seventeenth and eighteenth centuries criminalized the practice. The 1928 criminal code of the Weimar Republic in Germany made duels an offense punishable by imprisonment. In the U.S. the District of Columbia outlawed dueling in 1839, and since the Civil War all states have legislated against dueling, imposing punishments ranging from disqualification from public office to death.

Similarly the Hindu rite of sati (suttee), the practice of a widow burning herself to death on her husband's funeral pyre, was criminalized by the British government in India in 1821 at a time when the annual count of widow deaths in Calcutta was estimated to be about 500.[1] Sati was declared illegal and punishable by the criminal courts as culpable homicide amounting to manslaughter (ironically) punishable by death. Orthodox Hindus protested the new criminal law by appealing to the Privy Council in London. The Privy Council dismissed their appeal and upheld the colonial law. In Hindu areas outside the jurisdiction of British imperial power the practice continued, and in 1839 four of the wives and seven female slaves of the Maharaja Ranjit Singh of the Punjab burned to death on the funeral pyre with his corpse. Today however the practice has virtually disappeared.

In China the custom of foot-binding has come to an end. In the nineteenth century 40–50 percent of Chinese women had bound feet. For the upper classes the figure was almost 100 percent. Foot-binding was first outlawed by the Qing dynasty in 1912—government inspectors could levy fines on those who continued to bind their daughters' feet, and the communists issued their own ban a year after they came to power in 1949. Today the practice no longer exists.

It is not clear whether these laws were the catalyst for changes in society or if they were simply following preexisting developments. In the case of foot-binding, for example, social change was already well under way by the time the prohibition was enacted. The practice had virtually vanished when the communist government issued its ban. It seems that most of the change occurred between 1900 and 1920, when anti-foot-binding associations were formed in many parts of China. People who joined these associations took an oath that they would not bind their daughters' feet and, perhaps even more important, that they would not permit their sons to marry women with bound feet. This created a new marriage market unpredicated on tiny three-inch "lotus" feet in potential wives. Extinction of the practices of dueling and widow-burning also seem to have been more influenced by deep social changes rather than criminal laws and legal process. In fact historians of the Indian colonial period now suggest that sati was more likely a cultural rebellion against British colonization itself, rather than a deeply ingrained preexisting practice.

In a global context supporting a culture's own efforts to transform or reform itself to reinforce equality is complicated.[2] The right approach, many say, is social rather than legal. For example the Inter-African Committee on Traditional Practices Affecting the Health of Women and Children identifies as its objective the eradication of all forms of harmful traditional practices, including forced marriage and female genital cutting. The organization mounts seminars and workshops within communities to present alternative social practices. One former excisor said she had been so affected by the seminar that she changed her livelihood: she no longer performs female genital cutting but washes and irons clothes for a living. In another case in a school in Addis Ababa genital cutting was halted when girls about to undergo the ritual cutting were threatened with expulsion. Womankind Kenya, a grassroots group opposing the practice, seeks out excisors in order to convert them. The group enlists the help of religious leaders to denounce the practice and to teach instead that female genital cutting is equally as sinful in the eyes of God as cutting any other part the body.[3]

To Western governments it seems natural to use the law to prevent harmful activities. The data suggest however that forcing social change through legal sanctions may do nothing more than increase hostility and defiance among the target audience. For example some African women prominent in the movement against female circumcision have expressed a sense of alienation from the sensationalistic nature of the anti-cutting campaign coming from the first world. Human rights mean different things in different national contexts: Western feminists fight to change sexist stigma in the workplace, African women demand the removal of the bride price, and feminists of the Muslim world seek the relaxation of the dress code and regulations enforcing gender separation. Given the differences in attitudes towards controversial cultural practices, it seems unlikely that a purely legal solution such as criminal prohibition will bring cultural practices to a halt when the major forces behind them are deeply rooted in economic, religious, and social phenomena.

Civil society is touted by many as the best place for working out this conundrum by having nongovernmental organizations and transnational corporations replace some of the traditional roles of courts. Some of the empirical data support this contention. For example analysis of child labor rates around the world shows that membership in international nongovernmental organizations has a significant correlation with decreased child labor rates, whereas a government's ratification of International Labour Organization (ILO) conventions on child labor does not.[4] What I term here the "civil society critique" locates the impetus for human rights change outside traditional legal mechanisms. The civil society critique focuses on human rights as a negotiation between social movements and governments and takes the focus off courtrooms and legal argumentation. It raises the question whether law, and especially courts, may have outlived its usefulness in the era of globalization.

While it might seem that nongovernmental organizations (NGOs) and global trade practices challenge the singular centrality of society's legal institutions, I argue here that courts are crucial in translating political struggle into a language that will direct governments. The civil society critique makes a valid point that global actors today are different from those in earlier global movements such as the slavery abolitionists in the nineteenth century and women's rights advocates in the twentieth century. NGOs are a new source of social change that reflects the huge growth in civil society political activism in both rich and poor countries. These transnational and local social movements have become a powerful force that leverages the global information revolution to spread human rights ideas across the world.

In this chapter I argue that law is more important than ever under contemporary conditions. Civil society groups are political movements that respond to specific political and cultural issues. Their claims are frequently stated in the language of universal values. Similarly corporations are important actors that both threaten and advance human rights claims, and multinational corporations that influence national governments must have their activities scrutinized.

Civil society and market mechanisms on their own, however, are insufficient means for the resolution of conflicts. While it might seem that NGOs and global traders challenge the importance of legal institutions to society, in fact the role of courts is a vital complement. Law is needed as both supplement and backstop to social change. Legal institutions are places where the political struggles of social movements can be included in the debate about public values and the allocation of government resources. Human rights claims have greater impact when their claims are harnessed to legal institutions. As the field of human rights actors expands and diversifies, it becomes more important to have legal norms test those claims. Courts and judges have an important role in interpreting the human rights demands made by civil society.

At the same time, human rights need to be interpreted by a legal infrastructure that is equipped for cultural diversity. Courts offer special institutional competencies that have no counterpart in civil society. Courts have the proximity to a human rights conflict needed to articulate the separate elements of a cultural-diversity claim but also enjoy the political distance needed to assess interests that lie behind that claim.[5] Human rights claims of a minority can be balanced by courts against rights claimed by the majority. Courts can scrutinize claims made by elders and religious leaders who wish to maintain cultural practices and weigh them against the claims of nontraditionalists who claim the right to move away from traditional practices. Courts can use international standards as an absolute limit on any cultural-diversity claim that might involve massive violations of the human right to bodily integrity, such as torture or labor conditions resembling slavery. International human rights treaties provide a standard for change, a language of rights, and an expectation of an institutional remedy for human rights conflicts.

The way in which human rights are interpreted varies hugely however. Cultural diversity continues despite globalization, economic homogenization, and the emergence of a global civil society. How should courts that adjudicate human rights claims approach and understand their task? Here I wish to show that the complexity of human rights adjudication requires a self-conscious reexamination of judicial methods specifically tailored to balance the claims of cultural difference.

In what follows, the trajectory of globalization as a new international force for change is traced through three elements: nongovernmental organizations, trade conditions, and the expression of human rights norms in international treaties. Globalization—the lowered costs of communication and the transportation of labor, capital, and ideas across borders—has made these three elements more powerful. Responding to the civil society critique that these forces are powerful enough to shrink or even displace the role of courts, I argue that these developments instead reemphasize the need for courts. Adjudication has an important role in globalization. I describe how courts around the world are already carrying out the function of evaluating and coordinating the respective demands of nongovernmental organizations, economic activities, and international human rights treaties. In the last section of this chapter I focus specifically on how specialist human rights courts can best carry out this coordination and assessment function.

Global Society

"Globalization"

"Globalization" and "civil society" are terms that need close scrutiny when it comes to analyzing their impact on international human rights. When the UN Charter was drafted after World War II, the philosophical justification for human rights drew upon the idea of an essential human nature that is shared by everybody everywhere. Is this justification holding up under conditions of globalization? Literature about globalization has exploded over the past two decades but the jury is divided. The history customarily starts with the creation of the United Nations and is followed by an account of the Internet, electronic finance, and the disintegration of the Soviet Union.

There is little agreement however on the meaning and effects of globalization. Proponents and critics express themselves in substantively incompatible positions. Critics see globalization as perniciously magnifying global economic inequalities beyond the scope of governments to correct them.[6] They deploy apocalyptic terminology and point to growing economic disparities as their proof. They argue that the laws of states are becoming less relevant as global capital and sophisticated technologies expand. This critique tends to deemphasize the independent sovereignty of each state, instead stressing the dependencies between states and international organizations and among individuals. These dependencies—so goes this line of argument—erode the importance of territory to the state relative to its economic power, such as the ability to issue currency and influence the value of world markets.[7]

Others see the information age as revolutionizing political participation, which in turn pressures governments to honor their international human rights obligations.[8] For example it has been claimed that rising rates of primary school enrollment and literacy are beneficial results of globalization that increase general prosperity and decrease child labor and poverty.[9] Using as an indicator school and college curricula, there is today a universal citizen of the world who, ready-made, steps into a life of common values and shared understandings. Virtually everywhere, education materials downplay nationalism and emphasize "transcendent moral themes . . . [which] are seen from a universal and global, rather than a local and particular, perspective."[10] Where once a country's history books repeated cultural mythologies such as ethnic, racial, or tribal traditions, contemporary primary educational materials depict individualism as superseding nationality, gender, and social class. The nation-state is no longer depicted as a mother-country or heartland but instead as a standardized bureaucracy. A national government may differ from others somewhat in the details of its policies but it is presented as being part of a global trend, that of "carrying out standard policies that will help both individuals and national society participate successfully in a larger world economy and society."[11] Less affluent countries in particular are directed in their educational work by international organizations such as UNESCO and the World Bank and by international professionals.[12]

Does this mean that as globalization intensifies people the world over are becoming the same? Not necessarily. The number of bloody civil conflicts since the end of the Cold War that reflect ethnic and cultural cleavages would suggest not. Furthermore beginning in the 1960s a reverse intellectual trend has developed that professes a growing sense that common human identity or nature is nothing more than a fig leaf. Over the past decades scholarly critics of universal norms have emphasized alternatives to the universalist account of human nature. Some social theorists and philosophers have sought to differentiate universal human rights from local "narratives" that explain localized cultural practices and traditions. The psychoanalytic critique, for example, proposes that human identity is the temporary and fluid result of both external contexts and our subconscious. As Slavoj Žižek has put it, "multitude has been in, unity out; contingency in, necessity out; difference in, universality out; antinomy in, noncontradiction out; resistance in, revolution out."[13]

The paradox in these various arguments is that cultural identity is being claimed as a human right at precisely the moment when economic and technological forces appear to be creating a world culture. The result is contradicting justifications for human rights, making the interface between respect for human rights and isolationism seem more and more problematic. One approach might be to assert more strongly the universalism of Western individualism and identity. In some ways this seems the least complicated way out of the legal, political, and philosophical quagmire. The old twentieth-century intellectual assumptions of universal identity are simply now too contested by world events to be maintained. It seems clear that claims to culturally differentiated identities are likely to increase and indeed to garner greater political, even militant, support.

Amid this intellectual maelstrom a complex structure of international institutions now functions alongside state systems. These institutions have increased expectations among publics about the human rights performance of their governments, though they have not necessarily increased their governments' human rights performance. For example great inequality exists in many states although the globalization of school curricula portrays homogeneity. Only a very few individuals have any real prospect of achieving the equality and success depicted in their textbooks.[14] The same country that depicts gender equality in its school materials may also fail to prevent the illegal labor of women and children who are being trafficked across international borders.[15] Great cultural diversity and great inequality characterizes the real world, and societies continue on parallel trajectories defined by their own cultural heritages.[16] In reality while there has been a dramatic expansion in depictions of universal human rights values, cultural differences continue as drivers of human behavior.

Achieving Human Rights Through Nongovernmental Organizations

International nongovernmental organizations and transnational networks, coalitions, and movements push both domestic and international institutions to consider people and interests that previously have been neglected.[17] Slavery campaigns in the nineteenth century provided the earliest example of a broad social movement producing change through domestic and international agitation, as do the later global campaigns in the twentieth century for democracy and gender equality.

Similar effects can be seen in other contemporary social movements. In India for example a coalition of local, national, and international nonstate organizations has been able to reform and even stall the construction of several large dams on the Narmada River that would have displaced thousands of local farmers. Networks of NGOs from around the world have compelled the World Bank to alter its lending policies and priorities to take into account social and environmental concerns. Transnational human rights activists have campaigned against government human rights abuses in Chile. The 1973 Chilean military coup prompted international and domestic human rights groups to form a transnational advocacy network that set key precedents for later human rights networks. Monitoring, raising funds internationally for domestic opposition groups and research centers, and creating intergovernmental organizations that lobby powerful Western states to take action against errant governments are all products of the pioneering work of the Chilean transnational network.[18]

Other transnational collective actions have been less successful. A campaign to change the conditionality policies of the International Monetary Fund for example has yet to make much impact. As researcher Paul Nelson notes, "The efforts of NGOs to influence the World Bank, while in agreement on broad themes for reform (greater popular participation, accountability, transparency) are far from homogeneous. Despite the increasing conceptual integration of the networks' agendas, direct planning, information sharing, and joint advocacy among them is only recent, and their agendas remain distinct."[19]

American political scientist Kathryn Sikkink and other researchers looking at similar phenomena have demonstrated that the ability of civil society and NGOs to produce change depends on a number of factors, for example whether the issue is an international one as in the case of women's inequality or more a domestic concern as in the case of Chile's human rights abuses from a particular historical period.[20] There are also questions of timing, how the identity of the particular individuals who are involved in the campaign may influence outcomes, and how the involvement of international agencies representing other groups such as trade organizations may alter national responses. Because nongovernmental organizations are formed around civil society interests, the competing interests of the NGOs themselves (which may or may not be accountable to a particular demographic) can be significant. Sikkink notes: "NGOs and networks need to address their own asymmetries and questions of accountability and transparency so they can enhance their internal democracy while helping to democratize international institutions."[21]

At the same time while transnational capital and NGOs unquestionably play a new role in national and international affairs, the traditional activities of national governments remain central to the lives of citizens.[22] Empirical evidence shows that values change along with globalization, but traditional patterns of social organization continue.[23] In other words reliance on national political and legal institutions continues even as the global economy, global communication, and global institutions mushroom.

Achieving Human Rights Through Economic Transactions

In addition to interest group pressure through nongovernmental organizations, attaching human rights to trade and economic aid agreements can increase human rights protection by providing incentives to economic actors for good human rights performance. This technique has been used with respect to children's and minority rights with varying degrees of success.

For example, better human rights in the European Union have resulted from "conditionality," the policy by which Western Europe gives economic aid for improved governance to its eastern neighbors as they prepare to join the EU. Conditionality, that is, giving economic aid with stipulations and conditions, is a dance between national and external incentives. It works by connecting political values to economic improvements. It has played an indispensable role in some of the former communist countries of Eastern Europe by taking human rights off the moral wish list and making it an institutional reality.

European countries originally applied conditionality in 1990, when they included democracy and human rights clauses in financial aid and trade agreements with their former colonies in Africa.[24] Conditional agreements became the framework of integration for the ten countries admitted to the European Union in 2004 and then again for Bulgaria and Romania as they worked towards EU accession in 2007.[25] Internal incentives with such economic agreements come in the form of political payoffs for would-be EU countries; citizens want the benefits of EU membership and give support to the political parties that can deliver it. External incentives come from the EU itself: money, training, and equipment from the European Commission are powerful inducements for government reforms in would-be EU countries.

Economic incentives need not be an alternative to law however, and in fact the use of economic incentives in European Union expansion has relied heavily on legal institutions and processes. Upon entering the EU, countries accept the "acquis communitaire," the detailed laws and rules adopted as the basis of the EU's founding treaties.[26] When Western Europe began taking an interest in the development of its eastern neighbors after the fall of communism in 1989, it capitalized upon the political will of legislatures there to undertake programs of legal reform that met externally set standards. The EU has been generous in granting economic aid to help bring this about, but as a condition for aid it requires evidence of a commitment to create laws that institutionalize democratic government, free markets, and human rights. For example, before Hungary and Poland were admitted to the EU in 2004, they legislated extensive human rights reforms as part of their demonstration of readiness to be part of the European pact.[27] Bulgaria and Romania had to show that they were promoting Europe's values of the rule of law in order to gain EU admission in 2007.[28] As a consequence the core of Europe has grown from a postwar trading alliance of six countries into a vibrant union of twenty-seven countries and 450 million people. Legalizing human rights has been a crucial part of the EU's transformation and continues to be an issue in the hot debate over the future accession of Turkey.

International trade law and international human rights law were also employed in the UN embargoes in 1979 and 1986 that aimed at ending apartheid in South Africa.[29] Provisions of international trade treaties and constitutional documents such as the UN Charter, the General Agreement on Tariffs and Trade / World Trade Organization (GATT / WTO),[30] and the constitution and conventions of the International Labour Organization are often invoked today when discussing the protection of human rights that are endangered by international trade.[31]

The GATT/WTO system is the major international institution dealing with international trade. The GATT (the precursor to the WTO) did not incorporate specific provisions regarding workers' rights. Its primary focus was free trade, and its ability to promote better labor standards was restricted to trade-related labor standards.[32] After forty-eight years of activity the GATT was replaced in 1995 with the WTO,[33] which similarly does not prescribe human rights standards in its processes of treaty making.[34] On the other hand, the North American Free Trade Agreement (NAFTA) includes a 1993 side agreement on labor, and the 1991 Social Chapter of the European Union's Maastricht Agreement articulates labor standards for member countries. Human rights issues are a controversial topic at ministerial meetings of the World Trade Organization, where trade and labor standards are linked regionally and internationally.[35] Most of the discussion concerns human rights violations that directly result from international trade, such as child labor, trafficking in women, and direct harm to workers. General human rights, such as procedural guarantees and substantive rights such as freedom of religion, are not considered relevant to trade and are not included.

The list of opponents to linking trade to human rights performance is long and includes governments of developing countries, free-trade economists, and private enterprises operating from developing countries. All argue that making free trade conditional on human rights policy prevents developing economies from increasing export trade, which is one of the best routes to economic improvement: "connecting trade with human rights . . . deprive[s] the South of its key comparative advantage, namely the ability to use cheap labor. It is instead simply a guise for protectionism."[36]

On the other hand nongovernmental organizations agitate in favor of human rights as part of the international trade regime. They argue that globalization and trade liberalization are preventing national governments from devising national policies and are creating a "race to the bottom."[37] The UN has called on the WTO to shift international trade to a human rights–based approach because "promotion and protection of human rights is the first responsibility of Governments" and the "primacy of human rights law over all other regimes of international law is a basic and fundamental principle that should not be departed from."[38] Using the example of child labor, American scholar Joseph Langan explains the opposing arguments: "Labor activists and workers' organizations in the developed northern countries argue that the use of child labor by developing nations in the south is . . . akin to an unfair state subsidy. . . . Governments of the developing world respond [they] . . . do not agree . . . the standards espoused by the north . . . are 'international.'"[39]

Some have suggested linking the WTO's more than 150 members with human rights law through its dispute resolution mechanism or through Article XX of the GATT, which lists general exceptions available under the GATT for the purpose of public policy.[40] Article XX calls for the protection of public morals and the protection of human, animal, or plant life or health; prohibits prison labor; and measures compliance with GATT-consistent laws.[41] A more tenuous linkage might exist through Article XXI, which provides for a national security exception.[42] Given its purely economic focus, though, it seems unlikely that the WTO will apply a broad exception to the treaty provisions to include general human rights–based trade sanctions as a global mechanism.[43]

Individual states and regional trading blocs are able to employ such mechanisms, as the child labor example demonstrates. Child labor activists have argued that the International Labour Organization should be linked formally with the GATT / WTO system.[44] The ILO has been the principal international body for setting international standards and monitoring child labor since 1919, when it set fourteen as the universal age at which children could legally work. ILO labor standards are recognized and supported by many countries, and its triad of workers' organizations, employers' organizations, and governments helps the organization avert many of the political difficulties that beset the United Nations and other international organizations. ILO policies have become so much a part of mainstream thinking on the issue of child labor that the norm of regulating the type and duration of employment for children is now considered routine, even by those countries whose actual enforcement of the norm is poor.[45] Because the ILO has no jurisdiction in international trade, however, countries can ignore internationally accepted labor standards and receive no sanctions from the WTO. Moreover unilateral efforts by governments to set up trade sanctions in order to enforce international labor standards have been viewed as illegitimately protectionist and impermissible under the GATT.[46]

Some individual states are leveraging their domestic trade laws with international human rights standards. For example the U.S. prohibits the importation of products of indentured or forced child labor in accordance with baseline international standards under Section 301 of the U.S. Trade Act of 1974.[47] While on its face such an embargo against products made by forced labor represents a U.S. violation of its GATT / WTO obligations, the WTO has ruled that the U.S. Trade Act is consistent with U.S. GATT obligations.[48] The U.S. Tariff Act prohibits the importation of goods made in a foreign state by forced labor.[49] Implementation and enforcement of this legislation is difficult,[50] so in practice it has been applied sparingly and only to products of "convict labor."[51] Officially the U.S. Department of State stands against foreign child labor exploitation. Realistically the U.S. has taken few serious steps to curtail child labor. For example in 1994 Pres. Bill Clinton capitulated on an earlier U.S. position by renewing China's most-favored-nation status without the threatened requirement that China more thoroughly protect human rights, even though Chinese practices of abusive child labor continued.

As a corrective to problems in both international and national systems, several U.S. statutes provide for the granting of duty-free benefits to a developing country contingent on its taking steps to provide workers with internationally recognized workers' rights. In practice it seems that these statutes have attracted little attention to the problem of exploitation of child labor, nor are they consistently enforced. This has led to some self-regulation—U.S. corporations and industry bodies are creating their own policies to reduce their reliance on imported goods produced through child labor and unfair trade practices.[52]

When included in an economic agreement, minority rights have fared better than child labor. For example when the European Union was created at Maastricht in 1992, there was little mention of minority rights.[53] The 1997 Treaty of Amsterdam amended the 1992 treaty of the European Union, made substantial human rights changes, and put greater emphasis on matters of citizenship and the rights of individuals as conditions for countries seeking EU accession. Although the Treaty of Amsterdam did not explicitly designate proper treatment of minorities as a precondition for application for EU membership, from 2002 onward, the European Commission's regular reports began applying the European Framework Convention for the Protection of National Minorities.[54] This convention defines collective group rights, rights to cultural autonomy, and rights to political representation for groups within states that have a minority culture, language, or religion. It provides legal guarantees against discrimination, guarantees certain freedoms such as access to the media, teaching and use of minority languages and education, and encourages the participation of national minorities in public life.

Although EU law lacks a firm historical basis for minority rights, the introduction of such laws as part of a broader integration package for a prospective EU country has had a significant effect. Minority rights now figure prominently in accession discussions, as when Hungary and Slovakia were able to demonstrate better treatment of their Roma (Gypsy) populations prior to their admission to the EU in 2004. Admission of Romania and Bulgaria on the other hand was delayed in order to encourage reform, including human rights reform.[55] To pass the EU accession test these latter two countries needed to demonstrate that they could be more effective in stemming corruption and the trafficking of women and children. They had to prove that they had both the legislative will and sufficient institutional capacity to apply the integration package and improve their enforcement of minority rights. The human rights situation has improved as a result, and now minority groups in both countries have legal mechanisms to press for solutions to the many human rights problems that still remain.

The key point here is that, with the exception of failed states, most countries can improve their performance with the right combination of internal and external incentives. Human rights can be fostered by isolating external economic incentives, linking them to demonstrable human rights improvements, and giving outside institutions a role in assessing progress. In Europe the "carrots" for improved human rights performance are financial aid, technical assistance, and membership in a regional trading club. The "stick" is the loss of that package.

Europe has a unique system of economic levers formed in part because it has regional courts to back up its political values; its centralized lawmaking body in the European Parliament in Brussels is reinforced by the European Court of Human Rights in Strasbourg. This is discussed in more detail in Chapter 5. The EU has harnessed the continent's social and economic forces to political and legal institutions that in turn press for human rights improvements. These experiences illustrate the ongoing importance of courts as enforcement mechanisms for human rights policies that are incorporated into trade-related activities.

Human Rights Enforcement Through Global Law

Another version of the civil society critique stresses the role of international human rights treaties as part of a human rights familiarization process. Some see globalization as adding new ways for international movements to influence states. For example sociologists studying why countries sign onto human rights treaties tell a story of global trends.[56] They argue that even repressive governments with virtually total control over their populations are nevertheless influenced by the worldwide trend to support human rights. Others see new ways that individual national legal systems might influence those in neighboring countries. Princeton legal scholar Anne-Marie Slaughter for example sees evidence of "judicial globalization" in an increasing amount of constitutional cross-fertilization, where national constitutional courts look for guidance in the decisions of constitutional courts around the world.[57] She points to the rise of "judicial comity," with national judges citing the legal decisions of foreign courts and gradually creating a shared international set of legal norms and practices.[58] Others see globalization as a complex new order that has supplanted a world order dominated by sovereign states. Yale legal scholar Harold Koh describes the "age of globalization" as the "globalization of freedom," evidenced by the growing number of democracies that the United States especially has helped build.[59]

This approach risks overemphasizing the effect of international rhetoric on making human rights improvements on the ground.[60] Human rights improvements do not necessarily follow simply because a government signs a human rights treaty. For example U.S.-based legal scholar Oona Hathaway has suggested that the human rights standards of some states entering into the international human rights treaty system get no better after they ratify an international treaty.[61] In response American legal sociologists Ryan Goodman and Derek Jinks have argued that international human rights treaties operate more broadly, beyond either coercion or persuasion.[62] International human rights treaties, they suggest, gradually exert external normative pressures on governments. This alternative sociological approach argues that governments comply with higher human rights standards because of a distinctive social process, something that Goodman and Jinks label "acculturation."[63] It is not a state or a government that is socialized by international human rights, they argue. Rather individuals are socialized about human rights, then those individuals alter government practices.[64]

As Goodman and Jinks describe it, acculturation has three potential effects on promoting international human rights. First, structural reforms such as the ratification of an international human rights treaty or the enactment of a national constitutional rights provision can shift the domestic political dynamics of the reforming state.[65] These formal changes create opportunities for civil society to pressure the government to observe human rights even though the government itself has little or no intrinsic interest in human rights reforms. While these changes do not typically cause dramatic or immediate reductions in human rights violations, formal organizational changes do produce tangible effects.[66] Second, if a government links to a human rights system outside its own border it is subjected to "the civilizing force of hypocrisy." Over time it is increasingly difficult for governments to sustain the dissonance between their high-sounding human rights rhetoric and their lesser human rights reality. This provides incentives to individual government officials to implement the high-sounding human rights promises.[67] Third, Goodman and Jinks argue that acculturation can teach states that superficial or shallow human rights gestures will not be enough to satisfy either their constituency at home or their critics abroad.[68] Instead, each small reform will up the ante for the next reform.

Courts as the Necessary Link

Still missing in all of these accounts is the key role that courts play in the dissemination of human rights norms. Courts provide the connection between politics and practice, the bridge between the formal words of a treaty and the concrete changes necessary once a country has signed on to it. Arguably the most important feature of the acculturation approach to human rights set out by Goodman and Jinks is the opportunity for states to absorb international human rights standards through the influence of individuals who have human rights aspirations for their government and who have the opportunity to parlay that into the particularized needs of their country's population. This is where judges and courts play a crucial role. Judges are a conduit of human rights acculturation. Judicial decisions spell out the rights of politically powerless people and groups under human rights treaties and agreements and direct their decisions to governments. Courts apply abstract human rights principles to the peoples' everyday lives.

Courts and Human Rights

Human Rights as Legal Rights

Claims for human rights by individuals before courts substantially enhance the activities of human rights actors in civil society whether corporate or non-corporate. For example when Khalid Adem was brought before the court in Georgia in 2006 for cutting his two-year old daughter, the human rights at stake were his daughter's right to bodily integrity and his right to practice his own culture. The right to bodily integrity is a moral right that in the U.S. has taken political form. It was enforced in this instance by convicting Adem of assault, ruling out "the cultural defense" (something discussed in further detail in Chapter 6), and sentencing him to a term of imprisonment.

Human rights claims are a complex package of moral, political, and legal factors. When advanced as moral or political claims, human rights demands are usually directed at a government as part of a strategy to mobilize the public politically against the government. Sometimes the claim may be directed to a global public in the hope that external pressure—diplomacy, pressure on trade relations, even trade sanctions or UN Security Council resolutions—will encourage a government to improve its human rights. Human rights presented as legal claims however are different. They are directed at a government's specifically *legal* obligation to deliver a particular human right by altering the practices of government agencies and officials. A legal claim seeks specific performance of a legal obligation. This obligation may already exist as words in a constitutional document or in a piece of legislation that gives jurisdiction to a national court. Sometimes a claim may be made under a less well defined legal obligation in an international or regional human rights treaty. Courts take a general human rights directive and apply it to a particular fact, working from the particular historical and legal context that frames meaning of that right within that jurisdiction.

Judges and Human Rights Acculturation

A conflict between rights is at heart a conflict between values. Determining whether a human right ought to be recognized and then how it affects other competing human rights involves some degree of reflection about the normative values that underscore a rights claim. Legal reasoning is uniquely suited to elucidating the core principle of a human right, specifying its essential elements, and juxtaposing an individual human rights claim to its generalized human rights principle.[69]

Adjudication in courts offers three specific institutional qualities that complement civil society mechanisms. First, in each individual case human rights claims need to be particularized. Courts go beyond merely stating their recognition of a right found in a constitution or based in legislation or an international treaty. Legal reasoning encompasses both general principles and individual cases, and the human rights debate is at heart a process of this type of reasoning. It requires the systematic comparative evaluation of standards and the beliefs that underwrite standards. These beliefs may be justified for a particular individual but if generalized might present a human rights problem to society. Alternatively a general principle could cause undue harm to an individual. Adjudication applies that generalized principle to concrete circumstances to ascertain whether legal redress is available.

Second, the epistemological advantages of courts extend to their unique fact-finding function. Institutions that formulate and specify human rights norms must be able to identify and utilize properly the relevant empirical information. Legal reasoning requires a court to ascertain whether a human right is threatened by *particular* facts. It is an empirical assessment about causation that follows from the moral philosophical analysis of identifying the normative basis of the human right. The ability to identify relevant and reliable information is a key epistemic virtue of a court.

Third, courts offer a public reasoning process about conflicts between values that have particular advantages over debate conducted through either formal politics or informal civil society lobbying. Rights must be specified and justified through procedures that are publicly credible. Legal institutions are uniquely able to do this because they are constrained by public rules of legal process. A court's credibility derives from its conformity to procedural standards that aim to exclude facts that are not relevant while including reasonable moral and empirical positions. The most legitimate legal institutions—ones that can be viewed as sources of guidance about the existence and content of human rights norms—are those that publicly engage in such moral and empirical processes and also publicly demonstrate that they are constrained by procedural standards.

Legal reasoning is a special combination of moral philosophical reflection applied to a carefully delimited field of relevant circumstances and arguments. These structural features mean that properly functioning courts can provide credible public justification for the existence of a right, even when the legal outcome may be disputed by those who hold other values. Countries where the decisions of its courts are respected and upheld by governments have the clear advantage here. As the example of Pakistan in Chapter 1 demonstrates, however, legal pronouncements about human rights decisions can be highly valued by ordinary people when their governments are ignoring the rule of law. Even in those countries where courts have low status, courts can articulate a norm and provide civil society groups with specific grounds for complaint.

Human Rights and National Courts

Adjudication of international human rights standards by national courts in individual cases shows that legally expressed human rights principles are an important complement to civil society. Jurisprudence can be a powerful instrument for changing cultural habits and prejudices. For example the Colombian Constitutional Court and the Indian Supreme Court have expanded their equal protection guarantees to advance human rights, despite the difficulty of separating general constitutional principles from specific social and cultural conflicts. In its decisions on gender equality the Colombian Constitutional Court has demonstrated that it can conform to the original intent of the constitution as well as play a transformative role in human rights changes. India has also extended international human rights standards to gender equality and has also set standards for police custody of criminal suspects, prevention of abusive wiretapping, and improvements in juvenile justice. Colombia and India are just two examples of a pattern that is repeating worldwide, especially in those legal systems that allow individual petitions to the highest national court.

Colombia   The 1991 Colombian Constitution replaced the 1886 Constitution, which contained few fundamental rights. The new constitution encompasses a broad range of negative and positive provisions, including economic, cultural, and collective rights, as well as civil and political rights.[70] It contains several formal guarantees of equal rights for women and incorporates principles of the UN Committee on the Elimination of Discrimination against Women (CEDAW) and also provides two important new judicial mechanisms for the protections of rights and liberties—a separate Constitutional Court and the *tutela*.[71] The *tutela* is a citizen injunction that allows any person to seek immediate judicial protection when their constitutional rights are violated or threatened by either the government or a private person. All *tutelas* are forwarded to the Constitutional Court for discretionary review.

During the 1990s the Colombian court granted a series of injunctions that spurred the national legislature to enact new laws on domestic violence, employment equality, and sexual and reproductive rights.[72] For example the court ruled that a teacher could not be fired for teaching sex education to her third-grade class on the grounds that the sex information had been provided to teachers with the intention of reducing sexually transmitted diseases and undesired pregnancy. In the ruling, Justice Eduardo Cifuentes Muñoz, now president of the court, said, "ignorance and prejudice, in part, explain the subordinate position that some wrongly assign to women."[73] Subsequent rulings against discrimination of persons based on sexual orientation, particularly in the military, have cleared the way for the first Colombian same-sex marriage, in 1998.[74]

Of course the court's decisions enforcing fundamental rights have not necessarily ended all of Colombia's discriminatory practices.[75] Law plays an important role but cannot itself bring about social and cultural change. Women are still significantly underrepresented in both government and the private sector positions in Colombia. *Tutelas* however are especially beneficial for those who have been marginalized by the judicial system and have no other judicial avenues for their defense. Many women believe the *tutela* is the only hope for transformation in a country where the regular justice system has frequently reinforced discrimination and subjugation of women.[76] While some critics of the Constitutional Court's activist role claim that the *tutelas* have slowed down judicial processes, the Colombian public is generally in favor of them because they are often faster than other ordinary judicial procedures.

From the U.S. perspective this deliberate policy-making is seen as a dangerous departure from assumptions about the rightful role of the judiciary.[77] Judicial activism is often treated with suspicion in the U.S. because of the concern that judges may usurp the political role of a legislature. Selective application of higher human rights standards where victims have little or no political representation does not replace political action, however. As Justice Cifuentes of Colombia writes, the role of a constitutional court is, "without engaging in populism or demagoguery," to defend those at the margin of institutions: "Women, homosexuals, low-income workers, children . . . have been most advantaged by the decisions of the Constitutional Court . . . because . . . Court is aware that through the institutional mechanisms of political representation, the demands of these groups are not duly articulated. The Constitutional Court, at least with respect to the judicial system, that [sic] has to take responsibility for helping these groups in a much more direct and decided manner."[78]

India   Under the 1950 Constitution of India the Supreme Court has extensive jurisdiction to enforce fundamental rights. Primarily it is an appellate court that takes up appeals against judgments of the provincial high courts, but it also takes "writ petitions" from individuals in cases of serious human rights violations or very urgent cases. A writ petition to the Supreme Court can be started by any citizen simply by addressing a letter to the chief justice of the Supreme Court of India, who can then put the issue before the court because it concerns a question of public importance. The writ petition concept is unique to India and has played a critical role in promoting civil and political rights in the Fundamental Rights chapter of the Constitution. Writ petition Supreme Court decisions have also promoted many economic and social rights that are declared but not enforceable under the constitution, including the rights to free education, livelihood, a clean environment, food, and many other things.

For example the chief justice of the Supreme Court of India received a letter drawing attention to media reports about deaths in police lockups and the need for better "custody jurisprudence." The next time the court heard a case on the constitutional right to life under Article 21 it held that custodial deaths or any form of torture or cruel, inhuman, or degrading treatment fell within the right to life guarantees under the Constitution, whether during investigation, interrogation, or at any time during police custody.[79] The Supreme Court made extensive references to the human rights contained in the International Covenant on Civil and Political Rights (ICCPR). Even though when it first ratified the ICCPR in 1979 India had specifically exempted the government from any liability for compensation to victims of unlawful arrest or detention, the Supreme Court swept the exemption away, saying it had "lost its relevance in view of the law laid down by this Court in a number of cases awarding compensation for the infringement of the fundamental right to life of a citizen. . . . There is indeed no express provision in the Constitution of India for grant of compensation for violation of a fundamental right to life, nonetheless, this Court has judicially evolved a right to compensation in cases of established unconstitutional deprivation of personal liberty or life."[80]

In another writ petition regarding the gang rape of a social worker in the workplace, the Indian Supreme Court substantially extended the jurisprudence on gender equality.[81] At the time the case was brought, India had no domestic law on sexual harassment in the workplace, although it had ratified the Convention for the Elimination of Discrimination Against Women. The Supreme Court relied on CEDAW and on public statements the Indian government made at the 1994 Beijing International Women's Conference, saying, "We have, therefore, no hesitation in placing reliance on [this] for the purpose of construing the nature and ambit of constitutional guarantee of gender equality in our Constitution. . . . Independence of [the] judiciary forms a part of our constitutional scheme. . . . It is now an accepted rule of judicial construction that regard must be had to international conventions and norms for construing domestic law when there is no inconsistency between them and there is a void in the domestic law."[82]

The Supreme Court formulated guidelines to enforce gender equality and to guarantee against sexual harassment and abuse, including extensive workplace guidelines. These guidelines were enforced against employees until formal legislation was enacted through the usual parliamentary channels.

In another case of writ petition political wire-tapping has been stopped by reference to international human rights standards.[83] The Indian government had been using old (1885) pre-independence legislation to justify phone-tapping of its political opponents.[84] When the People's Union of Civil Liberties challenged the constitutional validity of the practice, the Supreme Court upheld the challenge, making extensive reference to the right to privacy under the International Covenant on Civil and Political Rights. Finally, juvenile rights also have been actively developed by the Supreme Court through a writ petition reference to standards under international human rights covenants and treaties.[85]

Adjudicating Cultural Difference

These case studies show that courts and judges can help in the diffusion of human rights norms to civil and political rights. The same advantages can also be applied to conflicts that are understood as "cultural." Disputants over cultural practices also question which human "self" should act as a stable and unbiased referent for assessing differing truth claims, an even more challenging inquiry than the traditional legal processes for assessment of accuracy and credibility.

Case by Case

In a homogenous society[86] adjudication has been seen traditionally as a scientific process—a gradual approach to truth, first forming a hypothesis and then attempting its empirical verification or falsification. This assumes philosophical agreement about the human capacity for objectivity and methodological agreement about the linear process of isolating one true account of a legal event.[87] The dominant view of adjudication emphasizes the objectivity (or at least the aspiration to objectivity) of legal judgment. Legal positivism as it is known sees the separation between law and morality as both feasible and ethical. This view argues that the role of judges is to act impartially by setting aside their own moral beliefs and applying the letter of the law. Legal positivism has been much criticized. American legal philosopher Ronald Dworkin is one such critic who argues that moral philosophy is an integral part of legal judgment.[88] Dworkin's alternative approach says that judges seek a resolution to legal disagreements by appealing to the political and moral narratives of their legal community. There seems little common ground between positivists and anti-positivists, emphasizing further how cultural conflicts in a heterogeneous society pose an acute problem for courts.

In human rights cases judges are often called upon to settle authoritatively legal contests where at least one party is drawing on a point of view that is culturally or historically determined. The judge may neither share such a perspective nor easily grasp it. For example British or French judges are not likely to share or easily comprehend the beliefs of the African women who practice female genital cutting. U.S. or Australian judges are not likely to share or easily understand the view that the main harm of rape is dishonor to a community. These are difficult tasks even in a relatively homogeneous society where judge and litigants may share some common sense of self. They are vastly more difficult in a heterogeneous society where shared understandings are hard to come by. The work of judges is especially complicated when complainants draw on culturally specific images of self to ground their claim for legal redress.

The shortcomings of both positivism and the Dworkin alternative can be seen when they are applied to conflicting visions of human rights of people sharing the same legal jurisdiction. Either approach is complete, or in any case adequate to the human rights challenge. Both fail to address fully how the substance and content of human rights has been written by history and power.[89] Neither positivism nor Dworkin's criticism of it can deal adequately with profound cultural difference where underlying values lie in direct conflict. Human rights claims by minorities and cultural groups have highlighted an important philosophical problem inherent in the very use of liberal human rights discourse, namely that an understanding of human rights rooted in ideals of liberal equality among individuals may eradicate certain cultures by radically transforming their cultural differences. When language like "human dignity," so weighed down with historical baggage, is being used, adjudication of human rights claims becomes increasingly complex.

Although there may not be agreement about the underlying philosophical assumptions of a legal right, or even its methodological practice, the job of judges is to pay close attention to evidence and its credibility using evidentiary and procedural rules. In each case a relationship must be found between general legal rules and concrete and particular facts within a standard legal process. This adjudicative approach to human rights claims need not necessarily be tethered to Western liberal individualism. Adjudication as structured and public process can, however, require different paradigms of human values to explain their claim in a common legal procedure.

Cultural Difference and Legal Process

The importance of legal proceduralism has been emphasized by those inside and outside the legal academy. For example historian Michael Ignatieff has suggested that international human rights norms will only have legitimacy if they are the product of "a commitment to respect the reasoned commitments of others and to submit disputes to adjudication."[90] Political theorists Amy Gutman and Denis Thompson have suggested that the moral authority of collective decisions depends upon the moral quality of the process by which those decisions are made.[91]

A more sustained philosophical analysis of legal proceduralism has been offered by German philosopher Jürgen Habermas in *Between Facts and Norms*,[92] where he develops the discourse ethics he had previously set out in *Theory of Communicative Action*.[93] It is an approach that captures the unique dilemma confronting a judge who must adjudicate a conflict between competing world views, while also providing a procedural guarantee to individuals who seem to be making vastly different, even completely opposite, claims. Habermas's point in *Theory of Communicative Action* is that the ethical way to resolve competing ideals and values is through rational discourse in the processes of democracy. In *Between Facts and Norms* he applies this discourse-based theory of ethics to legal institutions and suggests that both moral and legal norms depend implicitly upon the intuition to rightness contained within the discourse principle, or "the ideal speech situation." Along with Kant, Habermas sees law and morality as conceptually distinct. Legal validity is not a function of certainty of outcome in legal conflicts but rather the discursive clarification of the relevant facts and legal questions, so that "affected parties can be confident that in procedures issuing in judicial decisions, only relevant reasons will be decisive, and not arbitrary ones."[94]

Habermas's rationalization of the law does not predetermine its content but rather ensures that a country's law is the outcome of joint deliberations by legal actors about their ethical differences with one other. Indeed his emphasis upon the autonomy of each culture as a subset of a larger society provides clear recognition of the lack of universality among people, even if he also recommends a certain universality of bureaucratic processes. Implicit in this approach is the idea of a minimal commonality of beliefs, values, commitments, and emotions, even though there is no metaphysical *certainty* woven into Western thought of hearing the "other." Rather what we are left with is "a practical commitment to . . . communicative reason [as] the basis—perhaps the only honest basis—for hope."[95]

How might this approach be utilized in cultural conflicts between international human rights standards and localized beliefs and practice? Human rights inhabit the space between contingency and certainty, and courts need a method to put these into practice: contingency—in any event, part of life—formalized as the recognition and search for understanding of cultural difference; and certainty—at least enough for peaceable living amongst cultural difference—formalized out of a procedural framework that can articulate those differences.

Margin of Appreciation

The Need for a Standardized Theory

I describe here a method of adjudication already in use within the European regional human rights system and propose a modified version of it as a way for courts more generally to moderate between general human rights principles and local norms. The European Court of Human Rights deploys a legal doctrine called "the margin of appreciation" when deciding if governments are fulfilling their human rights obligations under the European Convention on Human Rights (ECHR).[96] The ECHR uses the principle of margin of appreciation, described as "room for maneuver," "breathing space," "elbow room," or "a doctrine of self-restraint,"[97] to strike a balance between national views on human rights and uniform application of the European Convention across the forty-seven member countries of the Council of Europe.[98] This principle allows the court to take into account unique cultural and social conditions within individual societies. With certain modifications outlined below, the margin of appreciation can be adapted as a legal method of cultural adjudication.

Two Applications of the Margin of Appreciation

The concept of margin of appreciation was originally used by the European Court of Human Rights in 1958 in *Greece v. United Kingdom*. Since then more than 110 cases have been based on it. The ECHR has yet to provide an authoritative definition of margin of appreciation, but a careful analysis of the cases in which it has been applied shows two approaches. The first is relatively straightforward: it looks to the interplay of individual rights with a country's national interest. The second is a more sophisticated approach that also analyzes the interplay of individual rights with the larger European regional structure. I argue that this second methodology has advantages and with some further tweaking could be adopted by the regional courts discussed in Chapter 5.

"Maintaining Public Order"   One interpretation of margin of appreciation gives priority to particular core rights under the European Convention on Human Rights—the right to privacy, freedom of religion, freedom of expression, freedom of association, and freedom of property ownership—and only allows a government to pass laws infringing upon these individual rights when it is crucial to maintaining public order.[99] Margin of appreciation was applied in this way in the Turkish headscarf case, discussed in detail in the following chapter, where the European Court of Human Rights upheld the Turkish government's ban on Islamic headscarves in universities. In the absence of a uniform European conception of "public order" the ECHR allowed Turkey to decide for itself how it needed to implement its status as a secular nation.[100] Another example is the ECHR's 1971 decision that upheld a Belgian law that detained vagrants in order to prevent crime.[101] In each case the ECHR gave way to a national law that imposed a restriction on an individual's rights and freedoms on the grounds that governments are also tasked with passing laws that will protect the rights of all of their citizens and not just one group or minority.

Such use of margin of appreciation is based principally on the content of regional human rights, and the key role of the court is ensuring that a government's limitation on core European Convention rights is proportionate to its national interests. It effectively argues that human rights under the European Convention are similar to a federal constitutional standard: the margin of appreciation is used as a device to allow necessary, case-by-case exemptions from a federal standard.[102] The broader European standard of the right remains in place with an onus placed on governments to demonstrate that they have good reason to apply the standard more narrowly.

In other words under this first application of margin of appreciation there is no absolute legal prohibition on national governments "interfering" with convention freedoms as long as they are pursuing legitimate aims such as national security, public safety, economic well-being, and the prevention of crime. Used in this way the margin of appreciation is a filter for the more obvious human rights mistakes of governments. It stands for the non-absoluteness of the freedoms in the European Convention on Human Rights when it can be shown that there are alternative compelling arguments about the integrity of the state itself. It is a static test in the sense that it does not interpret the meaning of a regional human right but instead looks for reason why a government may be able to derogate from it.

Best Use of Margin of Appreciation   The second approach is more sophisticated, using margin of appreciation to acknowledge the structural complexity of a regional entity and incorporating recognition that individual rights and freedoms are in a dynamic relationship with other collective regional goals. There is an emphasis on changes within the region itself: the idea is that states are contemporaneously sovereign and autonomous entities while they are also part of a larger regional unit.[103] In a small but subtle change of emphasis the role of legal adjudication becomes more nimble: at the same time that a regional judge is articulating the relationship between a citizen and the government, the judge is also articulating the relationship of states with each other within that region. This second approach necessitates a comparative analysis of what restrictions other states in the region have imposed on a particular human right as the following European example demonstrates.

In a line of cases starting with *Rees v. United Kingdom* in 1986, *Cossey v. United Kingdom* in 1990, and *Sheffield & Horsham v. United Kingdom* in 1998, the ECHR considered whether the right of privacy confers a duty on European governments to alter public records to recognize officially the new gender identity of postoperative transsexuals. Initially the court ruled against transsexuals having this particular right to privacy[104]; however the majority weakened progressively from a twelve-to-three vote against transsexuals' right to privacy in 1986 (*Rees*), to an eleven-to-nine vote against the right in 1998 (*Sheffield & Horsham*). In 2002 the balance shifted radically, and the court reversed its case law in *Goodwin v. United Kingdom* and *I. v. United Kingdom*, ruling unanimously in favor of the rights of transsexuals.[105] In these two almost identical rulings the judges said they had to note the changing conditions within Britain and across Europe and respond to any "evolving convergence as to the standards to be achieved."[106]

This dynamic approach is preferable to the static approach because it looks not only at national laws as indicative of community sentiment but also at regional attitudes toward current practices. Where there is little consensus

among governments on whether something counts as a human rights violation, the court is more likely to assume that national authorities are able to
assess "the requirement of morals [that] varies from time to time and from
place to place, especially in our era, which is characterized by a rapid and far-
reaching evolution of opinions."[107]

Margin of appreciation as dynamic regionalism is still a young doctrine
and requires further refinement. For example it could be argued that this approach would be enhanced if judges had even more leeway to examine the
concrete practices under adjudication. Also consensus or lack of consensus
among states within a region may be relevant to a judge's deliberation, but
consensus should not replace a careful judicial analysis of individual circumstances. If there is a growing consensus among states as evidenced by
an emerging body of similar human rights reforms that has improved on the
regional standard, then that consensus is relevant. If on the other hand the
regional consensus is reducing the human rights standard, margin of appreciation ought not to apply. Margin of appreciation should only operate to increase levels of human rights.

Finally, a lack of consensus among states should never diminish an individual right. This happened in a 2004 case in France concerning discrimination against homosexuals' eligibility to adopt children. In this case the ECHR
looked at whether there was consensus across the laws of Council of Europe
member states.[108] Only The Netherlands had legislation permitting marriage
and adoption of children by homosexuals; other European states had restrictive conditions on adoption by a homosexual whether living alone or with
a partner. The court used the lack of European consensus to give France a
wide margin of appreciation and concluded that there had been no rights
granted by the convention because these were "social issues on which opinions within a democratic society may reasonably differ widely."[109] The court
missed the point here. Where there is no consensus between states the task of
the regional judge ought to be to focus on the relationship between citizen and
government. A lower human rights standard ought not follow from a lack of
legislative consensus among states.

Regional Dynamism   The best use of margin of appreciation as a means for
courts to explain their decisions is one that prompts judges to spell out a general human rights standard and a government's specific obligation to provide
it. Any compelling reasons a government may have to infringe on an individual's human rights should be stated by explicit reference to its empirical

context. The judge's proper role in such situations is twofold: first, serving as guardian of the human rights "constitution" comprising the totality of human rights treaties and conventions and second, expressing qualifications to the general standard in very precise terms. The best use of margin of appreciation is one that assumes the supremacy of higher international and regional human rights standards and restricts local authority to the most necessary departures from those norms. The judge must articulate in ways understandable both to a government and the public what unique circumstances might merit a margin. As R. St. J. MacDonald notes: "If the Court gives as its reason for not interfering simply that the decision is within the margin of appreciation of national authorities, it is really providing no reason at all but is merely expressing its conclusion not to intervene, leaving observers to guess the real reasons which it failed to articulate."[110]

My suggestion here is based on the idea of adjudication being a negotiation of values. Using comparisons of what other states are doing on a particular human right is akin to pooling information and monitoring best practices. In civil society nongovernmental organizations play a role in this process by gathering local knowledge to inform courts about norms and how they can be best interpreted and implemented.

Margin of appreciation is not a magic bullet for judges—clearly, there are possible complexities to a multifaceted approach to human rights interpretation, especially where categorical boundaries have proven beneficial in avoiding conflicts in the past. The danger of margin of appreciation is that it becomes a way of letting governments off the hook by giving them too much latitude to depart from an international human rights standard.[111] The great advantage of margin of appreciation however is that it works off an initial assumption of a higher human rights standard that applies collectively to states but still allows room for specific cultural variations. The benefits to a multifaceted approach outweigh its disadvantages.

The Legal Virtues

Globalization has added new actors to the human rights debate. Neither the conservative claim about the superiority of national laws nor the liberal arguments about the overriding values of universal human rights can offer a complete adjudicative method for judges operating under such circumstances. Under the sovereignty paradigm only laws that are particular to a national legislature and judiciary have any legal standing. Multiculturalism, on the other hand, risks taking away standards by which to judge the harmful effects of local culture.

The more recent civil society critique has downplayed the role of judges and courts in international human rights, sometimes to the point that there seems to be little role for legal adjudication. I argue instead that judicial decisions that set out the boundaries of a government's human rights obligation can be seminal for framing political expectations about human rights. More than ever the newly influential social movements and civil societies require a legal institutional mechanism for interpreting, articulating, and enforcing rights and obligations. Courts can analyze both sides of a claim and specify when a government's own assessment of the country's human rights needs take precedence over a broader standard or vice versa. A judge can identify both general human rights norms and the claims of a particular subgroup, assess whether the minority is trying to impose its views upon others, and determine if there is a viable exit option for an individual who may not wish to participate in the subgroup's cultural practice. Courts can help provide the language, the procedures, and the structures through which these claimants reliably can enunciate their differences.

In some cases it will be impossible to avoid a direct engagement between different cultural systems with differing moral schemas. If a cultural group has an irreducible value or practice and its own distinctive ethical valence, it may simply be impossible to coexist peaceably without acknowledging an intractable disagreement with another's cultural commitment. To be meaningful, adjudication of human rights claims under the conditions of globalization requires a method for hearing those claims across lines of ideological and cultural difference. This in turn implies that there must be a flourishing discourse of democracy and public life so that people who are different from one another can convey their desires to others.

My sketch here of human rights adjudication incorporates a multidimensional view of the new social actors that contribute to human rights, which include nongovernmental organizations, corporations, and trade bodies. Law and courts have an ongoing role in globalization, because law offers a framework and particular institutional competencies that are uniquely suited for adjudicating human rights conflicts. A key question for courts and judges adjudicating human rights conflicts will be to decide how much deference should be given to the decisions of more community-based dispute-settling mechanisms, such as tribal courts and religious courts, an issue I discuss in Chapter 6.

Still missing from the human rights approach that I have outlined so far is an international mechanism that avoids the problems of UN-level human rights standard-setting on one hand and problems with national institutions on the other. In the following chapter I argue that regional human rights courts offer particular institutional advantages because of their situation between states and UN-level bodies.

Chapter 5

Regional Human Rights Courts

The Cultural Conundrum

In March 2002 a sharia court in the state of Katsina in northern Nigeria sentenced Amina Lawal to death by stoning for adultery.[1] Amina Lawal's pregnancy, five years after the death of her husband, was evidence of her crime. Because the woman had no witnesses in support of her claim that a neighbor had raped her, the court disregarded her statement. When the Nigerian Court of Appeal upheld her sentence, Amina Lawal's case became an international cause célèbre. Women's groups around the developed world lobbied their governments to pressure Nigeria to pardon her.

Several months later Amina Lawal *did* walk free from the Katsina court but not because international human rights law had overruled traditional sharia law. Instead she was saved by a careful and strategic use of local law that honored the local religious system. In her final appeal before the religious court—a curious mixture of the religious robes of the mullahs and the British-style horsehair wigs and thick black barrister's garb of the Nigerian lawyers—Amina Lawal's counsel, a Nigerian named Hawa Ibrahim, explicitly employed religious reasoning. Ibrahim pointed to phrases in the Quran that recognize a husband's paternity over his wife's children for years after his death. The mullahs were persuaded to let Amina Lawal go free.

Since 1999 twelve Nigerian states, primarily in the northern region of the country, have adopted the sharia legal system. Sharia courts now adjudicate several offenses not formerly within their jurisdiction, including theft, unlawful sexual intercourse, robbery, defamation, and drinking alcohol. These courts may impose punishments under the provisions of Sharia Penal Code Law (SPCL), including death, forfeiture of property, imprisonment, fine, flogging, and amputation. Many have argued that the SPCL violates basic human rights, particularly the right to equality before the law and the right to be free from torture or degrading and inhuman punishment.

Ibrahim advances different reasons to explain the interest in and implementation of sharia in northern Nigeria. One is that fundamentalist groups inspired by the successful Iranian revolution in 1979 became determined to reproduce the Islamic revolution in Nigeria. Ibrahim describes the efforts of Auwalu Hamisu Yadudu, a Harvard-trained lawyer and advocate of sharia, who played a pivotal role in facilitating the Islamic legal system in Nigeria by arguing that the country's 1999 constitution guarantees freedom of religion. Yadudu claimed that sharia embodies the totality of Islamic guidance and governs every aspect of a Muslim's life. As a complete way of life for believers Islam "knows not the dichotomy" of Western religion as the private affair of each individual. Yadudu's arguments that the Nigerian constitution did not declare Nigeria a secular state cleared the way for sharia to be promulgated, in January 2000.

Another possible explanation is that cultural self-determination and sharia "militancy" is a way for the northern, largely Muslim areas of Nigeria to assert their political autonomy within the federation. Still another is that the rise of sharia is a consequence of globalization. According to Ibrahim, "One of the repercussions of globalization worldwide has been to arouse cultural insecurity and uncertainty about identities. Indeed, the paradox of globalization is that it simultaneously promotes enlargement on an economic scale and stimulates fragmentation on an ethnic and cultural scale."[2]

Amina Lawal's story is a victory of justice for one individual. Her story also demonstrates the deep problem of international human rights that cultural and religious differences are an ongoing ever-growing feature of international human rights controversies. Unlike cases of *mass* human rights violations such as genocide, however, it is unthinkable that the international community would send in the troops for *individualized* human rights problems such as Amina Lawal's.

In a multicultural, multireligious world governments pursue or permit cultural and religious practices that seemingly fly in the face of international human rights standards. There appears to be little that the international community can do about it. Indeed international involvement may be counterproductive: Amina Lawal's lawyer later expressed concern that the overzealous interest of Western women's rights activists had made the task of finding a locally based legal solution more difficult. International attention to the woman's plight emphasized the cultural divide between Nigeria and the West and led to the worry that the mullahs might insist on a death sentence in defensive reaction to Western pressures.[3] Ibrahim counsels the international community to familiarize itself with local conditions and nonconfrontational interventions, because "outside pressure to annul [sharia in Nigeria] likely will be ineffective and may lead to antagonism and a defensive attitude."

Amina Lawal's case demonstrates another disturbing feature of the current international system of human rights. Non-Western and Western human rights seem to be utterly at odds, providing opposite stories about the proper limits of human behavior with seemingly little middle ground. Ibrahim's solution was savvy and successful—this time—but the hope that a humane resolution can be found again, when the clash of values is as profound as Amina Lawal's case, seems to leave a lot to chance in the hope that a clever and sensitive lawyer like Hawa Ibrahim will find the opportunity to tread the fine lines of multiculturalism.

The multicultural critique of international human rights asks whether universal standards of human behavior can have any real traction in a world of such diverse religious, cultural, and national beliefs. Like the sovereignty critique addressed in Chapter 3 and the civil society critique addressed in Chapter 4, the multicultural critique raises valid concerns about human rights. In Chapter 4 I argued that adjudication of individual rights in courts is an important supplement and backstop to other catalysts of human rights change, such as nongovernmental organizations, trade agreements, and human rights treaties. This still leaves open the question of where such courts should be positioned in the international human rights system. I argue in this chapter that regional human rights institutions offer particular advantages for adjudicating human rights disputes because they can fill gaps in the current United Nations system of human rights committees and in many national legal systems.

The UN human rights treaty system assumes "moderate" multiculturalism, a gradual progress of slow adaptation to universal human rights standards, but this conception has structural limitations. The limitations of the UN human rights system need an institutional response—one that honors local and national cultures but also enjoys enough local credibility and insight that states will heed the pressure to improve their human rights practices.

National courts on the other hand are too often captive to local cultural habits and political contingencies to apply consistent standards of justice to each individual case. As Amina Lawal's case shows, the very nature of cultural harms is their cultural, religious, or ethnic conditioning, which makes them seem unassailably a part of the acceptable course of life. Unlike mass harms, such as genocide and ethnic cleansing, cultural harms are directed toward an individual in a social context in which those practices are normalized. Given the extent of cultural variation within and across communities, it makes sense to develop institutions and mechanisms that allow for the dynamic interpretation of cultures and the application of legal rules.

Using the model of hybrid courts in international criminal law discussed in Chapter 2, I seek to demonstrate particular advantages to decentralizing the human rights court system below the UN level and show that such courts are ideally positioned within regional institutions. Regional human rights treaties, laws, and courts offer philosophical and practical advantages for adjudicating cultural conflicts. Their special value lies in their geographic proximity to the people they judge, those who are bound together by shared histories and special relationships such as longstanding social and economic ties. These epistemic, normative, and fact-finding features are especially valuable for mediating culture.

Three regional systems of law already exist: those of Europe, the Americas, and Africa. They are however an under-theorized and little-noticed part of the international human rights system. Europe's system is the best known because the post–Cold War expansion to include some of the former Soviet republics in the European Union raised a new awareness of that region. The EU is more than a regional trading entity because the European Court of Human Rights (ECHR) is playing a significant role in interpreting European human rights norms within European states. Less well known are the Organization of American States, which houses the Inter-American Commission on Human Rights and the Inter-American Court of Human Rights, and the African Union, home to the brand-new African Court on Human and Peoples' Rights. These regional human rights courts offer particular advantages and if developed in the right way could play a role in making cultural human rights adjudication both morally credible *and* practically attainable.

My argument for expanding the role and the reach of regional human rights institutions is not that what works in Europe can be replicated elsewhere. Europe has a unique set of economic factors that give governments strong incentives to conform to a centralized common European system of human rights. The two other regional systems, owing to their different histories, enjoy incentive structures that are distinctively different from those in the EU. There are institutional features of the regional systems that transcend any particular regional specificity, however. My point is that regional systems have important institutional features that translate into particular advantages in developing a regional human rights jurisprudence. I argue that these three regional systems, and also a regional human rights system comprised of the ASEAN countries in Southeast Asia that I urge be established, have benefits for human rights in the same way that regionalism has demonstrated effectiveness for states trading under such regional treaties as the North American Free Trade Agreement (NAFTA) and has improved security for states under regional defense organizations such as NATO.

Of course, the regional human rights apparatus cannot provide a total remedy for human rights violations. While I argue the need for law in adjudicating the obligations of governments to prevent cultural harms to individuals, law plays only one part in a panoply of mechanisms—economic, diplomatic, and civic. Nor do I suggest that regional institutions as they exist today necessarily display all the features they ideally should have; however there are intrinsic features of regionalism that suggest answers to some of the legitimacy problems of the international human rights legal system. These benefits lie equally in the unique role of courts in adjudicating conflict and in the unique epistemic advantages that come from geographic and cultural proximity to human rights harms.

In what follows I outline the benefits of an *institutional* response to the philosophical problem of human rights. I discuss the advantages of regional human rights courts as well as some of their potential pitfalls.

The Case for Regional Human Rights Courts

When the UN human rights system was established in the 1940s it was thought that people's sense of belonging began in their family and went no further afield than their national identity. The sociological concepts of *Gemeinschaft* (akin to "family" or "community") and *Gesellschaft* (something like "broader civil society"), in which were grounded nineteenth-century ideas about national institutions, were extended to the new UN system, and it was assumed that a new international *Gemeinschaft* and *Gesellschaft* would develop from universal human rights. Today's communities however are complex in ways that were unforeseen in the mid-twentieth century. They are the product of the global movement of people and capital and of the expansion of human rights as an international political movement. Regions are a particular kind of community that now lend themselves to human rights.

The regional rights institutions of Europe, the Americas, and Africa have features different from those of both national and international human rights bodies. Regional systems have jurisdiction over multiple states within a geographic region, a sway greater than one nation-state but lesser than the UN international system. Regions tend to be organized in groupings of states that have either been historically allied in some way or are grouped within a continental bloc. The geographic proximity of member countries in regions is evident from the many linkages of trade, communications, travel, and intellectual endeavors that put national neighbors into conversation with one another. Often (though by no means necessarily) people within a region share common characteristics, typified by the nation- and language-based ethno-cultural groups within regions.

In important respects regions are also communities of memory. Regions share history both good and bad. Modern Europe's "glue" is World War II, the Cold War, and the end of communism, to which may recently be added a shared security challenge from fundamentalist Islam. Latin American countries share a history of overcoming brutal military regimes and of being used as pawns in the Cold War. African states were similarly a remote site of Cold War machinations, before which they shared the long and devastating experience of colonization by European powers. These shared histories exert a powerful influence upon the behavior of countries towards each other within a region as evidenced for example by the conspicuous respect that African nations show to one another's national sovereignty, a reverence for national political autonomy that seeks to redress the shared experience of European colonization.[4] These histories do not necessarily create fellow feeling among those within a region, but they do create a knowledge and understanding that is less accessible to those from outside that region.

Although regional courts are related to the international system of human rights through their common genesis in the UN Declaration on Human Rights, each regional court has a human rights emphasis that is uniquely shaped by its own region's political and cultural history. Such commonalities create structural and epistemological advantages for human rights courts functioning in a regional context. These regional legal institutions coexist with the UN agencies, but they have been established in response to each region's desire to coordinate international human rights law within *its* region and with *its* particular regional perspective. This motivation was clear when for example the states of the American system were drafting their regional human rights convention, writing that "The need for, and the desirability of, a regional convention for the Americas [is] based on the existence of a body of American international law built up in accordance with the specific requirements of the countries of the hemisphere. That need and desirability also followed from the close relationship that exists between human rights and regional development and integration. Consequently the Inter-American Convention on the Protection of Human Rights should be autonomous rather than complementary to the United Nations covenants."[5]

While each of the three regional human rights frameworks established its jurisdiction under the rubric of international human rights treaties and conventions, each region has its own specific human rights instruments that add unique differences. Each region has a distinctive legal "character" that distinguishes it from other regions, from the international system, and from domestic systems. Nonetheless regional human rights also share much of the language and ideology of international human rights, and gross violations such as torture or slavery continue to be absolute legal constraints shared by all of the regional systems.

Regional Human Rights Bodies

Europe

The most firmly established regional rights system is Europe's, a story of astonishing success far exceeding its modest beginning as a trading bloc after World War II. The EU began in the 1950s as the European Coal and Steel Community, which comprised six contiguous states (Belgium, France, Germany, Italy, Luxembourg, and The Netherlands). Europe turned its attention to human rights when the Council of Europe adopted the European Convention of Human Rights (ECHR) in 1950. Today the ECHR exercises jurisdiction over twenty-seven members of the European Union and twenty more states that make up the Council of Europe, ranging from Spain in the west to Russia in the northeast and Turkey in the southeast.[6]

The European community is linked to a specific locality in a physical, geographical sense. It also shares common economic goals that are pursued by letting people, goods, and services move freely across shared borders.[7]

Europe has a long common history dating from the Enlightenment that includes the rise of the nation-state and secular politics, significant colonial interests on other continents, and more recently an influx of former colonials as immigrants.

The ECHR has established its credentials in adjudicating human rights and influencing human rights law and policy of European governments.[8] It currently has an overwhelming caseload; at the end of 2007 approximately 103,000 cases were waiting to be heard. In 2006 alone it received more than 50,000 new requests to judge cases, much of the increase coming from the newer democracies of Central and Eastern Europe, where there is less trust in local judicial systems than in Western Europe. Russia is the biggest single source of cases.

The Americas

Although it has issued fewer decisions than the European regional system, the human rights protection system in the Americas is older: it began in 1948 with the American Declaration of the Rights and Duties of Man.[9] The American Convention on Human Rights protects the same civil and political rights as the UN Declaration of Human Rights but does not include the UN declaration's economic, social, and cultural rights. The Organization of American States (OAS) includes all states in the Americas, including the U.S. and Canada, but most of its work relates to Latin American countries.

Like the European system the inter-American system has institutions for human rights adjudication. Unlike the European model, however, there are three levels of human rights commitment to the inter-American declaration and the convention. Among the thirty-five OAS member states, twenty-one[10] have brought themselves under the umbrella of the OAS human rights legal system by signing both the declaration and the convention and through binding themselves to the Inter-American Court's jurisdiction. The U.S., Canada, and nine Caribbean states[11] accept the American Declaration and the resolutions or recommendations of the Inter-American Commission on Human Rights (IACHR) but not the Inter-American Court of Human Rights. Three Caribbean states that have signed onto both documents do not accept the court's jurisdiction.[12]

The Inter-American Commission is the primary human rights monitoring body under the OAS Charter.[13] While its formal jurisdiction includes the U.S. and Canada, most of its cases concern Central and South America and

Mexico and focus primarily on the human rights violations connected with military coups. Because of Latin America's particular history, the principal inter-American human rights documents emphasize democracy, restrictions on arbitrary exercise of discretionary executive powers, and restrictions on military and police powers.

Africa

The African Union (its institutional title since 2002) grew out of claims to self-determination as African states struggled for independence from colonial rule. Today comprising fifty-three states, the African Union was initially formed in 1963 as the Organization of African Unity (OAU). Its original intentions were relatively modest, to support postcolonial countries in their transition to political autonomy. In 1987 under the African Charter the African Commission on Human and Peoples' Rights was created to provide a system through which one person, a group of individuals, or a nongovernmental organization could petition the commission about human rights violations.

In 1998 the OAU adopted the Protocol to the African Charter on Human and Peoples' Rights on the Establishment of an African Court on Human and Peoples' Rights. The first judges of the African Court were selected in 2006, and Arusha, Tanzania, the site of the International Criminal Tribunal for Rwanda, was selected as the seat of the court. In 2007 and 2008 administrative staff were being hired, but the court had yet to hear its first case.

The African Charter provides a distinctive regional perspective on human rights. It uses the African concept of *ubuntu* (community) and avoids the winner-takes-all attitude of adversarial adjudication.[14] It generally favors the interests of the community over those of the individual and emphasizes economic and social rights while striving to incorporate international normative standards. For example an African marriage is not only the coming together of two individuals but the union two families or two clans. Ownership and control of property traditionally is by the family, the clan, or the community. The African Charter also explicitly recognizes the right of peoples to exist, thereby asserting as a human right what had previously, under the UN Convention on the Prevention and Punishment of the Crime of Genocide, only existed in the form of a prohibition against genocide.

The new African Court on Human and Peoples' Rights differs from its American and European predecessors and from all other international and regional judicial bodies in that actions may be brought before the court on the basis of any treaty (including international human rights treaties) that has been ratified by an African state party to a human rights case before the court. Through this particular provision, even though very few international human rights agreements contain mechanisms for judicial implementation, all of these agreements are claimed as part of the African Court's jurisdiction. The African Court thus has the potential to develop a broader dispute settlement system than any other regional human rights system.

Regionality

Features of Regionality

Regional institutions are uniquely placed to acquire information and filter knowledge about the cultural, religious, and gender practices of a region. Being closer to local realities than UN human rights committees, regional institutions have a different relationship to the facts in a human rights claim. Like the hybrid criminal courts reviewed in Chapter 2, regional adjudicative bodies are typically staffed by people *from that region.*

Regional institutions therefore have a unique *epistemic* relationship to regional contextual factors such as variations of political culture, important features of social history, and the institutional capacity of a government to make human rights reforms. Unlike UN institutions that are bound to emphasize a lofty standard of human rights because of the UN's vantage point on global universalism, regional institutions can use particular histories as reference points to temper abstract formulations of human rights. At the same time, regional courts are likely to be less subject to (although not immune from) political manipulation by governments or local elites. These features mean that regional human rights courts undertake a qualitatively different exercise than international human rights committees attached to the UN.

Regional legal institutions have a distinct vantage point that derives from their position as *neither* national *nor* international. Regional institutions operate on a stratum between the state and the UN human rights treaty system, and they have an opportunity to play a unique interpretive role. They are well placed to identify rights associated with basic human interests that are neither parochial (the risk with national institutions) nor overreaching (the risk with international institutions) when interpreting international human rights standards. These factors can lend legitimacy to a regional institution in its support for claims about the existence of human rights and their content. Regional human rights courts are ideally positioned to do the work of cultural interpretation of human rights. They can be an important interlocutor between human rights claims and claims of culture, between the human right to be equal and the human right to be different.

The best way to demonstrate the point is through regional human rights cases themselves, the decisions of regional institutions that have grappled with the law and culture of countries in a specific region. These rulings show that regional systems are positioned to develop a human rights juris- prudence that is broadly compatible with the spirit of international human rights treaties but also able to respond to the ways that local cultures coexist with national politics and national economic capacity. Regional courts can- not be a perfect solution, and some of these cases demonstrate drawbacks of regional systems that need correction. Just as the hybrid criminal courts for Kosovo and Bosnia and Herzegovina have utilized legal methods and proce- dures to adapt to administering international humanitarian law at the local level, so expanded regional human rights courts can draw upon legal insti- tutional characteristics in their application of international human rights law at the local level.

Regional Court Decisions

Europe   Abortion is an issue that divides communities around the world. It has been a divisive issue in Ireland for a long time and has recently become even more prominent because of the numbers of Irish women traveling to the U.K. for abortions, which are legal there.[15] Ireland joined the European Union in 1973 and signed the European Convention on Human Rights, which pre- cipitated a debate between "pro-choice" and "pro-life" factions. Pro-life ad- vocates succeeded in introducing an amendment to the Irish Constitution in 1983 that defines a fetus as having the right to life from conception.

Europe has exerted a moderating influence on abortion politics in Ireland, haltingly, but the practical effect has been greater than the admonitions of the UN Committee on the Elimination of Discrimination against Women (CEDAW) to the Irish government to "commence a national dialogue" on women's right to reproductive health.[16] It has been a gradual process. Abor- tion remained a purely national issue for several decades after Ireland joined the EU. Irish courts banned family planning groups and student associations from offering abortion counseling, information, and aid in traveling abroad to terminate pregnancies. Then in 1992 the Irish Supreme Court relented and gave permission for a pregnant fourteen-year-old rape victim who was reported to be suicidal to travel outside Ireland to obtain an abortion. The court based its decision entirely on Irish law[17] and declared that "[n]o decision on any question of European law is . . . necessary to enable the Court to give its judgment."[18] Two constitutional amendments were enacted in 1993 so that Irish law would not contravene the European Convention's guarantee of the right to travel freely throughout Europe and the right to information. In 1997 the Irish High Court allowed a thirteen-year-old rape victim to travel to Britain for an abortion, but only because of her exceptional circumstances.[19] Abortion on demand continued to be illegal in Ireland, and the clear implication from the court's decisions was that only women who are suicidal or otherwise at risk of dying could travel abroad to terminate their pregnancy.

An Irish women's organization brought a case before the European Court of Human Rights in 1992, claiming that the Irish's government's ban on information about abortion clinics in England contravened the right to freedom of expression under the European Convention on Human Rights. The ECHR upheld the claim, and as a result information on abortion has since become legally available in Ireland.[20] The sort of information now available in Ireland about pregnancy and contraception is vastly different from what was available before the ECHR case, and attitudes are slowly changing. A 1997 poll in Ireland found that only 28 percent of those asked believed that "an abortion should be provided to those who need it." A 2005 poll found that 36 percent believed abortion should be legalized. In July 2007 people were asked the question, "Is it time to legislate for abortion in Ireland?" and 38 percent voted "yes."[21]

Ireland is at the crossroads of change on a woman's right to choose, not only because of social changes but also because it is within the legal jurisdiction of the European Court of Human Rights. Many thousands of Irish women travel to the U.K. each year seeking termination of a pregnancy.[22] Irish jurisprudence is gradually changing however. A 2007 ruling from the Irish High Court (a court that sits below the Irish Supreme Court) allowed a pregnant seventeen-year-old woman with a fetus suffering from an extremely severe deformity to travel legally to the U.K. for an abortion.[23] Not surprisingly pro-choice groups find the rate of Irish legal change too slow. Europe provides for Ireland a social comparison, a legal mechanism through which pro-choice individuals can articulate their human rights claims, and Irish social attitudes have begun to diverge from their traditional religious underpinnings.

Abortion is also a controversial topic in Poland, a relatively new EU member. Abortion was legalized in Poland in 1956, but the ruling was reversed in

1993 after communism ended, the traditional power of the Catholic Church was reasserted, and legislation was passed prohibiting abortion with only extremely restrictive exceptions. The 1993 law imposes criminal sanctions upon any doctor who terminates a pregnancy in breach of these conditions. The law has pushed abortion underground and made doctors reluctant to perform even legally permissible procedures.

In early 2007 a case was brought against the Polish government by a woman who was denied an abortion despite warnings by her doctors that pregnancy could put her at risk of blindness. Deciding in favor of the woman, the European Court of Human Rights looked at comparable systems in Bulgaria, Croatia, the Czech Republic, Denmark, Finland, Norway, Slovakia, Slovenia, and Sweden. The court declared that in a country where some form of therapeutic abortion is legally available the government must have procedures to allow women to access those abortions before it was too late to perform a termination. The comparable European procedures all have strict time limits on administrative review of abortion services, recognizing the inherently time-sensitive nature of these procedures.

The European Court directed Poland to create a system of adjudication and enforcement before an independent body competent to review the evidence. It ruled that not having such processes undermined women's right of access to reproductive health care and could have serious consequences for their lives and health. Once the legislature allows abortion, the court said, it must not structure the legal framework in a way that would limit real possibilities for a woman to obtain a termination. When time is of the essence, the legal system must protect and implement the rights of women who claim a need for therapeutic abortion: "the Convention is intended to guarantee not rights that are theoretical or illusory but rights that are practical and effective. . . . [The government has] positive obligations inherent in an effective 'respect' for private life. These obligations may involve the adoption of measures designed to secure respect for private life even in the sphere of relations between individuals."[24]

Another controversial issue is religious clothing and ornamentation. Religious headscarves and ornamentation have been the topic of fierce debate across Europe and have led to cases before national courts that have found their way on appeal to the European Court of Human Rights. There are more than thirty cases pending before the ECHR on this issue, including an appeal from the constitutional court of the German state of Bavaria, which in early

2007 upheld a 2003 law that bans teachers from wearing the *hijab* (Muslim headscarf) on the ground that doing so contravenes the gender equality guaranteed under the constitution.[25] Eight other German states have introduced similar laws. In 2004 and 2005 the European Court of Human Rights upheld the right of the Turkish government to ban women from wearing the *hijab* in schools and universities based on the need to maintain public order.[26] In the 2004 ECHR case the court found that banning the headscarf in Turkey is not an attack on religious freedom but is a legitimate method of countering Islamic fundamentalism. If students or teachers were allowed to wear headscarves in public schools it could put pressure on other students and threaten their religious freedom. In this circumstance the ban was merely a *restriction* on the fundamental right to religious freedom under the European Convention and not a direct violation of that right.

Having this human rights issue decided by the ECHR at the regional level gives valuable guidance to national courts. For example, in June 2008, Turkey's Constitutional Court ruled that the parliament had violated Article 2 of the Constitution when it passed amendments to lift the headscarf ban on campuses. Article 2 enshrines secularism in Turkey as a constitutional principle. The court decided that the parliament could not remove the constitutional guarantee of secularism simply by voting to amend it.

The 2004 ECHR headscarf decision draws a distinction between political Islam and religious Islam, with the headscarf seen as a symbol of political Islam and the oppression of women. The context of the human rights conflict is all-important and has led to different outcomes in similar situations. For example in a case decided in April 2007, the ECHR ruled that Turkey had violated the European conventions by banning an elected representative from parliament merely because she wore a Muslim headscarf.[27] In 1999 militant secularists had kept Merve Kavakçı from taking her seat in the Turkish parliament, shouting her down for hours and then ejecting her from the parliamentary chamber because she was wearing the *hijab*. Weeks later the Turkish government stripped Kavakçı of both her parliamentary seat and her citizenship.[28] The court said that Turkey's behavior violated the right to "the free expression of the opinion of the people in the choice of the legislature" under the European Convention for the Protection of Human Rights, and it awarded damages to Kavakçı.

The Americas   Like the European court decisions, human rights court decisions in the Americas are also making a regional impact.[29] The system in the

Americas does not have the formal economic structure of the European Union and the European Council, so there is much less incentive for the thirty-five American governments to comply with decisions from the Inter-American Court of Human Rights. Only twenty-one states are actually bound by all of the Inter-American Court's decisions although all thirty-five governments are supposedly bound by the Inter-American Commission's reports. There are also outliers in the American system, the United States being the prime example.[30] Over the past decade or so the Inter-American Court of Human Rights has handed down a series of bold decisions against Latin American governments.

In Guatemala relatives of "disappeared" children alleged the kidnapping, torture, and death of the children by members of the security forces.[31] The Inter-American Court of Human Rights decided against the government in 2001, saying that it had contravened the 1987 Inter-American Convention to Prevent and Punish Torture, as well as the International Convention on the Rights of the Child. The court ordered Guatemala to pay damages to the victims' families and to adjust its domestic regulations to comply with the rights of children under Article 19 of the convention. The court also issued ancillary directives: it ordered the government to give an educational institution a name that referred to the young victims, investigate fully the facts, identify and sanction those who were responsible, and adopt into its domestic law regulations that would ensure future compliance with the convention. Continuing in a watching role, the court in 2005 declared that Guatemala had complied with key aspects of the 2001 judgment, but it also decided to continue monitoring Guatemala's commitment to investigate and prosecute those responsible for the crimes.[32] This case marks the first time in twenty years that the court has decided a children's rights case, and it is the first time that a judgment involved the full panoply of legal, social, economic, and educational remedies. The Guatemala case was also remarkable because it heralded the subsequent advisory opinion issued by the Inter-American Court about the general rights of children.[33] National governments now have a template for legal reform.

In another case, in 2003 the Inter-American Court of Human Rights became the first international tribunal to declare that governments are subject to a general right of access to information through an interpretation of the right to freedom of expression under Article 13 of the American Convention on Human Rights.[34] Three environmental activists had requested information from the Chilean government regarding a controversial logging project. In addition to ordering the disclosure of information the court said that governments of the OAS must train their public officials on procedures for releasing information. Governments must be guided by the principle of "maximum disclosure," meaning that virtually all government-held information must be accessible to the public. Chile has since complied with the court's ruling by introducing draft access to government-held information legislation that is now before the Joint Commission of the Chamber of Deputies and the Senate for final review.[35]

The custody rights of lesbians have also come before the Inter-American Commission.[36] The case dates to 2003, when Karen Atala Riffo, a judge in Chile, lost custody of her three children by an order of the Chilean Supreme Court and was disbarred from her judicial post. Atala's representatives had presented psychological studies and decisions from the United States and other jurisdictions to show that sexual orientation has no bearing on a person's ability to be a good parent. They argued that depriving Atala of the custody of her children constituted discrimination on the basis of sexual orientation. Despite this evidence the Supreme Court ruled that by deciding to live with her female partner the mother had given preference to her own interests ahead of those of her children and that her children could be subject to discrimination because of the homosexual relationship of their mother. Atala has taken her case to the Inter-American Commission, where a "friendly settlement" process of negotiation between the parties is ongoing. If Atala succeeds it could mean significant law reform in Chile as well as monetary compensation for her.[37]

Most recently, in its first decision on a human rights violation related to people with mental disabilities, the court ordered the Brazilian government to pay compensation to the family of an individual with a psychiatric disorder who died in a government-run clinic, based on violations of the American Convention on Human Rights.[38] Brazil has complied; the president issued a decree in August 2007 ordering compliance and payment of monetary compensation to the victim's relatives. The government will report to the Inter-American Court on the measures undertaken to reform its health policy toward people with mental disabilities.[39]

Not all governments in the Americas comply with the decisions of the court and the commission. A convicted prisoner challenged Trinidad and Tobago for rights under the American Convention of Human Rights and the OAS Charter after he was punished with fifteen strokes of the cat-o'-nine-tails. The court upheld his case and fined the Trinidad and Tobago government. It also ordered the government to amend its constitution and its criminal punishment practices to bring them into line with regional national human rights standards. In finding Trinidad and Tobago in breach of its obligations the Inter-American Court relied on its own case law that had already construed the meaning of the right to physical integrity under the American Convention on Human Rights. The court complemented its analysis with reports from the UN Human Rights Commission, case law from the European Court of Human Rights, and even a controversial case from the Trial Chamber of the International Criminal Tribunal for the Former Yugoslavia, the *Čelebići* case, that had decided issues of command responsibility in Bosnian genocide camps in 1992.[40] Relying on all these external court decisions, the Inter-American court said that "the very nature of this punishment reflects an institutionalization [sic] of violence, which, although permitted by the law, ordered by the State's judges and carried out by its prison authorities, is a sanction incompatible with the [American Convention on Human Rights] . . . corporal punishment by flogging constitutes a form of torture and . . . is a violation . . . of the right . . . to have . . . physical, mental and moral integrity respected."[41] The Inter-American Commission on Human Rights has continued to provide information periodically on compliance with the orders issued by the court, reporting as recently as 2006.[42] Under the terms of the court's decision Trinidad and Tobago was required to pay compensation to the victim within a year from the notification of the judgment, but the government by 2008 had yet to comply with the order and nothing indicates this will change in the future. This adds to prior cases concerning death penalty issues in which Trinidad and Tobago has also not complied with reparations required by the Inter-American Court.[43]

In all these examples the regional court judges a national government on its human rights performance in a specific instance in the hope and expectation that a higher standard will be applied in the future by the national government. In fact this has occurred. Both the American Declaration and the American Convention now have constitutional status in Argentina.[44] In 1992 the Argentine Supreme Court, relying on an advisory opinion issued by the Inter-American Court, held that the American Convention creates directly enforceable rights in Argentina without the need to enact domestic Argentine legislation.[45] Then a major amendment to the Argentine constitution in 1994 made international and regional human rights legally binding at the national level.[46] In other words both the UN Declaration of Human Rights and the other seven main international human rights covenants and treaties, as well as the American Declaration of Man and the American Convention on Human

Rights, must guide Argentine law. These two regional documents are now much more regularly invoked by the Argentine Supreme Court than the UN human rights instruments. A comprehensive overview of the Supreme Court of Argentina's case law between 1992 and 2005 shows that inter-American human rights law is frequently cited by that court when it intercedes to prevent bad domestic practices.

The local incorporation of inter-American human rights is now even affecting Argentina's constitutional law. For example, a 1996 case called *Bramajo* concerning preemptive detention of a criminal defendant was the first time the Supreme Court of Argentina was faced with a directive issued by the Inter-American Commission about the compatibility of a piece of domestic legislation with a provision of the American Convention on Human Rights.[47] The court decided that the Argentine Constitution gives constitutional status to the American Convention and that the convention has a special "enhanced" status. The American Convention must be read by the Argentine authorities not as an isolated *corpus juris* but in accordance with the way the convention had been interpreted overtime by the regional monitoring bodies, the Inter-American Commission and the Inter-American Court. In other words the Supreme Court of Argentina tied its own hands as the primary interpreter of the Argentine constitution and acknowledged the existence of *concurrent* regional arbiters.[48]

In the 1995 *Giroldi* case the Supreme Court of Argentina concluded that inter-American regional jurisprudence should be a guide or interpretative aid in determining the scope of human rights law of regional origin in Argentina.[49] A key argument in *Giroldi* stated that "This Supreme Court, as a supreme body of one of the branches of the federal government, is required—as far as its jurisdiction is concerned—to apply the international treaties to which Argentina is a state party in the manner previously described . . . failure to do so might engender international responsibility of the Nation *vis-à-vis* the community of states."[50]

Most significantly the Argentine Supreme Court is increasingly deferring to decisions of the Inter-American Court of Human Rights as authoritative interpretations of the regional human rights standards that must be applied in Argentina.[51] This situation began in the 1990s, when the Supreme Court cited the so-called "advisory opinions" of the Inter-American Court, and has now evolved in a way that the Supreme Court applies decisions of the Inter-American Court that are directed at other OAS member states.[52] The Argentine

Supreme Court's interpretations of regional human rights law are superseded not only by the Inter-American Court's directives specifically against Argentina but also by regional decisions that apply to other OAS members.[53]

For example in a 2005 case concerning the right to appeal of a person accused of a criminal offense under the American Convention on Human Rights, the Argentine Supreme Court considered the precedential value of a decision of the Inter-American Court directed at Costa Rica. The Argentine Supreme Court held that because Costa Rica's criminal appeals system was similar to Argentina's and because the Inter-American Court of Human Rights had adopted an earlier UN Human Rights Committee standard, the Inter-American Court decision should be applied to Argentina. The Argentine Supreme Court ordered a full revision of a criminal conviction by an Argentine appeals court, including a reexamination of both the law applied to the case and the facts on which the judges had based the conviction.[54]

On the other hand decisions of the Inter-American Commission, which is not a court but simply a monitoring body, have been treated with less deference by the Argentine Supreme Court, particularly if compliance would mean reversing a previous Argentine Supreme Court decision. A 1998 decision in a habeas corpus case involving a group of prisoners demanding their release was taken to the Inter-American Commission from a domestic court in Argentina. The commission had issued a report the previous year recommending the immediate release of the prisoners. The case eventually reached the Supreme Court of Argentina, which refused to order the release, saying that commission decisions were a guide but were not binding decisions: "Even though Argentina has to undertake its best efforts in order to favorably answer to the recommendations suggested by the Inter-American Commission, in accordance with the principle of good faith that rules the fulfillment of Argentina's international duties; such a statement does not amount to affirm that the domestic judiciary is under an obligation to comply with the content of those recommendations."[55]

This points out the special saliency to national courts of court decisions relative to nonlegal bodies such as commissions and committees. The regional courts of Europe and the OAS are altering the human rights jurisprudence of national courts. Regional courts are in close proximity—geographic, cultural, historical, and economic—to human rights problems, which gives them an institutional advantage over distant UN human rights committees and a special position for the strengthening of human rights decisions of regional courts.

Creating an ASEAN Regional Human Rights Court

Asia as Exception

Europe, Africa, and the Americas have established regional human rights systems, leaving behind Asia and the Pacific as the largest and most populous region without an equivalent institution. (The Middle East too lacks a human rights court system.)[56] The idea that Asia or the Asia-Pacific region should follow the lead of others and establish a formal human rights system is not new—it has been suggested over the years by those within the region and supported more recently by the United Nations. My argument here is that the time is ripe for a regional human rights institution comprised of the ASEAN countries, complete with regional human rights charters, human rights courts, and commissioners and judges. Over time, it might also incorporate Australia and New Zealand, which both have significant trading and diplomatic ties with ASEAN countries.

Such an enterprise would not encounter smooth sailing. Like the development of the European Union a regional system in Southeast Asia would raise the question of which countries are in and which are out of the regional unit. This too is not a new consideration. The EU originally comprised only six Western European countries, and an expanded roster that included Romania and the Czech Republic would have been unthinkable in the 1960s. A human rights system for ASEAN would have to deal with the potential membership of China, Japan, and India, just as in the European Coal and Steel Community, Luxembourg, and Belgium had to deal with membership of France, Germany, and Italy. There would also be concerns about accepting as members states whose participation might be intermittent or even nonexistent, in the same manner as ad hoc participation of the U.S. in the inter-American regional human rights system. Nonetheless, the benefits of establishing an ASEAN court of human rights outweigh the liabilities—problems that other regions have demonstrated will likely diminish overtime.

Formalization and Expansion of ASEAN

Developments in the Asia-Pacific region seem to argue for the creation of regional rights institutions though the signs are at times contradictory. A regional economic organization already exists in Asia. The Association of South East Asian Nations (ASEAN) was formed in 1967 with five members—Indonesia, Malaysia, Philippines, Singapore, and Thailand. The spread of communism, particularly by Vietnam, was the threat at that time. Not surprisingly the earliest ASEAN documents emphasized principles of "self-determination, sovereign equality, and non-interference in the internal affairs of nations."[57] By the 1980s and with the end of the Cold War however, ASEAN's objectives became economic, meaning that at the onset of the Asian economic crisis of 1998 the association expended most of its energy on regional economic cooperation.

In 2008 ASEAN consists of ten member countries (now including Brunei Darussalam, Vietnam, Laos, Myanmar, and Cambodia, plus the original five members) that meet regularly together with other neighbors. The ASEAN Declaration gives the aims and purposes of the association as accelerating the economic growth, social progress, and cultural development of the region, promoting regional peace and stability through adherence to the principles of the United Nations Charter, and abiding in respect for justice and the rule of law in the relationship among countries in the region.[58] As was the case in other regions, what began with modest objectives has since expanded. In 2003 ASEAN established a plan with the objective of creating three institutions: the ASEAN Security Community,[59] the ASEAN Economic Community,[60] and the ASEAN Socio-Cultural Community.[61] Even so, its policies toward its member states may differ depending on the situation. For example, while ASEAN required Cambodia to demonstrate progress in making the transition to democracy to gain admission, it did not place the same requirement on Myanmar (Burma).[62]

Asian Sovereignty

As the countries of ASEAN have expanded their international economic and political presence they have also attracted international scrutiny and criticism of some of their human rights practices. They have bristled at this criticism, defending "Asian values"—a style of "constructive engagement" that uses "gentle persuasion and the wielding of 'economic carrots.'"[63] Although they are formally bound by the UN Charter, ASEAN states have adopted an indignant and united stance against foreign states or international organizations that have criticized their human rights. For example in 1994 the Philippine president banned forty foreign delegates from entering the country to attend the first Asia-Pacific Conference on East Timor because there had been critical reports in the international press about government repression.[64]

ASEAN countries view the implementation of human rights as a matter of national oversight that should not be subject to international supervision. Their preferred method of dispute resolution is nonconfrontational, carefully

avoiding human rights terminology and "addressed through discreet diplomatic channels . . . [that seek] not to embarrass . . . through isolation or condemnation. Change is induced through peer pressure . . . delinking human
rights from economic development issues, for example, through rejecting the
inclusion of a social clause in international trade agreements as a new form of
protectionism."[65]

This response could be interpreted partly as a reaction to Western criticism
of the human rights situation in Asia and as a continued response to colonialism.[66] Asian governments, with their self-confidence bolstered by economic
success, interpret Western propagation of capitalism, democracy, and Western
interpretations of human rights as "missionary" and a threat to their economic
interests, because international human rights agitation could repel prospective
financial and corporate investors. Similarly, making economic aid and trade
relations conditional upon human rights progress is seen by Asian nations as a
challenge to their sovereignty and national autonomy. Not surprisingly ASEAN's
stance has led to tension with the European Union, which wants human rights
and promotion of democracy to remain on the EU-ASEAN agenda.[67]

"Asian Values"

In many ways the ASEAN battles over universal standards of international
human rights exemplify the ideological battles over sovereignty and cultural
relativism. ASEAN states see Asian values as different from liberal ideology and
human rights that have their historical roots in the West. They point out that
most Asian countries did not have a role in the formation of the early international human rights documents because at that point they were either European
colonies or were newly emerging as sovereign states. Some Asian politicians
have also argued that international human rights are an alien culture that is in-
appropriate in the Asian context. Singapore's former prime minister Lee Kwan
Yew has argued this even while human rights activists in his own country accused him of using Asian values as a shield against valid criticism of the repressive practices of some ASEAN governments. Finally, proponents of Asian
values have argued that human rights can come only after a certain degree of
economic development has been achieved, even if this "economy first" approach
might reinforce the power asymmetry between ruling elites and citizens.[68]

Despite these arguments of some Asian leaders, human rights institutions
have been developing, inexorably pushed along by the energy of grassroots
lawyers and activists within Asian states on the one hand and encouraged by

UN leadership on the other. This combination of internal and external forces has produced a complex network of NGOs and quasi-governmental bodies at regional and national levels in Asia. Even governments that initially said there was little need for a regional human rights arrangement in the ASEAN region are gradually changing their views. Asian NGOs have responded to governments' lackadaisical approach to human rights by creating several organizations such as the Asian Legal Resource Centre (ALRC) and the Asian Human Rights Commission. The ALRC was founded in 1986 by a prominent group of jurists and human rights activists in Asia and now has general consultative status with the Economic and Social Council of the United Nations. Its agenda centers on legal self-reliance and empowerment of people; it emphasizes cultural, social, and economic rights and the right of development and works closely with regional, national, and local groups involved in this field.[69] The Asian Human Rights Commission (AHRC), an independent NGO also founded in 1986, actively promotes the UN, particularly its human rights agencies, and has stated that it seeks the development of regional human rights mechanisms.[70] It has created the Draft Asian Human Rights Charter, which sets out universally applicable rights that arise from an "Asian" perspective and incorporates many of the rights supported by most Asian states under various international treaties, including the rights of women and children. The charter also extends to areas not readily recognized by most Asian states, such as the rights to democratic government, peace, cultural identity, freedom of conscience, and social justice.

Asian governments have resisted the Draft Asian Human Rights Charter. They see the expansion of human rights as "a threat to state self-interest and sovereignty."[71] Despite this resistance, pressure for a regional institution is steadily growing among lawyers' associations and society groups. In 1996 the Asia Pacific Forum of National Human Rights Institutions was created after a meeting of national human rights institutions, regional governments, and nongovernmental organizations. It adopted the Larrakia Declaration, which sets out principles governing the function of national human rights institutions.[72] Governments, UN agencies, and human rights NGOs have been granted observer status. Some ASEAN states such as Indonesia and Malaysia have bowed under the pressure and established their own national human rights commissions.[73] These commissions make an important start, although they probably lack genuine independence and are still underfunded. The Philippines commission has not yet had much impact on redressing and reforming abusive government practices,[74] but the Indonesia commission has performed reasonably well. It has been successful at mediating land issues and has been critical of some actions of the Indonesian police force. This commission also undertook an inquiry into reports of mass rapes of ethnic Chinese women, eventually determining that these crimes had occurred and calling on the government to investigate and resolve all cases of human rights violations.[75] Commentators have optimistically suggested that: "the common citizen recognizes that the Commission is sufficiently independent from the government and sufficiently successful to be worth appealing to without fear of repercussions; it is not perceived as toothless. . . . As a vehicle for focusing attention and publicity on human rights violations on a larger scale through its public statements and investigations, the Commission may be able to check government abuses."[76]

The United Nations is playing an active role in encouraging the formation of human rights bodies at the regional level in southeast Asia with two objectives: the creation of structures for the protection and promotion of human rights at national and regional levels and the introduction of a coordination mechanism for human rights activities at national and regional levels.[77] Other organizations and international bodies such as the Asia Foundation also promote the establishment of a regional human rights system.[78] Among the programs that the Asia Foundation supports is the Working Group for an ASEAN Human Rights Mechanism (the Working Group), whose primary goal is to establish an intergovernmental human rights commission for ASEAN.[79]

A Coordinated Human Rights Approach

During the 1990s ASEAN began addressing many problems associated with human rights, including women and children's rights, HIV/AIDS, rural poverty reduction, illiteracy, drug trafficking, and environmental problems, including the haze from Indonesian forest fires. In 1997 the heads of government adopted a document called ASEAN Vision 2020. Although international human rights terminology was avoided ASEAN Vision 2020 articulates goals that correspond to socioeconomic rights. The most optimistic sign by far occurred in August 2007 at ASEAN's fortieth meeting. A substantial first draft of an ASEAN charter was tendered, which included the establishment of an ASEAN human rights body. At the meeting it was proposed that a high-level task force be created to ease the transition and that an enabling provision for the establishment of a regional human rights body be given high priority. The ASEAN foreign ministers expressed consensus in favor of the creation of an intergovernmental human rights commission, a move that one official considered "the most sig-nificant development to take place during the ongoing 40th ASEAN Ministerial Meeting in Manila, Philippines."[80]

While economic cooperation between ASEAN states will probably in-crease and internal tariff barriers perhaps be lowered, it seems unlikely that human rights protections will be significantly featured without the develop-ment of more cohesive human rights institutions. One suggestion would be to enhance the self-reporting scheme of the Asia-Pacific Forum, which mimics the procedures of the Inter-American Commission on Human Rights.

Political Factors

China, Japan, and India—each more powerful than all ASEAN nations com-bined—play an immense role in Asia, but their inclusion in an Asian regional human rights system seems inconceivable right now. Few in Europe in the 1950s however imagined today's European Union of twenty-seven countries, including some that once were part of the Soviet Bloc. As was the case with the expansion of the EU, in Asia global and regional trade are the likely conduits for reducing isolationism and increasing integration. An Asian human rights system could be part of such a development and is an issue that needs empirical research, institutional planning, and political will.

Asian governments' "hands-off human rights" approach is well known, both within the ASEAN group and beyond. It was seen in late 2007, when ASEAN leaders were conspicuously silent in the face of the crackdown by the military junta in Myanmar on Buddhist monks' demonstrating for democracy in the streets of Yangon. The same deaf ear was turned again in March 2008 when China brutally repressed protests by Tibetan monks. ASEAN's reticence pays heed to China's looming geopolitical presence.

Earlier some small signs indicated that ASEAN's hands-off policy might change. In 1998 Thailand had proposed reexamination of the noninterven-tion policy, arguing that "a stronger new approach was needed to handle the escalation of economic, environmental, and political crises in the latter half of the 1990s. ASEAN member states had to be able to criticize each other's policies more openly where these had regional repercussions."[81] Both Thai-land and Philippines had criticized Malaysia for its poor treatment of former deputy prime minister Anwar Ibrahim in 1999 when he was sentenced follow-ing a highly controversial trial to six years in prison for corruption and then in 2000 to another nine years for homosexual acts. Thailand and Philippines alleged that he had been denied due process of law; this was the first time that an ASEAN state had broken ranks to comment on a politically sensitive matter in another ASEAN member state. By couching Anwar's maltreatment in detention in terms of previously eschewed "human rights" terminology, even countries that have hitherto resisted it are becoming part of an international network of language and ideology.[82] Anwar Ibrahim has recently made a political comeback. In 2008 he won the *Permatang Pauh* by election and returned to parliament as leader of the Malaysian opposition.

The Way Ahead

ASEAN's modus operandi of pragmatism, mutual communication, and consensus-seeking is similar to the African system, which uses the African concept of *ubuntu* to incorporate community interests and needs into any analysis of individual claims. In the Asian context it continues to be important that political parties develop an understanding of the sovereignty as *relational*—that is, that governments derive their legitimacy from their protection and promotion of human rights—and that the international community too has a moral interest in a government's treatment of its people.

　　Like other regional systems an ASEAN human rights system would exist within the UN superstructure, each state being a signatory of the UN Charter and UN human rights treaties such as the Convention on the Elimination of All Forms of Discrimination against Women, the Convention on the Rights of the Child, and the Convention on the Prevention and Punishment of the Crime of Genocide. An Asian regional body could supplement UN human rights country reporting when it is delayed and also might issue advisory opinions as to whether reservations entered to the UN treaties by states counteract the underlying spirit and intent of the UN treaty. ASEAN's "economics first" argument could be leveraged for human rights by pointing out that civil and political rights can *promote* development. Most important, a regional human rights court could develop regional human rights jurisprudence that is free from the charge of Western bias and provide a human rights credibility that national courts in Asian countries rely upon.

Designing Regional Institutions to Maximize Human Rights

In this chapter I have suggested a reconceptualization of the work of regional human rights courts in adjudicating human rights conflicts. The regional approach is offered as a supplement to rather than a replacement of the international human rights apparatus; it assumes that the state continues as the principal delivery mechanism for human rights for the day-to-day needs of its people. There are potential advantages of regional human rights adjudication, and the creation of an Asian regional human rights system could apply these benefits to ASEAN countries and potentially also countries in the ASEAN neighborhood. This new system would inevitably face decisions on where the regional boundary lies in the same way that Europe is continually confronted with such decisions.

There are also risks involved in increasing the role of regional systems, despite the rich potential of doing so. One possible danger is that increased regional human rights autonomy might be used to create geographic human rights "ghettos" or, even worse, pockets of like-minded human rights abusers. Regional solidarity might become a cloak for a national government's oppression, as when the 1993 Bangkok Declaration on Asian values promoted a regional-value preference for economic advancement over civil and political rights. In fact it seems more likely that autocratic Asian leaders at that time were expressing their personal views and not those of their publics, which emphasized the problem of sovereignty that was discussed in Chapter 3.

The same problem could arise in the African Court on Human and Peoples' Rights.[83] African politicians often use the shield of culture as a barrier to criticism of practices that violate the most fundamental human rights and that their own citizens want stopped. At the other end of the spectrum, universalists have been criticized for transforming the discourse of human rights into "an intellectual battering ram," relentlessly chanting universal standards when deference to local norms could in some instances offer a solution that enhances the protection of human rights in the local community.[84] A regional concession to international standards must strike a balance. The outcome is likely to be controversial and places a heavy onus on a regional court to demonstrate through its written decisions that it has taken account of all reasonable positions.

A second risk is the "lead nation" phenomenon, in which one country spreads its political, economic, and social creed to its closest neighbors. This can be a double-edged sword. For example South Africa leads the African Union out of commercial self-interest and in the interests of stabilizing the region. For the most part this has been good for the region. As in the Asian values example however, in which Malaysia's lead against human rights in the Anwar Ibrahim case had the regrettable result of tipping the balance against rights implementation within ASEAN countries, so has South Africa's ambivalence about some human rights issues retarded the human rights performance of other African governments. South Africa's delay in taking a more critical stance toward Pres. Robert Mugabe's human rights violations in neighboring Zimbabwe is a case in point. In the nearly three decades of Mugabe's rule, South Africa's reluctance to criticize some of Mugabe's worst human rights violations openly at times seemed to signal tacit approval of them.

Third, gradual improvement of human rights standards can only happen if states play the game rather than opt out. Countries occasionally withdraw from the international human rights system; for example, Somalia, China, and the U.S. have each refused to sign or ratify certain international human rights treaties. States also opt out of regional systems; there was some evidence of this in the Caribbean when Trinidad and Tobago denounced the American Convention in 1998, and again when Barbados, Guyana, Jamaica, and Trinidad and Tobago announced plans to establish a Caribbean Court of Justice in order to avoid the higher standards of the Inter-America Court of Human Rights on due process in death penalty cases.[85]

Finally, regional human rights courts cannot obviate the need for moral and political decisions about the extent of permissible domestic variations from human rights norms, whether these norms are mediated regional standards or strict international standards. Juxtaposing local and regional needs and values with international human rights standards necessarily requires a more intense mediation between local and international human rights standards, which leads to subtly different interpretations of common texts. For example under the jurisprudence of the European Court of Human Rights families are seen as units with one or two parents who may or may not be heterosexual. In Africa however the furor evoked by cases of adoption of children across state borders has made it clear that the African concept of family is different from that of the West. The leadership of African families are seen as extending well beyond parents to include second cousins and others, which means that an African child who loses his or her birth parents is not considered orphaned in the same way that a European child would be.

In the future another example may be the practice of female genital cutting in many parts of Africa, an issue that is likely to test the new African Court on Human and Peoples' Rights. The African regional court is better placed than an international body to tread the line between gender equality and cultural autonomy and better equipped to emphasize that each culture has many markers of its own distinctiveness. An African court with women judges drawn from countries where cutting is practiced will carry greater cultural heft than an international body. A decision by the African Court to enforce efforts to end or limit the practice of genital cutting could at the same time make it clear that replacing such harmful practices with new standards does not negate a culture *as a culture*. Fortified with a better knowledge of the practical human rights capacity of individual states within the region, regional courts can make better judgments about rights standards.

Conclusion

Regional human rights courts have unique institutional advantages for resolving human rights conflicts. They can help reduce philosophical disagreements about international rights norms, which may increase compliance by states. Courts within regional institutions are closer than international bodies to the experiences of people in the jurisdiction and are uniquely placed to assess local human rights needs. They are better able to appreciate the practical constraints on governments in responding to those needs. Regional institutions are uniquely situated to formulate morally credible and practically attainable standards of human rights—a negotiation between reality and hope.

Chapter 6

Human Rights for the 21st Century

SINCE THE TERRORIST ATTACKS on the World Trade Center towers in New York in 2001 the international debate about universal human rights has intensified. News about oppressive authoritarian governments, murderous religious fanaticism, and brutal civil wars is reported daily, underscoring the potency of those who put themselves on the other side of international society. Many of the themes of this book—the long shadow of colonialism, the efficacy of international human rights institutions, the claims of national sovereignty and multiculturalism—have become vexing questions amid newly vivid fears about national security and violence motivated by religious fanaticism. One of the most demanding tasks of making sense of human rights is clarifying where the borders lie between criticism, contempt, and violence. What cultural practices should a society allow its people? For those outside a country's borders, how best to approach cultural practices that seemingly fly in the face of international human rights standards?

The response I have given here reaffirms the place of law and courts but modifies their role to account for contemporary realities. Chapter 1 demonstrated that European colonialism has deeply influenced the vision and scope of international human rights laws and institutions. This history provides a warning about adopting a simplistic universalist approach to human rights. Even the best-intentioned liberal rhetoric can slip into paternalism. In my own country of Australia, for example, generations of colonial and post-colonial politicians have crafted polices for the Aboriginal people on the basis of paternalistic assumptions about their community. Official policies justified the stigmatization of the native peoples, and Aborigines were turned into perpetual outsiders by actions designed to give them a new set of values "for their own good." Applying international human rights to the vast set of social, cultural, and economic problems that are the legacy of colonialism is fraught with difficulty. On one hand it is essential to avoid a repetition of past colonial interventions, even those that may be well intended. On the other hand national governments must fashion policies and laws that prevent human rights violations occurring right now.

Chapter 2 highlights the extraordinary achievement of the international system of international human rights treaties, committees, and courts. A complex web of international institutions has been established in just sixty years. Part of this great achievement is also part of its problem, however: the very fact that the system is international means that it struggles with a vast workload. It also struggles to prove its relevance to the everyday lives of those who are geographically and culturally removed from international institutions. Governments may use these problems as an excuse for their reluctance to implement human rights reforms.

Chapter 2 noted that despite these difficulties, the creation of international criminal tribunals has put courts back onto the agenda as institutions of human rights change. The two UN-backed ad hoc tribunals, the International Criminal Tribunal for Rwanda (ICTR) and the International Criminal Tribunal for the Former Yugoslavia (ICTY), should be closing their doors in 2010 because of their sunset provisions.[1] Part of the international controversy about these tribunals has been their cost (each has an annual budget of approximately $90 million), their delays, and the relatively few cases that they have decided.[2] An institutional variation—the hybrid criminal tribunal—provides a novel legal mechanism. One lesson learned from these courts is that criminal law as a subset of international human rights is still in its infancy and requires further development. The other lesson—much more the focus of this book—is that the hybrid criminal courts offer an intriguing institutional adaptation. Hybrid human rights institutions provide a response to the questions about the universal nature of human rights because they interpose a legal process between national courts and international human rights institutions.

In Chapter 3 I contend that in the post-9/11 years the international conversation about protecting human rights has been overdetermined by the rhetoric of domestic security at home and promotion of democracy abroad. International human rights have become linked, for better but mostly for worse, with international humanitarian intervention. A chain of evidence about international interventions leads to the conclusion that neither paternalism nor national self-interest necessarily produces human rights improvements in another country when they are delivered by coercive military intervention.

My point in Chapter 3 is that any intervention must be based overwhelmingly on humanitarian concerns. Intervention should improve human rights. I urge a much broader assessment of a human rights crisis than has been the case in the past, one that focuses more on the responsibility of governments in crisis to expend their available resources on their populations. There must also be a clear-eyed assessment of the post-intervention future that deals not only with current human rights violations but also the roots of civil conflicts. A country's history of social schisms and divisions will inevitably affect the prospects of the external interveners. Such an approach to international humanitarian intervention does not necessarily promote more interventions nor necessarily damn past interventions that can be seen as truly humanitarian. It does however de-emphasize the role of nation-building in international human rights.

A further point in Chapter 3 is that a better assessment of the pros and cons of an intervention strategy is likely to be made if it is done multilaterally and cross-checked among the intervening parties. Any decision to intervene militarily will be sounder if outside states have no economic or political agenda of their own for intervening on foreign soil. Then too, as the plight of The Sudan so tragically demonstrates, intervention may not help. In The Sudan a combined force of about 20,000 European Union and African Union military personnel had little effect because the international political will to act in *effective* ways seemed to be missing.

Taken together, Chapters 2 and 3 point out the limitations on the "hard" end of the international system: neither military intervention nor the formal application of criminal law necessarily improve human rights conditions on the ground. In Chapter 4 I go on to assess the "soft" end of the spectrum: nongovernmental organizations, trade, and treaties. As is the case with the system of international criminal courts, the human rights reforms wrought by the less coercive systems are promising though still patchy and inconsistent. The energy of nongovernmental human rights organizations has been a catalyst for action by national governments. Equally the human rights leverage of trade has put human rights reform on the international economic agenda, and the gradual spread of human rights ideas via "world society" pathways is altering the ways that people think about themselves and their governments.

Chapter 4 explores how these informal catalysts have been applied to the legal systems of states, then demonstrates the importance of adjudication in a world that uses legal definitions as standards for interactions across national borders and between societies. Margin of appreciation is a judicial technique that allows courts to incorporate evidence from nongovernmental human rights organizations, international trade accords, and human rights agreements as evidence of new human rights benchmarks. By allowing courts to review human rights standards in other fields, margin of appreciation makes judges the instruments of human rights rather than of the state.

Chapter 5 argues for a more comprehensive system of regional human rights courts. Regional courts offer an institutional way to straddle the border between legal and moral issues in cultural conflicts. Unlike the international war crimes tribunals, which are bound to some extent to serve political ends determined by states and especially the great powers, regional courts are uniquely positioned within the international system.[3] While no legal system can be completely cabined from political agendas, regional systems are less vulnerable to statist interests than national and international human rights mechanisms. They offer specific institutional features as a model to regions such as ASEAN that have yet to fully leverage their regional human rights potential.

Regional Human Rights Courts in a Globalized World

Putting international human rights into local contexts through regional courts' application of a margin of appreciation is a theory of gradualism. The premise is the knowledge that deep social change is incremental and that the role of law is inevitably small, through crucial. My aim here is to see an increase in the potency of law when it is deployed by making the law credible and relevant to those who use it.

Implicit in the model I have sketched is the assumption that one of the purposes of law is to communicate with those affected by legal processes. This means that if human rights laws, policies, and adjudicated decisions fail to take account of what might for some be a proper rationale for behavior, they fail in a significant way to communicate and thus fail in one of their purposes. Thinking intelligently about the relationship between laws, habits, and practices of different cultures requires deconstruction of crude oppositions and mythologies, whether of non-Western culture and Enlightenment views. The symbolic role of certain behavior or practices within culture requires legal understanding.

If this paradoxical idea is true—that universal law and universal rights are a way of setting the parameters for regional courts to define where at any moment those parameters apply to local circumstances—the implications are twofold. First, there is a plain procedural question about how existing courts function and what weight is properly given to the issues before it. There is a larger issue, however, about what it is to live under more than one jurisdiction. What degree of accommodation should be given by courts to minority communities that have strongly entrenched legal and moral codes and that, while no less "law-abiding" than other communities, relate to something other than international human rights standards alone?

While there may be a strong, even practically unbreakable international consensus about the wrongness of torturing prisoners or raping children, there is a much less clear sense of what is being "violated" in cases that are by some at least viewed as legitimate ways of expressing cultural identity. What is interpreted as cultural, religious, or gendered identity in one country or region may be interpreted as political values elsewhere. For some—especially outside the European or North American setting—cultural beliefs and practices are *the* marker of shared identity, accepted not as a matter of individual choice but as a cultural standard.

The death penalty and corporal punishment are issues that exemplify the fuzzy division between political and cultural values. Societies with a formal separation between politics and religion interpret as simply wrong the death sentence for blasphemy passed in Afghanistan in early 2008 on a journalism student after he questioned Islam's permission for men to have up to four wives when women can have only one husband. In the same way societies that observe equality between men and women interpret as plainly wrong the 2007 sentence of an unmarried woman to 200 lashes for adultery by a court in Saudi Arabia when proof of her crime was that she had been alone in a car with an unrelated man. Countries without the death penalty view as plainly wrong the 2008 decision of the U.S. Supreme Court not to require Texas to rehear a death-row case despite a ruling by the International Court of Justice that the U.S. had violated a prisoner's rights in contravention of its obligations under the Vienna Convention.

Each of these examples involves the use of domestic criminal laws to punish an individual. In the West criminal courts have occasionally permitted a "culture defense," either as mitigation of criminal liability or as factor in reducing the severity of the sentence passed. "Cultural" defendants ordinarily admit fault. They acknowledge having caused harm but seek to excuse their conduct on the ground that their motives are licensed by their culture. If successful such excuses can result in a criminal charge being changed to a lesser offence or reduction of a sentence. Like other arguments in criminal law such as "ignorance," "mistake of fact," or "compulsion," the culture defense, when assessing responsibility for the consequences of a person's conduct, takes into account that person's subjective state of mind.

The culture defense in criminal law is controversial, and courts have been reluctant to apply it. In 2007 an Laotian Hmong immigrant from an insular Minnesota community of 27,000 was charged with killing six white hunters in Wisconsin. The defendant used a "cultural defense" strategy, alleging that the hunters had used racial slurs when they ordered him off their property in an earlier hunting incident. His "culture defense" was unsuccessful and he was sentenced to a long prison term (Wisconsin does not have the death penalty). Other attempts to accommodate culture can be seen in the creation of separate courts in Canada, the U.S., and Australia for criminal sentencing of convicted individuals that belong to indigenous minority groups.

Advocates of the cultural defense in criminal law argue that it promotes commitment to individualized justice and fairness.[4] From a jurisprudential standpoint the philosophical basis for the cultural defense rests on moral relativism, the idea that every person's cultural values are as valid as any other's. Applied without limit the cultural defense conflicts with the international system's principles of universal human rights. Applied with limits it can mesh with regional variations of human rights standards and their implementation. Margin of appreciation follows this logic by envisaging cultural variation evaluated in its context by regional human rights courts through adjudicative principles. The key for a human rights court at the regional level is to create a system of judicial evaluation of cultural differences while working with built-in checks and balances that still incrementally improve compliance with international human rights standards. The logical first step for regional courts is to assess the authenticity and prevalence of a cultural practice. This requires courts to seek out ethnographic expertise to test the authenticity, legitimacy, and prevalence of cultural practices. A regional judge can review evidence about a culture's relevance to the particular facts, asking such questions as what is the individual litigant's place in a particular cultural group? What are that group's deep cultural practices? What are positive and negative consequences—social, economic, religious—

for an individual that participates in these cultural practices? How different are these particular cultural practices from the normative standards within that country, throughout the wider region, and under international human rights treaty standards?

Regional courts also need to hear the arguments of those who dispute the legitimacy and desirability of practices declared customary by inviting conflicting testimony from psychological and cultural experts. Some cultural practices, particularly those affecting women, may be contested even within cultural communities. Courts need to learn whether cultural dictates compel every member of a group and if susceptibility is conditioned by the strength of social identification with a cultural group. Courts also need to know if violations of cultural standards can result in ostracism, corporal punishment, or even death.

Delving into the background for cultural motivations in this way will enlarge the volume of cultural information. An effective argument for cultural exceptionalism ought to weave a comprehensible narrative from facts about a culture. The argument will need to persuade a court that in the particular context of the case before it, the relative benefits of a cultural practice outweigh its relative harms. Cultural identification on this view does not expunge individual agency or government responsibility; rather it puts both into the cultural context in which they are exercised.

My proposal for cultural exceptionalism articulated by regional human rights courts has some important variations in the use of the culture defense in Anglo-American criminal courts. First, it applies in the context of a civil, not a criminal, hearing. In other words a regional court would be hearing arguments from complainants (often represented by nongovernmental organizations) that they be compensated for their government's failure properly to protect or prevent a cultural practice. Second, the remedies offered by regional human rights courts are directed at governments and not individual litigants. Regional courts might recommend financial compensation as well as outline other steps that a national government should take, such as amending particular legislation or introducing a government policy that would affirm a culture but provide alternatives for harmful cultural practices. For example, female genital cutting is an issue that may be taken up by the new African Court on Human and Peoples' Rights. Adapting an approach already utilized by local nongovernmental organizations, the African Court can affirm the underlying culture in which cutting takes place, yet disaggregate a harmful practice by directing a government to establish a program that demonstrates alternative coming-of-age rituals. Alternatives are already in place in Kenya, where the objective of cultural inclusion for girls and young women is met and the rate of female mortality and infection is reduced.

Finally, whereas the culture defendant represents herself or himself in the criminal courts, my proposition for cultural exceptionalism in a regional human rights court also includes group claims to cultural practices and property. Group rights raise questions different from responsibilities of individuals. Individual litigants may invoke subcultural identity in order to limit the responsibilities they may have to assume, group litigants invoke subcultural identity claims to retain or augment a right. Regional human rights courts can carefully undertake the work of parsing ethnographic evidence of group identity, clarifying the features that merit protection and separating cultural habit from cultural necessity.

Adjudicating Culture

A judicially administered standard of cultural exceptionalism would transport judicial inquiry into barely charted territory. Adjudicating cultural conflict in a way that respects both divergent value systems and cultural beliefs but that also respects the objectivism of national legal systems raises challenges. A broader investigation of culture is called for. Even when a cultural claim can be shown to be true, deeper analysis may reveal ways in which cultural norms may be oppressive for powerless members of that group. Anthropologists and ethnographers will serve as expert witnesses and consultants to explain the mechanisms of motivation and reasoning that underpin culturally dictated action.

One objection to having a higher level of legal regard for communal identity is that it leaves legal processes at the mercy of vexatious appeals to cultural difference. An example might be forced marriages where it is crucial to distinguish among cultural, economic, and religious factors. Judges must have a recognized means for deciding the relative seriousness of identity-related claims—a way of distinguishing social habits and economic transactions from deeply rooted matters of culture and faith. Access is needed to recognized authorities acting for a cultural group, with a high degree of community recognition of those in the community who wish to change communal practices, so that vexatious claims can be identified and rejected. A court needs to know when a potential conflict is real and where it is grounded in nuisance.

The second issue—a very serious one—is that a margin of appreciation in some areas such as family issues could have the effect of reinforcing some of the most repressive or retrograde elements in minority communities, with particularly worrying consequences for the rights of women. The right to bodily autonomy is axiomatic in all Western conceptions of liberty. Bodily autonomy is given pride of place in international human rights treaties and covenants by taking precedence over other rights. Paradoxically, however, the very same principle of liberty undergirds the right to hold and express beliefs of cultural identity.

In legal terms this paradox invokes a tangle of issues around legal recognition of group rights, the claims of a community to sustain its own convictions and practices rather than those of merely one individual. This is a highly controversial area and questions are raised about assessment of the compatibility of a community's practices with the rights otherwise recognized for all citizens. Margin of appreciation for cultural practice applied by regional courts must have two firm limits: no jurisdiction can have the power to deny citizens' access to rights granted as "cultural" nor may a court sanction members of a cultural group for claiming those rights.

The Multicultural Challenge: Religion as the Microcosm

Margin of appreciation applied by regional human rights courts does not guarantee an absence of conflict, and it is not a panacea for the concerns of national security that have become prevalent in recent years. Anxieties in the West about the connections between fundamentalist Islam and terrorism have led to monolithic understandings of religion and culture and deemphasized the extent of variation between and within cultural subsets. Aggressive statements of overwhelming claims of universal and nonnegotiable liberties have led to increasingly heated and sometimes violent assertions of the right of other groups. The international human rights debate about Islam has fallen into the classic trap of cultural bias: Islam is perceived in the Western countries as an organized, coherent, and omnipresent danger.[5]

Such perceptions of sharia exemplify the worst features of the international debate on human rights. What most people think they know of sharia is that it is repressive towards women and partial to archaic and brutal physical punishments. This opinion powerfully reinforces the image of a premodern system in which human rights have no role. The effect of this reductionism is to propel both sides of the debate back into the worst form of universalism, one that brooks no connection between systems of thought and belief. It revives the intellectual trope described in Chapter 1 and leads Muslim scholars to note that "In the West, the idea of Shari'a calls up all the darkest images of Islam. . . . It has reached the extent that many Muslim intellectuals do not dare even to refer to the concept for fear of frightening people or arousing suspicion of all their work by the mere mention of the word."[6]

Regional human rights courts applying margin of appreciation can be interlocutors in this debate. A strategy that refuses from the start to accept that anyone could have reasons for thinking differently is a poor basis for disagreement; it is a way of denying the other a hearing and is the antithesis of legal procedural guarantees. Courts have at their disposal a suite of institutional processes and methods of reasoning that can help to delve below overly simplistic portrayals of religion and culture. Legal rules that ensure rights of rebuttal can embrace the debates within those cultures themselves as well as note the consequences of tendentious or misleading presentations upon both insiders and outsiders to a cultural or religious group.[7]

Courts are also able to delineate areas where there is complete disagreement between worlds. One such example is the Islamic prohibition against apostasy and the draconian penalties for transgressors. The approach of the West ought to be that in a society where freedom of religion is secured by law, it is wrong for any group to claim that conversion to another faith is disallowed or to claim the right to inflict punishment on a convert. In other words if applying the law of apostasy means that the only mode of contact between Muslim and non-Muslim people is open enmity, then such law oversteps its reasonable jurisdiction. It is one thing to say that a particular cultural practice may be deeply and dangerously wrong, and another to say or imply that if it is wrong it is because those who practice it are infantile, willfully blind, or perverse. Courts can put credible evidence into public circulation. More nuanced cultural evidence will generally reveal the extent to which differences exist *within* cultures. There is *in principle* no reason to spring to the conclusion that the whole of that world of non-Western jurisprudence and practice is somehow monstrously incompatible with human rights simply because it does not fit immediately with how Western minds understand it.

Notes

Chapter 1

1. General Musharraf alleged that Chaudhry had used rank to secure a police job for his son and had also enjoyed "unwarranted privileges," such as the use of government aircraft.

2. Makau Mutua, "Savages, Victims and Saviors: The Metaphor of Human Rights," *Harv. Int'l L. J.* 42 (2001): 201, 210.

3. The United States was only prevented from completely excluding so-called enemy combatants' access to the Geneva Convention by the U.S. Supreme Court's 2006 decision in *Hamdam*. *Hamdam v. Rumsfeld*. Secretary of Defense et al., Certiorari to the United States Court of Appeals for the District of Columbia Circuit, No. 05-184. Argued March 28, 2006; Decided June 29, 2006.

4. Jack L. Goldsmith and Eric A. Posner, *The Limits of International Law* (New York: Oxford University Press (2005), 13, 21–78. In their short, sharp book these American law professors argue that there are no normative principles of international law that bind states against their will. Neither treaties, nor customary international law or human rights norms have a moral force that binds states if those states never explicitly agreed to be so bound. International law, they argue, is a part of international politics. States enter into treaties and other international legal institutions when doing so serves their interests. Any cooperation among states is a byproduct of that rational act.

5. Pierre Proudhon, *La Guerre et la paix: recherches sur la principe et la constitution du droit des gens* (New York: Garland Publishers, 1972).

6. Jeremy Bentham, "Nonsense upon Stilts" (1843), reprinted in Philip Schofield et al., eds., *The Collected Works of Jeremy Bentham: Rights, Representation, and Reform* (Charlottesville, Va.: InteLex Corporation, 2002), 330.

7. Bentham rejected the dominant British natural rights tradition that went back at least to John Locke and that in Bentham's own lifetime had been embodied in the United States Constitution. Nevertheless, Bentham called it all "nonsense upon stilts."

8. Goldsmith and Posner, *Limits of International Law*.

9. Ibid., 3–17.

10. Wade M. Cole, "Sovereignty Relinquished: Explaining Commitment to the International Human Rights" (Ctr. Democracy, Dev. & Rule of Law, Stanford Inst. for Int'l Studies, Working Paper No. 21, 2004), citing Abram Chayes and Antonia Handler Chayes, "On Compliance," *Int'l Org.* 47 (1993): 175–205; Beth A. Simmons, "International Law and State Behavior: Commitment and Compliance in International Monetary Affairs," *Am. Pol. Sci. Rev.* 94 (2000): 819–35.

11. Oona Hathaway, "Do Human Rights Treaties Make a Difference?," *Yale L. J.* 111 (2002): 1935. Hathaway suggests that countries should be required to demonstrate compliance with human rights standards before they are permitted to ratify an international treaty, rather than the current system which aims for universal treaty membership.

12. Harold Hongju Koh, "The Globalization of Freedom," *Yale J. Int'l L.* 26 (2001): 305.

13. Anne-Marie Slaughter, *A New World Order* (Princeton: Princeton University Press, 2004), 65–103.

14. Ryan Goodman and Derek Jinks, "How to Influence States: Socialization and International Human Rights Law," *Duke L. J.* 54 (2005): 621.

15. John W. Meyer, Tricia Martin, and Francisco Ramirez, Working Paper, Department of Sociology, Stanford University (February 2008) (on file with the author).

16. Lewis H. Morgan, *Ancient Society* (1877) (Tucson: University of Arizona Press, 1985), 5, 11, 562.

17. Wade Cole, "The Social Construction of Indigenous People's Rights, 1500–2000." Paper presented at the Annual Meeting of the American Sociological Association (New York, 2007).

18. Antony Anghie and B.S. Chimni, "Agora: Third World Approach to International Law," *Chinese J. Int'l L.* 2 (2003): 77, 80.

19. Jürgen Habermas, "Interpreting the Fall of a Monument," *German L. J.* 4 (2003): 701, 707. Habermas notes that "non-Western cultures must appropriate the universalistic content of human rights from their own resources and in their own interpretation, one that will construct a convincing connection to local experiences and interests."

20. Charles Taylor, "Conditions of an Unforced Consensus on Human Rights," in Joanne R. Bauer and Daniel A. Bell, eds., *The East Asian Challenge for Human Rights* (New York: Cambridge University Press, 1999), 124; Daniel A. Bell, *East Meets West: Human Rights and Democracy in East Asia* (Princeton: Princeton University Press, 2000).

21. Helen Stacy, "Western Triumphalism: The Crisis of Human Rights in the Global Era," *Macquarie U. L. Rev.* 2 (2002): 193; Fareed Zakaria, "Culture Is Destiny: A Conversation with Lee Kuan Yew," *Foreign Aff.* 73 (1994): 109–26. For a more recent discussion see Michael Hirsh, Web Exclusive: "Rethinking Confucius: Lee Kuan Yew Recants," *Newsweek* (Jan. 28, 2001), http://www.singapore-window.org/sw01/010128nw.htm; accessed Oct. 13, 2008.

22. This is an interpretation shared by writers on both the left and the right. For example, Carl Schmitt, a German jurist discredited by his association with the Third Reich, wrote in 1950 that the European legal sensibility had first begun with expansion beyond Europe. Chantal Mouffe, ed., *The Challenge of Carl Schmitt* (New York: Verso, 1999), 65.

23. Thomas Hobbes, *Hobbes's Leviathan* (1651), reprinted in Sir William Molesworth,

ed., *The English Works of Thomas Hobbes of Malmesbury*, Volume XI (Bibliolife, 2008), 29; John Locke, "Two Treatises of Government and A Letter Concerning Toleration" (1689), reprinted in Ian Shapiro, ed. (New Haven: Yale University Press, 2003); Sir Ernest Baker, ed., *The Social Contract: Essays by Locke, Hume and Rousseau* (Oxford: Oxford University Press, 1962); Victor Gourevitch, ed. and trans., *Rousseau: "The Discourses" and Other Early Political Writings* (Cambridge: Cambridge University Press, 1997); Charles de Montesquieu, *The Spirit of the Laws* (1748) (Kitchener, Ont.: Batoche, 2001); Alexander Hamilton, James Madison, and John Jay, *The Federalist Papers* (1788) (Penguin Classics, 2003).

24. Anthony Pagden and Jeremy Lawrence, eds., *Francisco de Vitoria, Political Writings* (New York: Cambridge University Press, 1991).

25. I am indebted to Anghie's summary of fifteenth-century European perceptions of non-Europeans. Antony Anghie, *Imperialism, Sovereignty and the Making of International Law* (New York: Cambridge University Press, 2004).

26. Francisco de Vitoria, *De Indis et de Ivre Belli Relectiones* (1532) (Washington, D.C.: Carnegie Institution, 1917), 127, quoted in Anghie, *Imperialism, Sovereignty*, 20.

27. Anghie, *Imperialism, Sovereignty*, 32.

28. In *De Jure Belli*, Gentili wrote that a sovereign could justly wage war in self-defense or if a universal privilege such as freedom of the seas or free commerce were denied. Alberico Gentili, *De Iure Belli Libri Tres: On Defending the Subjects of Another Against Their Sovereign* (1612), trans. John C. Rolfe (New York: Oceana, 1964). The sovereign in his political role of representing the state was bound by universal morality. Sovereigns should also be guided by moral rules in their dealings with people who were not their subjects.

29. Gentili, *De Iure Belli*, 78.

30. Thomas Hobbes, witness to the violence of the Thirty Years' War in Europe and the Glorious Revolution at home in England, took the view that people are intrinsically driven to defend themselves from the selfishness of others, ensuring that life in the state of nature would be "solitary, poor, nasty, brutish and short." Hobbes, *Leviathan*, xiii.

31. James Brown Scott, ed., *Samuel Pufendorf, De Jure Naturae et Gentium Libri Octo* (1688) (New York: Oceana Publications Inc. & Willdy & Sons Ltd., 1964), 152.

32. James Brown Scott, *Samuel Pufendorf*.

33. Locke, Rousseau, and Diderot all recommended the inclusion of Pufendorf in law curricula, and Montesquieu relied heavily on his writings.

34. Micheline R. Ishay, *The History of Human Rights: From Ancient Times to the Globalization Era* (Berkeley: University of California Press, 2004), 110.

35. Mill, *Pace*: "the only purpose for which power can be rightfully exercised over any member of a civilized community, against his will, is to prevent harm to others. His own good, either physical or moral, is not sufficient warrant . . . over himself, over his own body and mind, the individual is sovereign." John Stuart Mill, *On Liberty* (1859), reprinted in David Broomwich and George Kateb, eds. (New Haven: Yale University Press, 2002). Mill wrote in nineteenth-century Britain at a time when the suffrage rule applied only to men. Male suffrage was guaranteed after the Civil War in the U.S. by the Fifteenth Amendment, although it was not enforced throughout the country until the Civil Rights Act of 1964.

36. *Code Napoleon; or, The French Civil Code. Literally Translated from the Original and Official Edition, Published at Paris, in 1804. By a Barrister of the Inner Temple*, trans. George Spence (London: William Benning, Law Publisher, 1827).

37. Women's rights are a good example. For example, the Code of Hammurabi, created around 1780 B.C. by Babylonian king Hammurabi, granted protection for women, though not equally with men, and slaves had fewer rights than free men and the rich. Hebrew laws dating from the fifth century B.C. abolished slavery for Hebrew slaves but not for foreign slaves. The Bible praises women but does not acknowledge their equality to men, often seeing them as property. Under ancient Hindu law, slaves and servants were given some restricted rights but were subject overall to a rigid division of society into four castes. While Buddha thought that hierarchy should only exist in regards to ranking of character and quality of a person, Buddhist universalistic notions of justice did not fully extend to women. Ancient Buddhists were more tolerant towards homosexuality than they were towards women. Confucius did not advocate slavery and homosexuality was not singled out for admonishment, but he did not believe that individuals were born with similar faculties or that they were equal in intelligence. Confucians believe wives should be servile towards their husbands. Christianity and the New Testament in particular support the subjugation of women and rationalize this by blaming Eve for the original sin. The Quran does not find Eve solely responsible for original sin and is relatively favorable towards women compared to "the later juristic tradition of Islam." Only Plato, in the fourth century B.C., encouraged fair treatment of women, a rarity among his contemporaries, and said they had the capabilities to fulfill the same tasks assigned to men.

38. Anne M. Cohler et al., eds., *Charles de Secondat Montesquieu, The Spirit of Laws* (1748) (New York: Cambridge University Press, 1989).

39. Adam Smith, "The Wealth of Nations" (1776), reprinted in James R. Otteson, ed., *Adam Smith: Selected Philosophical Writings* (Imprint Academic, 2004).

40. Adam Smith, "Theory of Moral Sentiments" (1759), reprinted in Otteson, *Adam Smith*, 121.

41. Margaret Wagner and Paul Finkelman, *The Library of Congress Civil War Desk Reference*, (New York: Simon & Schuster, 2002).

42. Dinesh D'Souza, *The End of Racism* (New York: Free Press, 1995), 105.

43. For example, the British legislation regulating factory labor such as the 1843 Ten Hours Act and the 1842 Mines Act.

44. In 1868 Tasmania became the first colony in the British Empire to introduce compulsory schooling. Britain introduced compulsory education in 1870; France did so in 1882.

45. At the same time Jews were still discriminated against, especially in the Eastern European countries and Russia, which instigated the rise of the Zionist movement. The Zionist movement began largely as a response to anti-Semitism in nineteenth-century Europe, and it sought the reestablishment of a Jewish homeland in Palestine. The UN partitioned Palestine into Jewish and Arab states following the Holocaust in 1947, and the Zionist goal was attained.

46. D'Souza, *End of Racism*, 158–59.

47. Emmerich de Vattel, "The Law of Nations or the Principles of Natural Law" (1758), reprinted in Murray Greensmith Forsyth, H. M. A. Keens-Soper, and Peter Savigear, eds., *The Theory of International Relations: Selected Texts from Gentili to Treitschke* (London: Allen & Unwin, 1970), p. xxx; Immanuel Kant, "Perpetual Peace" (1795), reprinted in Hans Reiss, ed., H. B. Nisbet, trans., *Kant's Political Writings* (New York: Cambridge University Press, 1970), 93.

48. Christian von Wolff, *The Law of Nations Treated According to a Scientific Method* (1749), Joseph H. Drake et al., trans. (Oxford: Clarendon Press, 1934).

49. Emmerich de Vattel, *The Law of Nations* (1758), trans. Charles G. Fenwick (Washington: Carnegie Institution, 1916).

50. Kant, *Perpetual Peace*; Immanuel Kant, *The Metaphysical Elements of Justice* (1797), John Ladd, trans. (Indianapolis: Bobbs-Merrill, 1965).

51. Kant, *Perpetual Peace*, 93.

52. The term derives from the Greek word *kosmos*, meaning "world," plus the word *polis*, meaning "city," "people," or "citizenry." It was widely used by ancient philosophers, notably the Stoics and Cynics, to describe a universal love of humankind as a whole, regardless of nation.

53. The literature on cosmopolitanism is now so vast that it is impossible to give a simple agreed-upon definition. The sense in which it is used here refers to Kant's original conception of an individual having simultaneous existence as a person, as a national citizen, and as member of a global society.

54. Reiss, ed., *Kant's Political Writings*, 5.

55. Kant's nation-state consisted of elected officials as representatives of the people, acting pursuant to a constitution that limits the government's power over citizens. He wanted to provide a philosophical justification for representative constitutional government that would guarantee respect for the political rights of all individuals within it. Kant combined freedom with reason by seeing freedom as the harmonization of individual will with universal reason—the reason for acting only if one's own action could be applied universally. To live in a society governed by laws was the true meaning of freedom, because the law would ensure equal political freedom for all.

56. Reiss, ed., *Kant's Political Writings*, 103.

57. Ibid., 46.

58. Ibid., 20.

59. For this description of the first professional organization of lawyers I am indebted to the carefully crafted history of Marti Koskenniemi, *The Gentle Civilizer of Nations: The Rise and Fall of International Law 1870–1960* (New York: Cambridge University Press, 2004).

60. Ibid., 41–51.

61. "Scramble for Africa" was a term coined by Sir Henry Campbell-Bannerman, a British Liberal politician who served as prime minister from 1905 to 1908. He used the term during his term as financial secretary to the War Office between 1871 and 1882, and he expressed outrage at the way the English were treating the Boers in the first Boer War (1880–81).

62. Koskenniemi, *Gentle Civilizer of Nations*, 93.

63. In Germany this meant defining the "nation" in ethnic terms through speaking German and (perhaps) having a German name. The most influential of the German nationalist philosophers, Georg Hegel (1770–1831), constructed in *Philosophy of Law and State* an elaborate dialectic system that culminated in the glorification of the national monarchic state and denied the validity of international law. In France the new nationalism meant that anyone who accepted loyalty to the French civil state was a "citizen." In England jurist John Austin in 1832 in *Province of Jurisprudence Determined* described law as a command emanating from a superior that could be enforced by a punitive sanction. International law therefore merely had the status of "positive morality"—"positive" because international law was practiced by nation-states as an observable fact, but "merely" morality because it was not backed with a sovereign's exclusive command. For a splendid historical account of this development see John Austin, *Province of Jurisprudence Determined* (1832), David Campbell and Philip Thomas, eds. (Brookfield, Mass.: Dartmouth Pub., 1998), 130.

64. Following the Napoleonic Wars, the British Empire included one quarter of the world's population and one third of the world's land area.

65. Montesquieu, *Spirit of the Laws*.

66. A Latin expression used in international law to mean "no-man's-land."

67. Koskenniemi, *Gentle Civilizer of Nations*, 92.

68. In Australia forced removal of Aboriginal children took place from the very first days of the European occupation and until the 1980s. Commonwealth of Australia, *Report of the National Inquiry into the Separation of Aboriginal and Torres Straight Islander Children from Their Families* (1997), available at http://www.humanrights.gov.au/pdf/social-justice/submissions-un-hr-commitee/6–stolen-generations.pdf. In Canada the residential school system was in place between the late 1800s until the mid-1980s. Indian and Northern Affairs Canada, *Royal Commission on Aboriginal Peoples, Report* (1996), available at http://www.ainc-inac.gc.ca/ch/rcap/sg/cg1_e.pdf.

69. Royal Commission on Aboriginal Deaths in Custody, *Report* (1991), available at http://www.austlii.edu.au/au/special/rsjproject/rsjlibrary/rciadic/. Statistics show that the rate of family violence victimization for indigenous women may be forty times the rate for nonindigenous women and also that despite representing just over 2 percent of the total Australian population, indigenous women accounted for 15 percent of homicide victims in Australia in 2002–3. Jenny Mouzas and Toni Makkai, "International Violence Against Women Survey" (2004), 48. Based on notifications (or reports) to child protection departments around Australia in 2001–2, 254 indigenous children under seventeen years had some form of abuse substantiated—that is, the statutory protection authority believed that abuse or neglect had occurred. Helen Moyle and Susan Kelly, eds., *AIHW: Children's and Family Services* (2003), 215. This rate of substantiation was on average 4.3 times higher (for all types of abuse) in the indigenous population than in the nonindigenous population.

70. Colonization was a tale of "slavery, plunder, war, corruption, land-grabbing, famines, exploitation, indentured labor, impoverishment, massacres, genocide and forced

resettlement . . ." Primyamvada Gopal, "The Story Peddled by Imperial Apologists Is a Poisonous Fairytale," (June 28, 2006), http://www.guardian.co.uk/commentisfree/story/0,,1807649,00.html.

71. Harvard legal historian Mary Anne Glendon credits the UN Declaration of Human Rights with "[c]onfirming the worst fears held in 1948 by the Soviet Union and South Africa [by] providing a rallying point for the freedom movements that spurred the collapse of totalitarian regimes in Eastern Europe and the demise of apartheid." Mary Ann Glendon, *A World Made New: Eleanor Roosevelt and the Universal Declaration of Human Rights* (New York: Random House, 2001), xvi.

72. Sixteenth-century French political and legal theorist Jean Bodin first described a "wise and well ordered . . . Commonweale" that, he said, "ought to be a lawfull or rightful government: for that name of a Commonweale is holy, as also to put a difference betwixt the same, and the great assemblies of robbers and pirats, with whome we ought not to have any part, commercement, societie, or alliance, but utter enmitie." Jean Bodin, *The Six Bookes of a Commonweale* (1576; reprint of 1606 ed.), Kenneth Douglas McRae, ed., Richard Knolles, trans. (Cambridge, Mass.: Harvard University Press, 1962).

73. *The Law of Peoples* does, however, make allowance for "reasonable pluralism" among the diversity of "reasonable peoples" that make up the society, "with their different cultures and traditions of thought, both religious and nonreligious." For Rawls it might be possible, even though such groups may hold fundamentally incompatible views on theology, metaphysics, and human nature, that each would use their own conceptions to arrive at consensus on the norms, even while disagreeing on the underlying beliefs that got them there. John Rawls, *The Law of Peoples* (Cambridge, Mass.: Harvard University Press, 1999), 17.

74. Jack Donnelly, "Human Rights, Democracy, and Development," *Hum. Rts. Q.* 21 (1999): 608–32.

75. Christopher Clapham, "Sovereignty and the Third World State," *Pol. Stud.* (Special Issue) 47 (1999): 522.

76. Helen Stacy, "Equality and Difference: Regional Courts and Women's Human Rights" (Ctr. Democracy, Dev. & Rule of Law, Stanford Inst. for Int'l Studies, Working Paper No. 18, 2004): 39–40.

77. Ibid., 58.

78. Albert Venn Dicey, *An Introduction to the Study of the Law of the Constitution* (London: MacMillan, 1908).

79. See the excellent work of the Centre on Housing Rights and Evictions (COHRE), at www.cohre.org; the European Roma Rights Centre (ERRC), at www.errc.org; and Human Rights Watch, at www.hrw.org/doc/?t=esc.

80. Cited in Nasser Hussain, "Towards a Jurisprudence of Emergency: Colonialism and the Rule of Law," *Law and Critique* 10 (1999).

81. Stephen Humphreys, "Are Social Rights Compatible with the Rule of Law? A Realist Inquiry" (Hauser Global Law School Program, Global Working Paper GLWP 10/06, 2006).

82. Ibid.

83. Amartya Sen, *Development as Freedom* (New York: Anchor Books, 1999).

84. Russel Hardin notes, "The oddity of group 'rights' is that they are characteristically coercive more than they are enabling, whereas classical individual rights are typically enabling by protecting us from coercion." Cultural group rights "seem to entail not the support of living communities, but the museum-like preservation of mummified cultures. . . . Oddly, few if any liberals who advocate static preservation of minority cultures would demand such preservation of mainstream cultures." Russel Hardin, "Group Boundaries, Individual Barriers" in Terry Nardin and David Miller, eds., *Boundaries, Ownership, and Autonomy: Diverse Ethical Perspectives* (Princeton: Princeton University Press, 2000), 288.

85. There can be support for such a claim while also acknowledging that the mutable nature of cultural groups and conflicts within groups means it is often difficult to determine rights. Chandran Kukathas, "Are There Any Cultural Rights?," *Pol. Theory* 20 (1992): 105.

86. When Kukathas refers to the party that is granting rights, it is unclear if he means to indicate the international human rights community, the surrounding dominant society, or liberal, rights-granting society.

Chapter 2

1. Taylor arrived in the U.S. in 1972 to attend college in Boston. He returned to Liberia in 1980, after Samuel Doe mounted the first successful coup d'état in Liberia, but left Liberia again in 1983 when Doe accused Taylor of embezzling almost one million U.S. dollars. Taylor fled back to the United States, where he was detained under a Liberian extradition warrant and locked up for fifteen months at the Plymouth County House of Correction in Massachusetts. Taylor escaped from prison by sawing through the bars on his cell window and spent the next four years receiving military training in Libya. Taylor returned to Liberia on Christmas Eve in 1989 at the head of a guerilla force of 100–500 men called the National Patriotic Front of Liberia (NPFL).

2. "Coalition to Stop the Use of Child Soldiers, Child Soldier Use 2003" (2004) (briefing for the 4th UN Security Council open debate on children and armed conflict).

3. Taylor had met Foday Saybana Sankoh, the leader of the RUF, while in Libya learning guerrilla tactics from Muammar Qaddafi. Sankoh was indicted by the Special Court for Sierra Leone in March 2003 and died of complications from a stroke while awaiting trial. The chief prosecutor for the trial said Sankoh's death granted him "a peaceful end that he denied to so many others."

4. Liberia, *Report to the U.N. Committee to the Convention on the Rights of the Child* (2002).

5. Only days after Taylor's arrest his son (also named Charles Taylor) was arrested in Miami on charges of passport fraud. He was subsequently indicted by the U.S. on charges of conspiracy and of committing torture while chief of a paramilitary unit during his father's regime, marking the first time a twelve-year-old federal anti-torture law had been used. The indictment said that in 2002 a man was abducted from his home and Taylor (Jr.) and others burned him with a hot iron, forced him at gunpoint to hold scalding water, applied electric shocks to his genitals and other body parts, and rubbed

salt in his wounds. In 2008 Taylor was in custody in Miami, awaiting sentencing for falsifying his father's name to get the passport he used to enter the United States. He faced a potential life prison sentence.

6. The government of Sierra Leone and the UN agreed in 1992 to establish the Special Court for Sierra Leone pursuant to Security Council Resolution 1315 (2000). The statute of the court gives it jurisdiction over crimes against humanity, common Article 3 of the Geneva Conventions, serious violations of international humanitarian law, and criminal law of Sierra Leone. See Statute of the Special Court for Sierra Leone (2002).

7. Taylor is charged with, first, individual criminal responsibility for planning, instigating, ordering, aiding and abetting by providing military training and support to the Revolutionary United Front and Armed Forces Revolutionary Council, and participating in the execution of a plan to take control of Sierra Leone during which the crimes were committed. Second, he allegedly was a superior to perpetrators of the crimes and failed to take reasonable measures to prevent or punish the crimes while knowing or having reason to know about them.

8. Six UN member states, including Nigeria, are helping underwrite the costs.

9. The remaining three justices are from Canada, Ireland, and Austria.

10. Criminal trials against individuals from each of the three factions involved in Sierra Leone's long civil war (the CDF, or Civil Defence Forces; the RUF, or Revolutionary United Front; and the AFRC, or Armed Forces Revolutionary Council) were ongoing in 2008 in Freetown before the Special Court for Sierra Leone.

11. A report by the War Crimes Unit of the University of California, Berkeley, in September 2008 criticized some procedural aspects of a 2007 trial: UC Berkeley War Crimes Center.

12. Thomas M. Franck, *Fairness in International Law and Institutions* (New York: Oxford University Press, 1995); Ryan Goodman and Derek Jinks, "How to Influence States: Socialization and International Human Rights Law," *Duke L. J.* 54 (2004): 621, 636 (citing Laurence R. Helfer and Anne-Marie Slaughter, "Toward a Theory of Effective Supranational Adjudication," *Yale L. J.* 107 (1997): 273; and "Measuring the Effects of Human Rights Treaties," *Eur. J. Int'l Law* 13(2003): 171.

13. Glendon, *World Made New*, 40.

14. Inclusion of both in the UN Charter was by dint of Eleanor Roosevelt's lobbying: "Taking care not to further polarize the issue, [Mrs. Roosevelt] observed: 'It seems to me that in much that is before us, the rights of the individual are extremely important. It is not exactly that you set the individual apart from his society, but you recognize that within any society the individual must have rights that are guarded. The [Human Rights] Commission might not have to decide with absolute certainty whether government exists for the good of the individual or the group, but I think we do have to make sure, in writing a bill of rights, that we safeguard the fundamental freedoms of the individual.'" Glendon, *World Made New*, 40.

15. The UN's treaty-based bodies are: Human Rights Committee (HRC); Committee on Economic, Social and Cultural Rights (CESCR); Committee on the Elimination of Racial Discrimination (CERD); Committee on the Elimination of Discrimination

against Women (CEDAW); Committee against Torture (CAT); Subcommittee on Prevention of Torture; Committee on the Rights of the Child (CRC); Committee on Migrant Workers (CMW); and Committee on the Rights of Persons with Disabilities (CRPD).

16. Hersch Lauterpacht, *International Law and Human Rights* (New York: F. A. Praeger, 1950), 417.

17. Daniel N. Posner and Daniel J. Young, "The Institutionalization of Political Power in Africa," http://www.journalofdemocracy.org/articles/gratis/PosnerandYoung-18-3.pdf; accessed Nov. 2, 2007. Other states with new constitutions include Ukraine, Macedonia, Slovakia, Slovenia, Serbia, San Marino, Montenegro, Moldova, Latvia, Georgia, Estonia, Eritrea, Czech Republic, Bosnia and Herzegovina, Armenia, Andorra, South Africa, and Argentina.

18. U.S. Institute of Peace, Truth Commissions Digital Collection, http://www.usip.org/library/truth.html; accessed Nov. 3, 2007.

19. Some of the newer national constitutions, such as that of Argentina in 1994, articulate the "doctrine of direct effect," which confers the status of binding domestic law on international human rights standards. European Union law also operates in this way upon EU member states.

20. See http://www.state.gov/g/drl/rls/hrrpt/2006/78759.htm (accessed Oct. 17, 2008), and http://www.state.gov/g/drl/rls/hrrpt/2006/78885.htm (accessed Oct. 17, 2008).

21. *The Prosecutor v. Julio Hector Simon*, Supreme Court of Argentina, Case No. 17.768, judgment of June 14, 2005 (Fallos 2005–328), citing I/A Court H.R., Case of Barrios Altos v. Peru. Merits. Judgment March 14, 2001. Series C No. 75.

22. In the case of *Roper v. Simmons*, 543 U.S. 551 (2005), in which the U.S. Supreme Court struck down the death penalty for juvenile offenders, Justice Anthony Kennedy stated, "Our determination that the death penalty is disproportionate punishment for offenders under 18 finds confirmation in the stark reality that the United States is the only country in the world that continues to give official sanction to the juvenile death penalty. This reality does not become controlling, for the task of interpreting the Eighth Amendment remains our responsibility. Yet . . . the Court has referred to the laws of other countries and to international authorities as instructive for its interpretation of the Eighth Amendment's prohibition of 'cruel and unusual punishments.'" In the same case Justice Antonin Scalia's dissenting opinion stated, "the basic premise of the Court's argument—that American law should conform to the laws of the rest of the world—ought to be rejected out of hand. In fact the Court itself does not believe it." Similarly in *Atkins v. Virginia*, 536 U.S. 304 (2002), in which the application of the death penalty to mentally retarded offenders was challenged, Chief Justice William Rehnquist dissented, stating, "While it is true that some of our prior opinions have looked to 'the climate of international opinion' to reinforce a conclusion regarding evolving standards of decency, we have since explicitly rejected the idea that the sentencing practices of other countries could 'serve to establish the first Eighth Amendment prerequisite, that [a] practice is accepted among our people.'" (internal citations omitted). Justice Kennedy also cited a decision of the European Court of Human Rights in *Lawrence v. Texas* striking down Texas' sodomy law. *Lawrence v. Texas*, 539 U.S. 558 (2003).

23. Transparency International, *Global Corruption Report: Corruption in Judicial Systems* (New York: Cambridge University Press, 2007).

24. A report by Human Rights Watch International, a New York–based human rights nongovernmental organization, criticized eleven out of twenty of these commissions as either flawed or ineffective. For example, the Benin Commission has been criticized as "lethargic," having "a credibility problem," "unknown to the population," and "in paralysis." Human Rights Watch, "Protectors or Pretenders? Government Human Rights Commissions in Africa, Benin" (2001), available at http://www.hrw.org/reports/2001/africa/benin/benin5.html.

25. India's Declaration ii reads, "With regard to article 16 (2) of the Convention on the Elimination of All Forms of Discrimination Against Women, the Government of the Republic of India declares that though in principle it fully supports the principle of compulsory registration of marriages, it is not practical in a vast country like India with its variety of customs, religions and level of literacy." See the UN Web site at http://www.un.org/womenwatch/daw/C.E.D.A.W./reservations-country.htm; accessed Sept. 27, 2007.

26. Mexico's declaration reads, "In signing *ad referendum* the Convention on the Elimination of All Forms of Discrimination Against Women, which the General Assembly opened for signature by States on 18 December 1979, the Government of the United Mexican States wishes to place on record that it is doing so on the understanding that the provisions of the said Convention, which agree in all essentials with the provisions of Mexican legislation, will be applied in Mexico in accordance with the modalities and procedures prescribed by Mexican legislation and that the granting of material benefits in pursuance of the Convention will be as generous as the resources available to the Mexican State permit." See the UN Web site at http://www.un.org/womenwatch/daw/C.E.D.A.W./reservations-country.htm; accessed Sept. 27, 2007.

27. Micheline R. Ishay, *The History of Human Rights: From Ancient Times to the Globalization Era* (Berkeley: University of California Press, 2004), 295.

28. "Before 1989 most of the foreign prostitutes working in Western Europe were recruited from Asia, South America and Africa. Virtually none were from East Bloc countries. By 1994 however the former Soviet Union and its satellites had become the major suppliers of prostitutes for Germany, Belgium, the Netherlands and Switzerland, among others. It is now believed that half of Germany's 200,000 prostitutes are from Eastern Europe. In the Netherlands, authorities say that nearly seventy percent of the foreign prostitutes come from Eastern Europe, mainly Russia, Ukraine, Poland and Hungary." Tom Hundley, "Eastern European Women Exploited in Sex Business," *Chicago Tribune* (May 7, 1996): 1.

29. Human Rights Watch states that "[s]ince 2001, the participation of child soldiers has been reported in 21 on-going or recent armed conflicts in almost every region of the world." It also reports that, "[d]enied a childhood and often subjected to horrific violence, an estimated 200,000 to 300,000 children are serving as soldiers for both rebel groups and government forces in current armed conflicts." See the Human Rights Watch Web site at http://www.hrw.org/campaigns/crp/fact_sheet.html, and at http://www.hrw.org/campaigns/crp/index.htm; accessed Sept. 27, 2007.

30. Committee on the Elimination of Discrimination against Women, *CEDAW Report of the Secretariat, Twenty Ninth Session*, 17–18, U.N. Doc. CEDAW/C/2003/II/4 (May 14, 2003), available at http://www.bayefsky.com/reform/C.E.D.A.W._c_2003_ii_4.pdf.

31. Convention on the Elimination of All Forms of Discrimination against Women, G.A. Res. 51/68, §6, U.N. GAOR, 51st Sess., Supp No. 49, U.N. Doc. A/Res/51/68 (Dec. 12, 1996) (extending two annual CEDAW sessions of three weeks each).

32. Aida Gonzales Martinez, "The U.N. and Protection of Human Rights: Human Rights of Women," *Wash. U. J. L. & Pol'y* 5 (2001): 157, 173.

33. Julie A. Minor, "An Analysis of Structural Weaknesses in the Convention on the Elimination of All Forms of Discrimination Against Women," *Ga. J. Int'l & Comp. L.* 24 (1994): 137, 148.

34. "Naming and shaming" as a tactic to produce changes in governance policies, however, succeeded in the global campaign to ban landmines that resulted in the Ottawa Process and the 1997 U.S. Convention on the Abolition of the Use, Stockpiling, Production and Transfer of Anti-Personnel Mines and their Destruction.

35. The way China and Russia use the war on terror to legitimize repression in their countries is routinely singled out by the State Department because "the existence of human rights helps secure the peace, deter aggression, promote the rule of law, combat crime and corruption, strengthen democracies, and prevent humanitarian crises. Because the promotion of human rights is an important national interest, the United States seeks to . . . hold governments accountable to their obligations under universal human rights norms and international human rights instruments." U.S. Department of State, *Human Rights*, http://www.state.gov/g/drl/hr/; accessed Oct. 31, 2007.

36. For the UN report see Anna Kajumulo Tibaijuka, *U.N., Report of the Fact-Finding Mission to Zimbabwe to Assess the Scope and Impact of Operation Murambatsvina* (2005), available at http://news.bbc.co.uk/1/shared/bsp/hi/pdfs/zimbabwe_22_07_05.pdf. For the U.S. call to end Zimbabwe's slum-clearance campaign see Press Statement, Sean McCormack, U.S. State Department Spokesman, "Government of Zimbabwe Destroying Informal Markets and Housing" (June 16, 2005), available at http://www.state.gov/r/pa/prs/ps/2005/48199.htm. For the U.S. State Department's Human Rights Report on Zimbabwe, see *U.S. Department of State, Zimbabwe—Country Reports on Human Rights Practices—2006*, available at http://www.state.gov/g/drl/rls/hrrpt/2006/78765.htm.

37. Blessing Zulu and Ndimayake Mwakalyelye, "U.S. State Department Human Rights Report Raises Hackles in Harare," *Voice of America* (Apr. 17, 2007), http://www.voanews.com/english/archive/2007–04/2007–04–17–voa69.cfm?CFID=197662024&CFTOKEN=30104985.

38. The world keeps watching, however. Following a five-day mission to Zimbabwe, the Geneva-based International Commission of Jurists (an international body of sixty lawyers, including senior judges, attorneys, and academics) produced a report in June 2007 critical of the Zimbabwe government for "interfering with the proper functioning of the administration of justice, the role of lawyers and their independence." Muchena Zigomo, "Judges 'Shocked' by Zim Rights Abuses," *Mail & Guardian* (June 11,

2007), http://www.mg.co.za/articlePage.aspx?articleid=310967&area=/breaking_news/breaking_news__africa/.

39. Michael Wines, "Zimbabwe: Mugabe to Pursue Nationalization," *New York Times* (July 25, 2007): 7.

40. *Filártiga v. Peña-Irala*, 630 F.2d 876, 884 (2d Cir. 1980).

41. Regina v. Bartle and the Commissioner of Police for the Metropolis and Others, Ex Parte Pinochet; Regina v. Evans and Another and the Commissioner of Police for the Metropolis and Others, Ex Parte Pinochet [1999] UKHL 17.

42. Given that honor killings often remain a private family affair, no official statistics are available on the practice or its frequency. According to a November 1997 report by the Woman's Empowerment Project, published in the official Palestinian daily, *Al-Hayat Al-Jadida*, there were twenty honor killings in Gaza and the West Bank in 1996. One representative of the group added, "We know there are more but no one publicizes it." Similarly an unofficial report given to the Palestinian Women's Working Society stated that "recently" forty women had been killed for honor in Gaza. The report defined neither the period in which these murders took place nor their exact circumstances. During the summer of 1997, Khaled Al-Qudra, then attorney general in the Palestinian National Authority, told *Sout Al-Nissa'* (Women's Voices), a supplement published by the Women's Affairs Technical Committee, that he suspects that seventy percent of all murders in Gaza and the West Bank are honor killings.

43. The honor killing emerged in the pre-Islamic era, according to Sharif Kanaana, professor of anthropology at Birzeit University in Palestine. It is, he believes, "a complicated issue that cuts deep into the history of Arab society." He argues that the honor killing stemmed from the patriarchal and patrilineal society's interest in maintaining strict control over designated familial power structures. "What the men of the family, clan, or tribe seek control of in a patrilineal society is reproductive power. Women for the tribe were considered a factory for making men. The honor killing is not a means to control sexual power or behavior. What's behind it is the issue of fertility, or reproductive power. Punishment for relationships out of wedlock is stipulated as 100 lashes if the woman is single, or if married, death by stoning. In both cases, however, there must be four witnesses willing to testify that the sexual act took place; conditions which make punishment of the perpetrator of the rape difficult, if not impossible." See Suzanne Ruggi, "Commodifying Honor in Female Sexuality: Honor Killings in Palestine," *Middle East Report*, No. 206 (spring 1998): 12–15, available at http://www.merip.org/mer/mer206/ruggi.htm.

44. Annan established the High-Level Panel on Threats, Challenges and Change in November 2003 in order to examine new dangers to international security and recommend ways of strengthening institutions of collective security. For more on the High-Level Panel on Threats, Challenges and Change, see http://www.un-globalsecurity.org/panel.asp; accessed Sept. 27, 2007.

45. Edward Said, *Culture and Imperialism* (New York: Knopf, 1993); Gayatri Spivak, *The Postcolonial Critic: Interviews, Strategies, Dialogues*, Sarah Harasym, ed. (New York: Routledge, 1990).

46. See, for example, *People v. Chen*, No. 87–7774 (N.Y. Sup. Ct. Mar. 21, 1989), in which a Chinese immigrant to the U.S. was charged with second-degree murder for bludgeoning his wife to death with a claw hammer after she told him that she had an affair. He subsequently argued that cultural pressures had provoked him and that in his culture husbands were permitted to take out their shame on their wives. Because of this defense the original charge of second-degree murder was reduced to second-degree manslaughter, resulting in a sentence of five years probation.

47. Alison Dundes Renteln, *The Cultural Defense* (New York: Oxford University Press, 2004).

48. See the list of human rights treaties appearing in United Nations, *Multilateral Treaty Framework: An Invitation to Universal Participation—Focus 2005: Responding to Global Challenges* (2005), 136–37.

49. Adopted in New York on March 7, 1966, the convention came into force in 1969 after twenty-seven states had ratified or acceded to it. At the end of 1990 the convention had been ratified or acceded to by 128 states—more than three-quarters of the membership of the United Nations. It is the oldest and most widely ratified United Nations human rights convention.

50. Adopted in New York on Dec. 16, 1966.

51. Adopted in New York on Dec. 16, 1966.

52. The former Commission on Human Rights had adopted distinctive human rights strategies, but none of them made the commission an effective actor in producing human rights reforms within domestic human rights systems. Initially it followed a policy of strictly observing national sovereignty by not investigating or condemning violators, only promoting human rights and helping states elaborate treaties. Then, as countries in Africa and Asia began to build their postcolonial legal and human rights frameworks, they pressed for a more active UN policy on human rights issues, especially in light of massive violations in South Africa under apartheid. Their influence led the commission to create panels of experts to investigate domestic human rights and produce reports on violations. Later, geographic workgroups were created that concentrated on violations in a given region or even a single country, as, for example, Chile under Pinochet. Later still, theme-oriented workgroups were formed that specialized in specific types of abuses.

53. The number of UN committees overseeing human rights mushroomed in the 1980s, partly in response to criticism of the International Court of Justice as difficult to access, erratic, and increasingly tending to focus on specific subgroups of particularly vulnerable groups.

54. Between 1970 and March 1991, CERD received 882 reports, including 73 that it had requested in order to obtain additional information.

55. For example, Article 11(1) of the International Convention on the Elimination of All Forms of Racial Discrimination states, "If a State Party considers that another State Party is not giving effect to the provisions of this Convention, it may bring the matter to the attention of the Committee. The Committee shall then transmit the communication to the State Party concerned. Within three months, the receiving State shall

submit to the Committee written explanations or statements clarifying the matter and the remedy, if any, that may have been taken by that State." This provision thus allows state-to-state complaints. Another example is Article 21(1) of the Convention against Torture and Other Cruel, Inhuman or Degrading Treatment or Punishment, which states, "A State Party to this Convention may at any time declare under this article that it recognizes the competence of the Committee to receive and consider communications to the effect that a State Party claims that another State Party is not fulfilling its obligations under this Convention."

56. The UNCESCR Committee, for example, has held discussions on the right to food (1989); the right to housing (1990); economic and social indicators (1991); the right to take part in cultural life (1992); the rights of the aging and elderly (1993); the right to health (1993); the role of social safety nets as a means of protecting economic, social, and cultural rights, with particular reference to situations involving major structural adjustment and/or transition to a free market economy (1994); human rights education (1994); the interpretation and practical application of the obligations incumbent on states party to the convention (1995); and a draft optional protocol to the covenant (1995). Committee members are experts who serve for a term of several years. They are elected in their personal capacity by the states party to the convention, taking into consideration geographical, civilization, and legal diversity. The committees work with the UN Secretariat in the preparation of UN General Assembly sessions, represent the committees at international conferences and other intergovernmental meetings of the United Nations, and conduct open dialogue between the committee, nongovernmental organizations, and others.

57. Wade M. Cole, "Sovereignty Relinquished? Explaining Commitment to the International Human Rights 1966–1999," *Am. Soc. Rev.* 70 (2004): 472–73; Oona A. Hathaway, "Do Human Rights Treaties Make a Difference," *Yale L. J.* 111 (2002): 1870; Oona A. Hathaway, "Why Do Countries Commit to Human Rights Treaties?," *Journal of Conflict Resolution* 51, 4 (2007): 588–621.

58. Tanja Borzel and Thomas Risse, *When Europe Hits Home: Europeanization and Domestic Change* (European Integration Online Papers, No. 15, 2000), available at http://ieop.or.at/ieop/texte/2000-015.htm; Goodman and Jinks, "How to Influence States."

59. Cole, "Sovereignty Relinquished?," 472–73.

60. Ibid., 13.

61. Miariam Abu Sharkh, History and Results of Labor Standard Initiatives. An Event History and Panel. Analysis of the Ratification Patterns, and Effects, of the International Labour Organization's First Child Labour Convention. Freie Universität Berlin, 2002.

62. Hathaway, "Do Human Rights Treaties Make a Difference?"

63. Comm. on the Elimination of Racial Discrimination, *Consideration of Reports Submitted by States Parties under Article 9 of the Convention* (2007), available at http://www.unhchr.ch/tbs/doc.nsf/0ac7e03e4fe8f2bdc125698a0053bf66/829ed701fb71ac04c1 2572ed00464d21/$FILE/G0741703.pdf.

64. For a statement on this matter see Amnesty International, *Egypt: Time to Implement the U.N. Committee against Torture's Recommendations* (2003), available at http://web.amnesty.org/library/index/engmde120382003.

65. Goodman and Jinks, "How to Influence States," 173 (citing Andrew Moravcsik, "The Origins of International Human Rights Regimes: Democratic Delegation in Post-war Europe," *Int'l Org.* 54 [2000]: 217).

66. Goodman and Jinks, "How to Influence States," 640 (citing Robert Axelrod, "Promoting Norms: An Evolutionary Approach to Norms," in Robert Axelrod, ed., *The Complexity of Cooperation* [Princeton: Princeton University Press, 1997, 44]).

67. Goodman and Jinks, "How to Influence States," 30–31 (citing Martha Finnemore, "Institutional Organizations as Teachers of Norms: The United Nations Educational, Scientific, and Cultural Organization and Science Policy," *Int'l Org.* 47 [1993]: 565).

68. Convention on the Prevention and Punishment of the Crime of Genocide (signed on Dec. 2, 1948, entered into force on Jan. 12, 1951) and Convention against Torture and Other Cruel, Inhuman or Degrading Treatment or Punishment (signed on Dec. 10, 1984, entered into force on June 26, 1987).

69. Based on data from the UN Department of Peacekeeping Operations, http:// www.un.org/Depts/dpko/dpko/index.asp; accessed Oct. 31, 2007, and reproduced in the 2005 UN Human Security Report, *U.N. Peacekeeping Force, U.N. Human Security Report* (2005), available at http://www.un.org/Depts/dpko/dpko/pub/year_review05/ printable_version.htm.

70. UN Charter, arts. 7 & 92; Statute of the International Court of Justice, art. 1, June 26, 1945, 59 Stat. 1055. Article 93(1) of the UN Charter declares that all the members of the United Nations are ipso facto parties to the Statute of the International Court of Justice. States that are not members of the UN however can access the court by virtue of article 35 of the court's statute. Nauru and Switzerland, which are not members of the United Nations, filed with the court's registrars declarations of acceptance of the court's jurisdiction on July 28, 1948, and Sept. 9, 1992, respectively. 1995–1996 International Court of Justice Year Book, 68.

71. Statute of the I.C.J., art. 38(1).

72. The ICJ also gives advisory opinions on legal questions submitted by international organs and agencies. Its judgment is final, and should one of the states involved fail to comply with it the other party may have recourse to the United Nations Security Council. Of its fifteen judges, each elected to a nine-year term by the UN General Assembly and the Security Council, the court's composition has in practice always included the five permanent members of the Security Council—China, France, Russia, the United Kingdom, and the United States. Judges sit as independent magistrates and not as representatives of their governments, and there may be no more than one judge of any nationality. International organizations such as the UN General Assembly, or one of the specialized UN agencies such as the World Health Organization, can request advisory opinions of the court. In principle the court's advisory opinions are consultative in character and are therefore not binding as such on the requesting bodies. Certain instruments or regulations can, however, stipulate in advance that the advisory opinion shall be binding. The bodies at present authorized to request advisory opinions of the court are four organs of the United Nations (General Assembly, Security Council, ECOSOC, and Trusteeship Council) and 16 specialized agencies of the United Nations

family (ILO, FAO, UNESCO, WHO, IBRD, IFC, IDA, IMF, ICAO, ITU, IFADI, WMO, IMO, WIPO, UNIDO, IAEA). The court can only hear a case if the states concerned in a cross-border dispute have accepted its jurisdiction. States can also opt in and out of ICJ jurisdiction through the reciprocal effect of "optional declarations," whereby a disputing state accepts the jurisdiction of the court as compulsory in the event of a dispute with another state that has made a similar declaration. In fact only sixty-six countries have entered such declarations, and some of these further narrow the court's reach by excluding certain categories of dispute. "The decision of the Court has no binding force except between the parties and in respect of that particular case." Statute of the I.C.J., art. 59. "The judgment shall be read at a public sitting of the Court and shall become binding on the parties on the day of the reading." Rules of the Court, 1979, I.C.J. Acts & Docs., art. 94.2, available at http://www.icj-cij.org/documents/index.php?p1=4&p2=3&p3=0. "If a party fails to perform the obligations incumbent upon it under a judgment rendered by the Court, the other party may have recourse to the Security Council, which may, if it deems necessary, make recommendations or decide upon measures to be taken to give effect to the judgment." UN Charter, art. 94.

73. Press Release, A. J. G. Downer, Minister for Foreign Affairs of Australia, *Declarations Recognizing as Compulsory the Jurisdiction of the Court* (Mar. 22, 2002).

74. "[T]he International Court of Justice is still towering in the international judicial arena. The ICJ is one of the six principal organs of the United Nations. It is the principal judicial organ of the cardinal international organization the only one with universal scope and membership. This grants the ICJ a crucial edge over all other international judicial bodies and explains why, in different epochs, scholars have envisioned for it the role of international constitutional court, or ultimate appellate jurisdiction." *Project on International Courts & Tribunals, International Court of Justice*, http://www.pict-pcti .org/courts/ICJ.html; accessed Nov. 2, 2007.

75. For example, in *Qatar v. Bahrain* the court held that Qatar has sovereignty over Zubarah and Janan Island and that the low-tide elevation of Fasht ad Dibal falls under the sovereignty of Qatar. It found that Bahrain has sovereignty over the Hawar Islands and the island of Qit'at Jaradah, and it drew a single maritime boundary between the two states. *Qatar v. Bahrain*, 2001 I.C.J. 40 (Mar. 16). Similarly in *Nigeria v. Cameroon* the court held that the Bakassi Peninsula and its oil reserves should be handed over to Cameroon. *Nigeria v. Cameroon*, 1999 I.C.J. 101 (Mar. 25).

76. For example, in *Nicaragua v. U.S.* the court ruled that the U.S. was not responsible for most of its actions in Nicaragua in the 1970s and 1980s because Washington did not have "effective control of the military or paramilitary operations in the course of which the alleged violations were committed." *Nicaragua v. United States*, 1986 I.C.J. 14 (June 22); "Genocide by Proxy: The World Court Weighs In, Worldview Commentary No. 256" (Chicago Public Radio broadcast, Feb. 28, 2007).

77. *Avena and other Mexican Nationals (Mex. v. U.S.)*, 43 I.L.M. 581 (2004).

78. *Democratic Republic of Congo v. Belgium* (2002); Pieter H. F. Bekker, "World Court Orders Belgium to Cancel an Arrest Warrant Issued Against the Congolese Foreign Minister," *ASIL Insights* (February 2002), http://www.asil.org/insights/insigh82.htm.

79. Michael J. Matheson, Council Comment: "The ICJ's Decision in *Bosnia and Herzegovina v. Serbia and Montenegro*," *Am. Soc. Int'l L. Newsl.* (Am. Soc. Int'l L., Washington, D.C., spring 2007): 9, available at http://www.asil.org/newsletter/councilcomment/. See also Application of the Convention on the Prevention and Punishment of the Crime of Genocide (Bosnia-Herzegovina v. Serbia and Montenegro), case 91, International Court of Justice (ICJ), Feb. 26, 2007.

80. The court held that the state responsibility created by the convention is not of a criminal nature and rejected the idea that ethnic cleansing may constitute genocide. Gregory H. Fox, "Council Comment: The ICJ's Decision in *Bosnia and Herzegovina v. Serbia and Montenegro*," *Am. Soc. Int'l L. Newsl.* (Am. Soc. Int'l L., Washington, D.C., spring 2007): 8, available at http://www.asil.org/newsletter/councilcomment/.

81. The court ordered Serbia and Montenegro to transfer to the ICTY individuals indicted for genocide and to cooperate fully with the tribunal. *Bosnia and Herzegovina v. Serbia and Montenegro*, Feb. 26, 2007, http://www.icj-cij.org/docket/files/91/13685.pd f?PHPSESSID=d3dcf6dba7552c69c6ce7f1e1fa718e0; accessed Oct. 18, 2008.

82. Many scholars have criticized the ICJ and call for it to be reformed. One target has been the fact that only states can be parties in cases of the court. This requirement rules out individuals and non-state institutions from using the court and prevents the ICJ from offering a comprehensive international dispute resolution forum. Ernst-Ulrich Petersmann, "Constitutionalism and International Organizations," *NW. J. Int'l L. & Bus.* 17 (1997): 398, 462–63. In addition some see the limited acceptance by state parties of Article 36(2) of the Statute of the ICJ as a sign of their mistrust of the adjudication of the Court. Michla Pomerance, *The United States and the World Court as a "Supreme Court of the Nations": Dreams, Illusions and Disillusion* (The Hague, Netherlands: M. Nijhoff, 1996). The court has also been criticized for its lengthy judgments and inefficient operation. Robert Y. Jennings, "The International Court of Justice after Fifty Years," *Am. J. Int'l L.* 89 (1995), 493, 497–505.

83. For example, requests by a state to intervene under Article 62 with a concern about a dispute before the court have been denied, while a chamber of the court and the full court both allowed a limited intervention in two separate cases. Similarly third-party state requests for intervention under Article 63 (in a dispute about construction of a convention) have been rejected by the court in one instance but allowed in another. Continental Shelf (Tunisia/Libyan Arab Jamahiriya), Application for Permission to Intervene by Malta, 1981 I.C.J. 3 (Judgment of Apr. 14); Continental Shelf (Libyan Arab Jamahiriya/Malta), Application for Permission to Intervene by Italy, 1984 I.C.J. 3 (Judgment of June 3); Nuclear Tests (*Austl. v. Fr.*), Application for Permission to Intervene by Fiji, 1973 I.C.J. 320 (Order of July 12); Nuclear Tests (*N.Z. v. Fr.*) Application for Permission to Intervene by Fiji, 1973 I.C.J. 324 (Order of July 12); Land, Island and Maritime Frontier Dispute (*El Sal. v. Hond.*), Application for Permission to Intervene, 1990 I.C.J. 3 (Order of Feb. 28); Land and Maritime Boundary between Cameroon and Nigeria (*Cameroon v. Nig.*), 1999 I.C.J. 275 (Order of Oct. 21); Military and Paramilitary Activities in and Against Nicaragua (*Nicar. v. U.S.*), (request by El Salvador) Declaration of Intervention, 1984 I.C.J. 215 (Order of

Oct. 4); Haya de le Torre (*Colom. v. Peru*), (request by Cuba), 1951 I.C.J. 71 (Judgment of June 13).

84. International Status of South West Africa, Advisory Opinion, 1950 I.C.J. Pleadings 324 (July 11). In the advisory proceedings on the *International Status of South West Africa* the court clarified that the General Assembly could receive petitions from the inhabitants of South West Africa submitted by the International League for Human Rights. Although the International League for Human Rights was granted standing to file information, ultimately it failed to do so within the time limit.

85. Advisory Proceedings on the Legal Consequences for States of the Continued Presence of South Africa in Namibia (South West Africa) Notwithstanding Security Council Resolution 276 (1970), 1970 I.C.J. Pleadings 639–40, 644, 672, 678–97 (Aug. 5).

86. Legality of the Use by a State on Nuclear Weapons in Armed Conflict, Advisory Opinion, 1996 I.C.J. 226 (July 8). This case held that a threat or use of nuclear weapons should also be compatible with the requirements of the international law applicable in armed conflict, particularly those of the principles and rules of international humanitarian law, as well as with specific obligations under treaties and other undertakings that expressly deal with nuclear weapons. With the president's vote breaking a seven-to-seven tie, the court held that it follows that the threat or use of nuclear weapons would generally be contrary to the rules of international law applicable in armed conflict and in particular the principles and rules of humanitarian law. In view of the current state of international law and of the elements of fact at its disposal, however, the court did not conclude definitively whether the threat or use of nuclear weapons would be lawful or unlawful in an extreme circumstance of self-defense, in which the very survival of a state would be at stake.

87. For a historical analysis of international justice developments, see Ruti G. Teitel, "Transitional Justice Genealogy," *Harv. Hum. Rts. J.* 16 (2003): 69.

88. For more on the ICTR see Virginia Morris and Michael P. Scharf, *The International Criminal Tribunal for Rwanda* (Irvington-on-Hudson, N.Y.: Transnational Publishers, 1998).

89. See data from the ICTY Web site, http://www.un.org/I.C.T.Y./glance-e/index.htm; accessed Oct. 31, 2007.

90. See the ICTR Web site, http://69.94.11.53/default.htm; accessed Oct. 31, 2007.

91. Milošević had served as president of Serbia from 1989 to 1997 and as president of the Federal Republic of Yugoslavia from 1997 to 2000. He was one of the key figures in the Yugoslav wars during the 1990s and also in the 1999 Kosovo war in which several thousand people died and 100,000 Kosovo Albanians were made homeless. He was indicted by the ICTY in May 1999 during the Kosovo war on charges of violating the laws of war and crimes against humanity in Croatia and Bosnia. Genocide charges in relation to Bosnia were added in 2000. Following the disputed Yugoslavian presidential election in October 2000, Milošević conceded defeat and resigned. Yugoslavia finally handed him over to The Hague when the U.S. threatened to withhold economic aid to Yugoslavia.

92. Anne Bodley, "Weakening the Principle of Sovereignty in International Law: The International Criminal Tribunal for the Former Yugoslavia," *N.Y.U. J. Int'l L. &*

Pol. 31 (1999): 417; Claude Jorda, "The International Criminal Tribunal for the Former Yugoslavia: Its Functioning and Future Prospects," *Hofstra L. & Pol'y Symp.* 3 (1999): 167; Gabrielle Kirk McDonald, "Reflections on the Contributions of the International Criminal Tribunal for the Former Yugoslavia," *Hastings Int'l & Comp. L. Rev.* 24 (2001): 155; Susan W. Tiefenbrun, "The Paradox of International Adjudication: Developments in the International Criminal Tribunals for the Former Yugoslavia and Rwanda, the World Court, and the International Criminal Court," *N.C. J. Int'l L. & Com. Reg.* 25 (2000): 551; Patricia Wald, "The International Criminal Tribunal for the Former Yugoslavia Comes of Age: Some Observations on Day-to-Day Dilemmas of an International Court," *Wash. U. J. L. & Pol'y* 5 (2001): 87.

93. More important, the capture of Mladić may be advanced by a video showing killings of Srebrenica captives. The video shocked many Serbs who until now had simply not believed a massacre had taken place in Srebrenica in 1995.

94. Franca Baroni, "The International Criminal Tribunal for the Former Yugoslavia and Its Mission to Restore Peace," *Pace Int'l L. Rev.* 12 (2000): 233; Claude Jorda, "The International Criminal Tribunal for the Former Yugoslavia," 167.

95. Robert F. Van Lierop, "Report on the International Criminal Tribunal for Rwanda," *Hofstra L. & Pol'y Symp.* 3 (1999): 203; Susan W. Tiefenbrun, "The Paradox of International Adjudication," 551.

96. Victor Peskin, "Courting Rwanda: The Promises and Pitfalls of the I.C.T.R. Outreach Programme," *J. Int'l Crim. Just.* 3 (2005): 950–61.

97. For a range of views, see Roger S. Clark & Madeleine Sann, eds., *The Prosecution of International Crimes: A Critical Study of the International Tribunal for the Former Yugoslavia* (New Brunswick, N.J.: Transaction Publishers, 1996). For a similar comment on the ICTR, see Stuart Beresford, "In Pursuit of International Justice: The First Four-Year Term of the International Criminal Tribunal for Rwanda," *Tulsa J. Comp. & Int'l L.* 8 (2000): 99.

98. Makau Mutua, "Never Again: Questioning the Yugoslav and Rwanda Tribunals," *Temp. Int'l & Comp L. J.* 11 (1997): 167.

99. S.C. Res 1503, ¶8, U.N. doc. S/RES/1503 (Aug. 28, 2003) (concerning the completion strategy).

100. See the ICTY Web site at http://www.un.org/I.C.T.Y./glance-e/index.htm; accessed Oct. 31, 2007.

101. See the ICTR Web site at http://69.94.11.53/default.htm; accessed Oct. 31, 2007.

102. The presidency of the court is composed of Judge Philippe Kirsch (Canada) as president, Judge Akua Kuenyehia (Ghana) as first vice president, and Judge Elizabeth Odio Benito (Costa Rica) as second vice president.

103. Although the U.S. is not among the seventy-eight countries participating in the I.C.C., Ocampo has taught at Stanford University and Harvard University.

104. Authoritarian governments such as Somalia's may fear participation in the ICC, but the U.S. has little reason to do so. U.S. constitutional values are in every practical sense enshrined in the ICC's structure, and it is virtually impossible that U.S. nation-

als would be tried before the ICC without U.S. consent. While individual U.S. military personnel may commit isolated war crimes, they are unlikely to come before the ICC, which will try war crimes "only when committed as part of a plan or policy or as part of a large-scale commission of such crimes." Press Release, "U.N. Diplomatic Conference, Meeting of Key Conference Committee Shows Continuing Differences on Important Provisions of International Criminal Court Statute," L/ROM/16, (July 13, 1998), available at www.un.org/I.C.C./pressrel/lrom16.htm. In addition, the I.C.C.'s jurisdiction is limited by the principle of complementarity, which prevents the I.C.C. from accepting jurisdiction unless the suspect's country is unwilling or unable to do so. Douglass Cassel, "With or Without U.S., World Court Will Debut," *Chicago Tribune* (May 12, 2002), 1.

105. Sean Sinclair-Day, "The Invisible Majority" (Internet radio broadcast Nov. 16, 2006; available at www.thatradio.com).

106. An example of such opposition is Henry Kissinger, "The Pitfalls of Universal Jurisdiction," *Foreign Aff.* 80 (2001): 86.

107. The International Court of Justice has refused to rule on whether or not universal jurisdiction claimed by a state is valid under international law. An arrest warrant was issued in 2000 under the Belgian law against the then minister of foreign affairs of the Democratic Republic of the Congo. The warrant was challenged before the ICJ in *The I.C.J. Arrest Warrant Case. Congo v. Belgium*, 2002 I.C.J. 2 (Feb. 14). The ICJ's decision, issued in 2002, found that it did not have jurisdiction to consider the question of universal jurisdiction; the court instead decided the question on the basis of the immunity of high-ranking state officials. The ICJ held by a 13–3 vote that sitting foreign ministers, like heads of state and government, are immune from criminal process in other countries. The court emphasized that foreign ministers need to be able to travel the world to represent their countries, free from the constant fear of arrest. The ruling effectively derailed several pending Belgian cases, such as one against Israeli Prime Minister Ariel Sharon. Several of the judges, however, considered the matter in separate and dissenting opinions, such as the separate opinion of Pres. Gilbert Guillaume, who concluded that universal jurisdiction exists only in relation to piracy, and the dissenting opinion of Judge Shigeru Oda, who recognized piracy, hijacking, terrorism, and genocide as crimes subject to universal jurisdiction.

108. A group of scholars from Princeton University published *The Princeton Principles on Universal Jurisdiction* in 2001 in order to clarify the jurisdiction of courts by adopting a universal approach towards jurisdiction. *Princeton Univ. Program in Law & Pub. Affairs, The Princeton Principles on Universal Jurisdiction* (2001), available at http://www1.umn.edu/humanrts/instree/princeton.html. In their view the crimes giving rise to universal jurisdiction include slavery, war crimes, crimes against peace, crimes against humanity, genocide, and torture. The alleged crime need not have taken place within the relevant state, nor do the victims or perpetrators need to be citizens—rather the jurisdiction stems from the severity of the alleged practice, the necessity to prevent such crimes, and the willingness of a national court to bring the issue to trial. Other principles espoused by the Princeton group include: (1) government officials—including heads of state—should not be immune from prosecution based on the defense that

they were acting in an official capacity; (2) there should be no statute of limitations on the prosecution of these crimes; (3) a state should refuse to extradite an alleged perpetrator when that person is likely to face the death penalty or any cruel, degrading, or inhuman punishment or would face sham proceedings with no assurance of due process; and (4) blanket amnesties generally are inconsistent with a state's obligation to hold individuals accountable for these crimes.

109. Laura Dickinson, "The Relationship Between Hybrid Courts and International Courts: The Case of Kosovo," *New UK L. Rev.* 37 (2003): 1059, 1062 (citing Wendy S. Betts, Scott N. Carlson, and Gregory Gisvold, "The Post-Conflict Transitional Administration of Kosovo and the Lessons Learned in Efforts to Establish a Judiciary and the Rule of Law," *Mich. J. Int'l L.* 22 [2001]: 371, 381).

110. For more on the understaffing of the court, see Organization for Security and Co-operation in Europe, Mission in Kosovo, *Report 9—On the Administration of Justice* (2002), available at http://www.osce.org/documents/mik/2002/03/863_en.pdf.

111. See the ICTJ Web site at http://www.ictj.org/static/Prosecutions/Kosovo.study. pdf; accessed Oct. 17, 2008.

112. For more on the court, see East Timor Judicial System Monitoring Programme, *Digest of the Jurisprudence of the Special Panels for Serious Crimes*, 6–16 (2007), available at http://www.jsmp.minihub.org/Reports/2007/SPSC/SERIOUS%20CRIMES%20 DIGEST%20(Megan)%20250407.pdf.

113. Laura Dickinson, "Note and Comment: The Promise of Hybrid Courts," *Am. J. Int'l L.* 97 (2003): 295, 298 (citing Richard Dicker, Mike Jendrzejczyk and Joanna Weschler, "Human Rights Watch: East Timor: Special Panels for Serious Crimes" [2002], available at http://www.hrw.org/press/2002/08/etimor-ltr0806.htm; and David Cohen, "Seeking Justice on the Cheap: Is the East Timor Tribunal Really a Model for the Future?," *Asia Pacific Issues* [Analysis from the East-West Center No. 61, 2002], available at http://www.ewc.hawaii.edu/stored/pdfs/api061.pdf).

114. Barry E. Carter, Phillip R. Trimble, and Allen S. Weiner, *International Law*, 5th ed. (New York: Aspen Publishers, 2007), 1194.

115. Each was found guilty on eleven of the fourteen counts: Count 1: acts of terrorism; Count 2: collective punishment; Count 3: extermination; Count 4: murder, a crime against humanity; Count 5: murder, a war crime; Count 6: rape; Count 9: outrages against personal dignity; Count 10: physical violence, a war crime; Count 12: conscripting or enlisting children under the age of fifteen years into armed forces or groups, or using them to participate actively in hostilities; Count 13: enslavement; and Count 14: pillage.

116. "Human Rights Watch, Justice in Motion: The Trial Phase of the Special Court for Sierra Leone" (2005).

117. Ibid.

118. Carter, Trimble, and Weiner, *International Law*, 1192–93 (citing Patricia M. Wald, "Iraq, Cambodia, and International Justice," *Am. U. Int'l L. Rev.* 21 [2006]: 541, 552).

119. Dickinson examines the problem of norm penetration, noting that purely

international and/or purely local mechanisms may have little impact on substantive norms. This is because penetrating norms depends on networks among professionals, as well as links from those networks to the broader population. Interaction through the hybrid mechanism can lead to the creation of such networks and the subsequent cross-fertilization of norms. Dickinson, "Promise of Hybrid Courts," 304 (citing Anne-Marie Slaughter, "Judicial Globalization," *Va. J. Int'l L.* 40 [2000]: 1103).

120. Dickinson, "Hybrid Courts and International Courts," 1067.

121. Sara Kendall and Michelle Staggs, *Interim Report on the Special Court for Sierra Leone. From Mandate to Legacy: The Special Court for Sierra Leone as a Model for "Hybrid Justice"* (The War Crimes Studies Center at the University of California, Berkeley, Apr. 2005).

122. In Aug. 2007 two defendants, Allieu Kondewa and Moinina Fofana, were convicted of murder, cruel treatment, pillage, and collective punishments, and Kondewa was also found guilty of use of child soldiers. Their trial was perhaps the most controversial of those before the court because the many Sierra Leoneans who were members of the CDF believed their party was protecting them from the supporters of the RUF, Charles Taylor's party. In October 2007 the court sentenced Kondewa to eight years imprisonment, and Fofana to six years, even though prosecutors had asked for thirty years for both. The court's lesser sentences were based on mitigating factors of the defendants' having: "contributed immensely to re-establishing the rule of law in this Country where criminality, anarchy and lawlessness . . . had become the order of the day."

123. Kendall and Staggs, *Interim Report*, 1066.

124. Christina M. Carroll, "An Assessment of the Role and Effectiveness of the International Criminal Tribunal for Rwanda and the Rwandan National Justice System in Dealing with the Mass Atrocities of 1994," *B.U. Int'l L. J.* 18 (2000): 163; Ivana Nizich, "International Tribunals and Their Ability to Provide Adequate Justice: Lessons from the Yugoslav Tribunal," *ILSA J. Int'l & Comp. L.* 7 (2001): 353.

Chapter 3

1. Jeremy Weinstein, *Inside Rebellion: The Politics of Insurgent Violence* (New York: Cambridge University Press, 2007), 4.

2. Ibid.

3. *Internal Displacement: A Global Overview of Trends and Developments in 2005* (Internal Displacement Monitoring Centre, Geneva, March 2006), available at http://www.internal-displacement.org/idmc/website/resources.nsf/(httpPublications)/07E155A5F6DA0DA6C1257138004691BD?OpenDocument; accessed Oct. 17, 2008.

4. James Mayall, "Sovereignty, Nationalism, and Self-Determination," *Pol. Stud.* 47 (1999): 474.

5. In Europe, for example, states increasingly combine their functions among governments. National laws and regulations are negotiated by thousands of officials through hundreds of multilateral committees. Decisions of the European courts interfere in each country's domestic affairs, and as a single political unit the European Union

has substantial external powers vis-à-vis the rest of the world to guarantee mutual security. When the states of the former Soviet Union apply for admission to the EU, they need to show evidence of their "good" sovereignty by accepting the European Human Rights Convention and its associated legal frameworks.

6. Hans Reiss, ed., H. B. Nisbet, trans., *Kant's Political Writings* (Cambridge: Cambridge University Press, 1970), 29; Immanuel Kant, "Critique of Judgment," in Pauline Kleingeld, ed., David L. Colclasure, trans., *Toward Perpetual Peace and Other Political Writings on Politics, Peace, and History* (New Haven: Yale University Press, 2006), 37.

7. Reiss, *Kant's Political Writings*, 29.

8. Ibid., 104.

9. Ibid., 31.

10. Ibid., 14.

11. U.N. Charter, art. 2(1).

12. U.N. Charter, art. 2(3).

13. Geneva Convention for the Amelioration of the Condition of the Wounded and Sick in Armed Forces in the Field, Aug. 12, 1949, 6 U.S.T. 3114, 75 U.N.T.S. 31; Geneva Convention for the Amelioration of the Condition of the Wounded, Sick and Shipwrecked Members of Armed Forces at Sea, Aug. 12, 1949, 6 U.S.T. 3217, 75 U.N.T.S. 85; Geneva Convention Relative to the Treatment of Prisoners of War, Aug. 12, 1949, 6 U.S.T. 3316, 75 U.N.T.S. 135; Geneva Convention Relative to the Protection of Civilian Persons in Time of War, Aug. 12, 1949, 6 U.S.T. 3516, 75 U.N.T.S. 287; International Covenant on Civil and Political Rights, G.A. res. 2200A (XXI), 21 U.N. GAOR Supp. (No. 16) at 52, U.N. Doc. A/6316 (1966), 999 U.N.T.S. 171 (entered into force March 23, 1976); and International Covenant on Economic, Social and Cultural Rights, G.A. res. 2200A (XXI), 21 U.N. GAOR Supp. (No. 16) at 49, U.N. Doc. A/6316 (1966), 993 U.N.T.S. 3 (entered into force Jan. 3, 1976).

14. Joseph Reese Strayer, *On the Medieval Origins of the Modern State* (Princeton: Princeton University Press, 1970), 57; Leo Gross, "The Peace of Westphalia 1648–1948," *Am. J. Int'l L.* 42 (1948): 20, 24–30; Eric Lane, "Demanding Human Rights: A Change in the World Legal Order," *Hofstra L. Rev.* 6 (1978): 269–76.

15. Steve Krasner describes three different elements of sovereignty: international legal sovereignty, which recognizes juridically independent territorial entities; Westphalian sovereignty, which prohibits intervention in the internal affairs of states; and domestic sovereignty, which describes the extent to which domestic authority structures are able to control activities within a state's boundaries. Krasner argues that Westphalian sovereignty—that is, the exclusion of external actors from domestic authority—has been overtaken by international legal sovereignty. In other words, sovereignty has become a Hegelian function of mutual recognition of states by other states in the international system. Steven D. Krasner, *Sovereignty: Organized Hypocrisy* (Princeton: Princeton University Press, 1999), 9. Daniel Philpott sees a similar dynamic of the international community defining the legitimacy of sovereignty. Philpott claims that the conception of sovereignty attained at the end of the twentieth century derived from revolutions in what he calls the "constitution of international society," which arises from "a set of

norms, mutually agreed upon by polities who are members of the society." Daniel Philpott, *Revolutions in Sovereignty* (Princeton: Princeton University Press, 2001), 12.

16. Thomas Hobbes, *Leviathan* (1651) (Oxford: Clarendon Press, 1909, 1958).

17. John Locke, "An Essay Concerning the True Original, Extent and End of Civil Government" (originally published anonymously in 1689), in E. Barker, J. Locke, D. Hume & J. Rousseau, eds., *Social Contract: Essays by Locke, Hume and Rousseau* (London: Oxford University Press, 1948).

18. Victor Gourevitch, ed. and trans., *Rousseau: "The Discourses" and Other Political Writings* (1750) (New York: Cambridge University Press, 1997).

19. Australian Aboriginals, for example, were simply overlooked as legal subjects because, with no apparently permanent settlements and no visible signs of agrarian cultivation, they did not fit the European prototype of sovereign people. They had no claim to land and no ability to vote for the first 150 years of colonial settlement. See *Mabo v. State of Queensland* (1992) 107 ALR 1.

20. Convention Revising the General Act of Berlin, Feb. 26, 1885, and the General Act and Declaration of Brussels, July 2, 1890, *Am. J. Int'l L.* 15 (1921): 314; available at http://www.homestead.com/wysinger/berlin-conference-doc.html.

21. *General Act of the Conference of Berlin, February 25, 1885.*

22. Mark Dummet, "King Leopold's Legacy of DR Congo Violence," http://news.bbc.co.uk/2/hi/africa/3516965.stm; accessed Oct. 4, 2007.

23. Isaak I. Dore, "Constitutionalism and the Post-Colonial State in Africa: A Rawlsian Approach," *St. Louis L. J.* 41 (1997): 1301, 1305.

24. This conception of sovereignty extended to both internal and external relations: a state exercises extensive control over its people within its territory, but at the same time it must respect the authority of other states within their territorial borders. This is a "thin" conception, because it concentrates on the state's right to govern its citizens, and not on the state's responsibilities towards its citizens. For more on this subject, see Jonathan H. Marks, "Mending the Web: Universal Jurisdiction, Humanitarian Intervention and the Abrogation of Immunity by the Security Council," *Colum. J. Transnat'l L.* 42 (2003): 445, 477.

25. John Ladd, trans., *Immanuel Kant, Metaphysical Elements of Justice: Part One of the Metaphysics of Morals/Imannuel Kant* (1780), 2d ed. (Indianapolis: Hackett Publishing Co., 1999).

26. Kant, *Critique of Judgment*, 122. Early philosophizing about sovereignty—Grotius' humanism and Kant's vision of cosmopolitanism and even the beliefs of the contractarians—presupposed human rationality and human agency to be a universal characteristic shared by all people, or at least by European people. By extension it framed beliefs about nation-states, which were also given the attribute of rational agency, as if a state were a person.

27. Hersch Lauterpacht, "States as Subjects of International Law," in Elihu Lauterpacht, ed., *International Law: Being the Collected Papers of Hersch Lauterpacht* (Cambridge: Cambridge University Press, 1977), 5.

28. Lauterpacht, "States as Subjects."

29. Lauterpacht, "States as Subjects."

30. Louis Henkin, "Human Rights and State 'Sovereignty,'" *Ga. J. Int'l & Comp. L.* 25 (1995): 31; Louis Henkin, "The Mythology of Sovereignty," *Am. Soc. Int'l L. Newsl.* (Am. Soc. Int'l L., Washington, D.C., March 1993): 1. Henkin's point is that sovereignty as it applies to states in the international system is inappropriately seen as an expression of the values of the state rather than representing the values of its people.

31. Gerard Delanty, *Inventing Europe: Idea, Identity, Reality* (Basingstoke, UK: Macmillan, 1995).

32. Jack L. Goldsmith and Eric A. Posner, *The Limits of International Law* (New York: Oxford University Press, 2005).

33. Betsy Baker Röben, "The Method Behind Bluntschli's 'Modern' International Law," *J. Hist. Int'l L.* 4 (2002): 249–92.

34. Intervention has never occurred in response to ongoing human rights violence such as rape in marriage, honor killings, or slavery, even though the numbers of such violations may be similar to the number of people being killed on the basis of ethnicity.

35. Goldsmith and Posner, *Limits of International Law*.

36. Jackson suggests evaluating the elements of traditional sovereignty in order to decide which elements should be preserved under the current global circumstances. He also is concerned with how sovereignty's "real policy values" can be identified and then divided from outmoded Westphalian ideals of sovereignty. Jackson proposes "sovereignty modern," as distinguished from older, monolithic notions of sovereignty. John H. Jackson, "Sovereignty-Modern: A New Approach to an Outdated Concept," *Am. J. Int'l L.* 97 (2003): 781–85.

37. Stanley Hoffmann, *The Ethics and Politics of Humanitarian Intervention* (Notre Dame, Ind.: University of Notre Dame Press, 1996): 12–13.

38. Hoffman, *Humanitarian Intervention*, 15.

39. For more about the erosion of sovereignty due to economic and technological developments, see Jackson, "Sovereignty-Modern," 785.

40. Kofi A. Annan, "Two Concepts of Sovereignty," *The Economist* (Sept. 18, 1999): 49, available at http://www.un.org/News/ossg/sg/stories/kaecon.html.

41. East Timor provides a good example. East Timor declared its independence from Portugal on Nov. 28, 1975. Nine days later it was invaded and occupied by Indonesian forces, who killed 60,000 Timorese in the initial assault. At the time the international community did not initiate any actions to protect the Timorese people. More than twenty years later, on Aug. 30, 1999, in a UN-supervised popular referendum, an overwhelming majority (78.5%) of the people of East Timor voted for independence from Indonesia. By this time the region's aspirations for independence were a focus of the United Nations, which had agreed to send a multinational peacekeeping force to the region in the pre-referendum phase, at the request of Indonesia. Soon after the referendum, anti-independence Timorese militias—organized and supported by the Indonesian military—commenced a large-scale, scorched-earth campaign of retribution against the East Timorese. On Sept. 20, 1999, Australian-led peacekeeping troops of the International Force for East Timor deployed to the country and brought the

violence to an end. On May 20, 2002, East Timor was internationally recognized as an independent state.

42. Fernando Teson, *Humanitarian Intervention: An Inquiry into Law and Morality* (Irvington-on-Hudson, N.Y.: Transnational, 1997), 117, 123–25.

43. Matthias Lutz-Bachmann, "Kant's Idea of Peace and the Philosophical Conception of a World Republic," in James Bohman and Matthias Bachmann, eds., *Perpetual Peace: Essays on Kant's Cosmopolitan Ideal* (Cambridge, Mass.: MIT Press, 1997), 68.

44. Vattel regarded intervention as being in the interests of a humane society; it should be collective because only the community of nations is competent to prevent violations. Giulio Diena, *Derecho internacional público* (Barcelona: Bosch, 1948), 147–48; Pasquale Fiore, *Tratado de derecho internacional público* (Madrid: Tomo Segundo, 1894), 24.

45. Thomas P. Brockway, *Basic Documents in United States Foreign Policy* (Princeton: Van Nostrand, 1957), 55–59.

46. Pres. William McKinley, in providing reasons for the U.S. intervention in Cuba, gave importance to humanitarian reasons and the desire to "end barbarism, killings and massacres which were taking place and which parties in conflict were very reluctant to stop." He stated that it would not be a right response to say that the problem was in another country, belonged to another country, or was not our concern. It was a special duty of ours and therefore intervention was just. Brockway, *Basic Documents*.

47. Article 51 of the UN Charter reads, "Nothing in the present Charter shall impair the inherent right of individual or collective self-defence if an armed attack occurs against a Member of the United Nations, until the Security Council has taken measures necessary to maintain international peace and security. Measures taken by Members in the exercise of this right of self-defence shall be immediately reported to the Security Council and shall not in any way affect the authority and responsibility of the Security Council under the present Charter to take at any time such action as it deems necessary in order to maintain or restore international peace and security."

48. Article 42 of the UN Charter states, "Should the Security Council consider that measures provided for in Article 41 would be inadequate or have proved to be inadequate, it may take such action by air, sea, or land forces as may be necessary to maintain or restore international peace and security. Such action may include demonstrations, blockade, and other operations by air, sea, or land forces of Members of the United Nations."

49. Article 2(4) of the UN Charter reads, "All Members shall refrain in their international relations from the threat or use of force against the territorial integrity or political independence of any state, or in any other manner inconsistent with the Purposes of the United Nations." See also Article 2 of the 1948 United Nations Convention on the Prevention and Punishment of the Crime of Genocide, which states, "In the present Convention, genocide means any of the following acts committed with intent to destroy, in whole or in part, a national, ethnical, racial or religious group, as such: (a) killing members of the group; (b) causing serious bodily or mental harm to members of

the group; (c) deliberately inflicting on the group conditions of life calculated to bring about its physical destruction in whole or in part; (d) imposing measures intended to prevent births within the group and (e) forcibly transferring children of the group to another group." For a definition of ethnic cleansing see the entry in Britannica Online Encyclopedia, available at http://www.britannica.com/EBchecked/topic/194242/ethnic-cleansing. According to this source "ethnic cleansing as a concept has generated considerable controversy. Some critics see little difference between it and genocide. Defenders, however, argue that ethnic cleansing and genocide can be distinguished by the intent of the perpetrator: whereas the primary goal of genocide is the destruction of an ethnic, racial, or religious group, the main purpose of ethnic cleansing is the establishment of ethnically homogenous lands, which may be achieved by any of a number of methods including genocide."

50. On the matter of intervention in Somalia see Security Council resolution S.C. Res. 794, U.N. Doc. S/RES/794 (Dec. 3, 1992). On the matter of intervention in Rwanda, see Security Council resolution S.C. Res. 929, U.N. Doc. S/RES/929 (June 2, 1994). On the matter of intervention in Haiti see Security Council resolution S.C. Res. 940, U.N. Doc. S/INF/50 (Dec. 15, 1994). On the matter of intervention in Bosnia and Herzegovina see Security Council resolutions S.C. Res. 770, U.N. Doc. S/RES/770 (Aug. 13, 1992), and S.C. Res. 816, U.N. Doc. S/RES/816 (March 31, 1993).

51. The massacre led to Washington's coercive diplomacy under which the Dayton Agreement was hammered out. For more on the Bosnian atrocities and the Dayton Agreement see Elizabeth M. Cousens, "Making Peace in Bosnia Work," *Cornell Int'l L. J.* 30 (1997): 789, 791–92.

52. John Norton Moore, "Grenada and the International Double Standard," *Am. J. Int'l L.* 78 (1989): 145, 154–55; Celeste Poltak, "Humanitarian Intervention: A Contemporary Interpretation of the Charter of the United Nations," *U. Toronto Fac. L. Rev.* 60 (2002): 1; Michael Reisman, "Sovereignty and Human Rights in Contemporary International Law," *Am. J. Int'l L.* 84 (1990): 866, 869. For more on the veto system preventing humanitarian intervention see Jules Lobel, "American Hegemony and International Law: Benign Hegemony? Kosovo and Article 2(4) of the U.N. Charter," *Chinese J. Int'l L.* 1 (2000): 19.

53. Michael Akehurst, "Humanitarian Intervention," in Hedley Bull, ed., *Intervention in World Politics* (New York: Oxford University Press, 1984), 99; Ian Brownlie, *International Law and the Use of Force by States* (Oxford: Clarendon Press, 1963); Lori F. Damrosch, "Commentary on Collective Military Intervention to Enforce Human Rights," in Lori F. Damrosch and David J. Scheffler, eds., *Law and Force in the New International Order* (Boulder, Colo.: Westview Press, 1991), 215, 217–21; Louis Henkin, "The Use of Force: Law and U.S. Policy," in Louis Henkin et al., eds., *Right v. Might: International Law and the Use of Force*, 2d ed. (New York: Council on Foreign Relations, 1991), 37, 41–44; Natalino Ronzitti, *Rescuing Nationals Abroad Through Military Coercion and Intervention on the Grounds of Humanity* (Boston: Martinus Nijhoff Publishers,1985).

54. Rawls, *Law of Peoples*. Rawls categorizes "decent il-liberal societies" as those that

have decent consultation hierarchies that allow all people to participate in some sort of consultation process; Rawls stops short of requiring democratic institutions. Charles Beitz, like Thomas Franck, argues that a right to democratic institutions ought be included in a list of moral entitlements leading to human rights. See Charles R. Beitz, *Political Theory and International Relations* (Princeton: Princeton University Press, 1999, rev. edition); Charles R. Beitz, "Human Rights and the Laws of Peoples," in Deen K. Chatterjee, ed., *The Ethics of Assistance: Morality and the Distant Needy* (Cambridge: Cambridge University Press, 2004), 193; and Thomas M. Franck, "The Emerging Right to Democratic Governance," *Am. J. Int'l L.* 86 (1992): 46.

55. On the opposition of Mexico, Cuba, Uruguay, Venezuela, and Brazil (which was a member of the UN Security Council at the time) see the Security Council's discussions for July 31, 1994, when representatives of Mexico, Cuba, Uruguay and Venezuela, among others, were invited to participate in the discussion without the right to vote. U.N. SCOR, 43rd Sess., 3413d mtg., at 4 (Mexico), 5 (Cuba), 6 (Uruguay), 8 (Venezuela & Brazil), U.N. Doc. SIPV 3413 (July 31, 1994).

56. U.N. Secretary-General Kofi Annan, press conference at the U.N. Headquarters (Sept. 10, 1999), available at http://www.unis.unvienna.org/unis/pressrels/1999/sg2360.html.

57. Annan warned that if Jakarta refused to accept the international community's assistance, it could not "escape the responsibility of what could amount . . . to crimes against humanity." Annan, press conference (Sept. 10, 1999). Or in the words of the Geneva Conventions Indonesian leaders would be left open to international prosecution because they had not taken "all feasible measures" to stop the violence. Geneva Convention on Civilians, art. 68.

58. U.N. Secretary-General Kofi Annan, Speech to Open the General Assembly (Sept. 20, 1999), available at http://www.un.org/News/Press/docs1999/19990920.sgsm7136.html).

59. Independent International Commission on Kosovo, *The Kosovo Report: Conflict, International Response, Lessons Learned* (2000). The commission's report warned that the gap between legal and legitimate humanitarian interventions was dangerous, leaving too much room for either failures to intervene on one hand or illegitimate interventions on the other. Conditions for humanitarian intervention need to be clearly specified.

60. In his national address of March 19, 2003, President Bush stated, "More than thirty-five countries are giving crucial support—from the use of naval and air bases, to help with intelligence and logistics, to the deployment of combat units. Every nation in this coalition has chosen to bear the duty and share the honor of serving in our common defense." U.S. President George W. Bush, Address to the Nation (Mar. 19, 2003), available at http://www.whitehouse.gov/news/releases/2003/03/20030319-17.html. Of these thirty-five nations, according to recent data from the U.S. Department of Defense reported by the online database Statemaster, the U.S. has sent approximately 133,000 troops; the U.K. approximately 8,000; South Korea 3,200; Italy 2,600; Poland 1,400; Australia, Romania, Japan, Georgia, and Denmark each sent 500–900 troops; and an additional 1,850 troops come from Albania, Armenia, Azerbaijan, Bosnia and Herzegovina,

the Czech Republic, El Salvador, Estonia, Kazakhstan, Latvia, Lithuania, Macedonia, Moldova, Mongolia, Netherlands, Portugal, Slovakia, and Ukraine. For more on these statistics, see the graph at http://www.nationmaster.com/graph/mil_ira_coa_for_tro_ str-iraq-coalition-forces-troop-strength; accessed Nov. 2, 2007. Global Policy Forum reports that "the United States alone provided more than 75 percent of the troops and a still higher proportion of the naval, air and ground-based weapons." *Global Policy Forum, The Coalition,* http://www.globalpolicy.org/security/issues/iraq/coalitionin-dex.htm; accessed Oct. 29, 2007. By April 2006 however many coalition members had already withdrawn their troops: "Among the countries that have exited the coalition are Singapore (in January 2004); Nicaragua (February 2004); Spain (Apr. 2004); Dominican Republic (May 2004); Honduras (May 2004); Norway (June 2004); Philippines (July 2004); Thailand (Aug. 2004); New Zealand (September 2004); Tonga (December 2004) Hungary (December 2004); Portugal (February 2005); Moldova (February 2005); Netherlands (June 2005); Ukraine (December 2005); and Bulgaria (January 2006)." John Nichols, "Bush's Crumbling 'Coalition' in Iraq," *Nation* (Apr. 11, 2006), http://www .thenation.com/blogs/thebeat?bid=1&pid=76457.

61. "Full text of Colin Powell's speech," *Guardian* (Feb. 5, 2003), http://www .guardian.co.uk/Iraq/Story/0,,889531,00.html; accessed Oct. 13, 2008.

62. Colin Powell's speech (Feb. 5, 2003).

63. U.S. President George Bush, *Address* at swearing-in ceremony for his second term (Jan. 20, 2005), available at http://www.whitehouse/gov/news/releases/ 2005/01/20050120-1.html ("with the ultimate goal of ending tyranny in our world").

64. Marek Antoni Nowicki, "The Intervention Syndrome" (Oct. 2005), available at http://www.project-syndicate.org/commentary/nowicki1; accessed Dec. 1, 2008.

65. While still unclear, the reasons for the fighting appeared to have had to do with the distribution of oil funds, while the fighting was colored by the poor organization of the Timorese army and police.

66. Such concerns are not new in international law. Similar criticisms were made at other historical periods, as when in 1938 international jurist Hersch Lauterpacht criticized the "positivism" that framed aggressive U.S. foreign policy, which in Lauterpacht's view had contributed to tensions building up to World War I. Hersch Lauterpacht, "The League of Nations," in Elihu Lauterpacht, ed., *International Law: Being the Collected Papers of Hersch Lauterpacht* (Cambridge: Cambridge University Press, 1978), 575.

67. Teson, *Humanitarian Intervention,* 117, 123–25.

68. Reisman, "Sovereignty & Human Rights," 240, 245.

69. U.N. Universal Declaration of Human Rights, art. 21, G.A. Res. 217A (III), 71, U.N. GAOR, 3d Sess., U.N. Doc. A1810 (Dec. 10, 1948).

70. Amartya Sen, "Democracy as a Universal Value," *Journal of Democracy* 10, 3 (1999): 3–17, 4.

71. Rawls, *Law of Peoples.*

72. Immanuel Kant, *Perptual Peace* (Filiquarian Publishing, 2007), 14.

73. Thomas Franck constructs a legal and political standard of civilization by insisting that "the right of each state to be represented in international organs, and to share in

the benefits of international fiscal, trade, development, and security programs should be dependent upon its government satisfying the system's standard for democratic validation." In fact he is even prepared to go so far as to consider the idea of "limit[ing] collective security measures to cases of attack against democratic states." Asking "Would it help Kuwait to establish democratic internal order if its future protection by UN-authorized collective measures depended upon such a transformation?" he acknowledges that it "is a change in the system's rules which is unlikely to come about in the near future," but he thinks that "it is worth contemplating." Thomas M. Franck, "Legitimacy and the Democratic Entitlement," in Gregory H. Fox and Brad R. Roth, eds., *Democratic Governance and International Law* (New York: Cambridge University Press, 2000), 25, 28.

74. Article 21 reads, "(1) Everyone has the right to take part in the government of his country, directly or through freely chosen representatives; (2) Everyone has the right of equal access to public service in his country; (3) The will of the people shall be the basis of the authority of government; this will shall be expressed in periodic and genuine elections which shall be by universal and equal suffrage and shall be held by secret vote or by equivalent free voting procedures."

75. Franck, "Emerging Right," 46.

76. Franck, "Emerging Right," 25, 28.

77. José E. Álvarez, "Do Liberal States Behave Better? A Critique of Slaughter's Liberal Theory," *Eur. J. Int'l L.* 12 (2001): 183, 189-90.

78. W. Michael Reisman, "Sovereignty and Human Rights in Contemporary International Law," *Am. J. Int'l L.* 84 (1990), 866; W. Michael Reisman, "Sovereignty and Human Rights in Contemporary International Law," in Fox and Roth, eds., *Democratic Governance*, 240, 245.

79. While conceding that there are cases in which it is difficult to determine who it is that the people wish to rule them, "a jurist rooted in the late twentieth century can hardly say that an invasion by outside forces to remove the caudillo and install the elected government is a violation of national sovereignty." Reisman, "Sovereignty and Human Rights," 240, 245. Reisman argues that a right of intervention has, in certain circumstances, become indisputable, especially when the wishes of a people have been clearly expressed in internationally supervised and validated elections and this expression of popular sovereignty is ignored by a domestic usurper. Reisman, "Sovereignty and Human Rights," 240, 245.

80. Immanuel Kant, "Idea for a Universal History with a Cosmopolitan Purpose," in Reiss, ed., *Kant's Political Writings*, 45.

81. Ibid., 46.

82. Weak states aren't necessarily poor states, but of the world's more than seventy low-income countries, about fifty of them—excluding well-armed hostile states such as North Korea—have been identified by the U.S. administration as weak in a way that threatens U.S. and international security. See http://www.dhs.gov/index.shtm (accessed Oct. 15, 2008) and http://www.state.gov/ (accessed Oct. 15, 2008).

83. Stuart E. Eizenstat, John Edward Porter, and Jeremy M. Weinstein, "Rebuilding Weak States," *Foreign Aff.* (Jan.–Feb. 2005): 135.

84. Elizabeth F. Drexler, *Aceh, Indonesia: Securing the Insecure State* (Philadelphia: University of Pennsylvania Press, 2008).

85. John Pendergast, "Intervention, Hailed as a Concept, Is Shunned in Practice," *New York Times* (Jan. 20, 2008).

Chapter 4

1. S.R. Sharma, *The Making of Modern India from A.D. 1526 to the Present Day* (Bombay, India: Orient Longmans, 1951), 478.

2. Bonnie Honig, "My Culture Made Me Do It," in Joshua Cohen et al., eds., *Is Multiculturalism Bad for Women?* (Princeton: Princeton University Press, 1999), 35–40.

3. Sophia Abdi Noor, the founder of Womankind Kenya, remarked that it was very difficult to convince Ms. Shuriye, who turned them away several times before they enlisted the help of religious leaders. Marc Lacey, "Genital Cutting Shows Signs of Losing Favor in Africa," *New York Times* (June 8, 2004): A3.

4. Miriam Abu Sharkh, "History and Results of Labor Standard Initiatives, An Event History and Panel Analysis of the Ratification Patterns, and Effects, of the International Labor Organization's First Child Labor Convention." Ph.D. dissertation, Freie Universität Berlin, 2002.

5. Eva Brems, Address at the Tenth Annual Conference on "The Individual vs. The State: Reconciling Universality and Diversity in International Human Rights Law" (June 14, 2002): 18.

6. Saskia Sassen, for example, worries that economic citizenship in the new global order does not belong to citizens anymore but to "firms and markets, particularly the global financial markets, and it is located not in individuals, not in citizens, but in global economic actors." Saskia Sassen, *Losing Control? Sovereignty in an Age of Globalization* (New York: Columbia University Press, 1996), 38.

7. Michael Hardt and Antonio Negri, *Empire* (Cambridge, Mass.: Harvard University Press, 2001), 44.

8. Timothy Brennan, "The Empire's New Clothes," *Critical Inquiry* 29 (2005): 337, 341.

9. Jagdish Bagwati, *In Defense of Globalization* (New York: Oxford University Press, 2004), 68.

10. John W. Meyer, "World Models, National Curricula, and the Centrality of the Individual," in Aaron Benovat and Cecilia Braslavsky, eds., *School Knowledge in Comparative and Historical Perspective* (Hong Kong: Springer, 2006), 261.

11. Meyer, "World Models," 7.

12. See, for instance, UNESCO's Literacy Initiative for Empowerment 2006–2015 (LIFE), available at http://portal.unesco.org/education/en/ev.php-URL_ID=53813&URL_DO=DO_TOPIC&URL_SECTION=201.html (accessed Oct. 17, 2008), as well as World Bank's Education for All-Fast Track Initiative (FTI), available at http://web.worldbank.org/WBSITE/EXTERNAL/TOPICS/EXTEDUCATION/0,content MDK:20278663~menuPK:617564~pagePK:148956~piPK:216618~theSitePK:282386,00.html (accessed Oct. 17, 2008).

13. Slavoj Žižek, "Critical Responses—A Symptom—Of What?," *Critical Inquiry* 29 (2003): 499.

14. Meyer, "World Models," 267.

15. Bagwati, *In Defense of Globalization*, 72.

16. Ronald Inglehart and Wayne E. Baker, "Modernization, Cultural Change, and the Persistence of Traditional Values," *Am. Soc. Rev.* 65 (2000): 19, 49.

17. Beth A Simmons and Lisa L. Martin, "International Organizations and Institutions," in *Handbook of International Relations* (London: Sage Publications, 2002): 192–211.

18. Darren Hawkins, "Human Rights Norms and Networks in Authoritarian Chile," in Sanjeev Khagram, James V. Riker, and Kathryn Sikkink, eds., *Restructuring World Politics—Transnational Social Movements, Networks, and Norms* (Minneapolis: University of Minnesota Press, 2002), 48.

19. Paul J. Nelson, "Agendas, Accountability, and Legitimacy among Transnational Networks Lobbying the World Bank," in Khagram et al., *Restructuring World Politics*, 144.

20. Kathryn Sikkink, "Conclusion," in Khagram et al., *Restructuring World Politics*, 301.

21. Ibid.

22. Jeremy Weinstein, "Autonomous Recovery and International Intervention in Comparative Perspective," Working Paper 57, Centre for Global Development, 2005.

23. Meyer, "World Models," 264.

24. Historically the European Union's development policy had been pursued informally through trade and financial agreements with the former colonies of member states. Breaking with this tradition, the fourth Lomé Agreement, in 1990, coupled economic aid and political conditionality clauses related to democracy, human rights, and the rule of law. Article 5 of the Lomé Agreement implemented a two-track approach for development: on the one hand, the active promotion of these values through financial aid, and on the other, reactive sanctions in case of violations. During the 1990s the European Council invoked suspension clauses against Nigeria, Rwanda, Burundi, Niger, and Sierra Leone. In other cases it withheld 30 percent of the funds until better implementation of human rights policies had taken place. The Cotonou Agreement of 2000, which replaced the Lomé system, strengthens conditionality by adding references to cultural and environmental dimensions of development. The Cotonou Agreement is more cooperative—instead of dictating development policies, it seeks to develop initiatives with the input of the developing country and jointly to evaluate progress. Tanja A. Börzel and Thomas Risse, "One Size Fits All! EU Policies for the Promotion of Human Rights, Democracy and the Rule of Law" (2004), http://iis-db.stanford.edu/pubs/20747/Risse-Borzel-stanford_final.pdf; accessed Oct. 13, 2008.

25. The treaty of accession was signed in 2003 and came into force on May 1, 2004, which was the day of enlargement.

26. The primary treaties are those of Rome (signed on March 25, 1957, entered into force on Jan. 1, 1958); Maastricht (signed on Feb. 7, 1992, entered into force on Nov. 1,

1993); Amsterdam (signed on Oct. 2, 1997, entered into force on May 1, 1999); and Nice (signed on Feb. 26, 2001, entered into force on Feb. 1, 2003).

27. Negotiations were initially concluded with Cyprus, the Czech Republic, Estonia, Hungary, Latvia, Lithuania, Malta, Poland, Slovakia, and Slovenia in December 2002. They were admitted to the EU in 2004.

28. Bulgaria and Romania signed the Treaty of Accession on April 25, 2005, and became members of the EU in January 2007. Marise Cremona, "Values in the EU Constitution: The External Dimension" (Center on Democracy, Development & Rule of Law, Working Paper No. 26, 2004): 12–13, available at http://iis-db.stanford.edu/pubs/20739/Cremona-Values_in_the_EU_Constitution-External__Relations.pdf.

29. On Dec. 12, 1979, the UN General Assembly adopted resolution 34/93 F, putting in place an embargo against South Africa. The resolution requested that all states enact legislation prohibiting the sale and supply of petroleum and petroleum products to South Africa. In 1986 the General Assembly called upon all states to broaden the scope of the oil embargo and established the Intergovernmental Group to Monitor the Supply and Shipping of Oil and Petroleum Products to South Africa.

30. General Agreement on Tariffs and Trade, Oct. 30, 1947, 61 Stat. A-11, 55 U.N.T.S. 194.

31. For a similar statement, see Janelle M. Diller and David A. Levy, Note and Comment: "Child Labor, Trade and Investment: Toward the Harmonization of International Law," *Am. J. Int'l L.* 91 (1997): 663, 665–66.

32. Salman Bal, "International Free Trade Agreements and Human Rights: Reinterpreting Article XX of the GATT," *Minn. J. Global Trade* 10 (2001): 62, 66.

33. Agreement Establishing the World Trade Organization, Apr. 15, 1994, 33 I.L.M. 1144 (1995). The WTO Agreement entered into force on Jan. 1, 1995. The WTO and the various Uruguay Round agreements have replaced the GATT, but maintained its legal norms by incorporating the current version of GATT, designated as GATT 1994. John H. Jackson, *The World Trade Organization: Constitution and Jurisprudence* (London: Chatham House Papers, Royal Institute for International Affairs, 1998), 12–29.

34. Thomas Cottier, Joost Pauwelyn, and Elisabeth Bürgi, "Linking Trade Regulation and Human Rights in International Law: An Overview," in Thomas Cottier, Joost Pauwelyn, and Elisabeth Bürgi, eds., *Human Rights and International Trade* (New York: Oxford University Press, 2005), 16; Joseph Langan, "Did Your Jeans Enslave Children? Child Labour in International Trade," *Asper Rev. Int'l Bus. & Trade L.* 2 (2002): 159, 164.

35. For more about the connection between human rights and international trade, see Robert Howse and Makau Mutua, "Protecting Human Rights in a Global Economy, Challenges to the World Trade Organization" (January 2000), http://www.dd-rd.ca/site/publications/index.php?id=1271&page=2&subsection=catalogue&print=true&show_all=true; accessed Oct. 13, 2008.

36. Bal, "International Free Trade Agreements," 665.

37. Tatjana Eres, "The Limits of GATT Article XX: A Back Door For Human Rights?," *Geo. J. Int'l L.* 35 (2004): 597, 599–600.

38. Ibid.

39. Langan, "Did Your Jeans Enslave Children?," 168–69.

40. Eres, "The Limits of GATT," 598.

41. GATT, art. XX.

42. GATT, art. XXI.

43. Frank J. Garcia, "The Universal Declaration of Human Rights at 50 and the Challenge of Global Markets: Trading Away the Human Rights Principle," *Brooklyn J. Int'l L.* 25 (1999): 51, 78–79.

44. Langan, "Did Your Jeans Enslave Children?," 166.

45. Miriam Abu Sharkh, "Time Bound Programmes: A Review of Experiences and Lessons Learned" (IPEC, ILO, 2006).

46. D. M. Smolin, "Conflict and Ideology in the International Campaign Against Child Labour," *Hofstra Lab. & Emp. L. J.* 16 (1999): 383, 390. Langan, "Did Your Jeans Enslave Children?," 166–67. Daniel S. Ehrenberg of Yale Law School has suggested a detailed mechanism through which labor standards and the international trade system could be linked. Ehrenberg argues that "in adopting the [Convention on the Rights of the Child] and other international conventions that disallow many aspects of exploitative child labor, most nations have undertaken an international legal duty to ensure the eradication of child labor within their own borders. Violations of these and other internationally accepted labor standards due to a state's failure adequately to police violations and enforce laws could therefore be construed to constitute illegal state subsidies. According to the system of international trade, illegal subsidies constitute an unfair comparative advantage and are actionable under the GATT/WTO enforcement regime. By linking the ILO and the WTO systems, expert analysis on whether labour standards have been infringed and how those infringements affect international trade could allow labour standards and trade to be joined. . . . In this way, the compilation of the ILO and the WTO would allow for an efficient and fair approach to enforcing child labour rights. . . . It has also been proposed that linkage of labour standards with the GATT could be done through the imposition of a social clause in the GATT." Daniel S. Ehrenberg, "The Labor Link: Applying the International Trading System to Enforce Violations of Forced and Child Labor," *Yale J. Int'l L.* 20 (1995): 361, 377.

47. Trade Act of 1974 (codified as amended at 19 U.S.C. §2411 [2000]).

48. Nevertheless because the U.S. Trade Representative has never invoked this power, the practical repercussions are unknown. Benjamin James Stevenson, Comment: "Pursuing an End to Foreign Child Labor Through U.S. Trade Law: WTO Challenges and Doctrinal Solutions," *UCLA J. Int'l L. & For. Aff.* 7 (2002): 129, 146–47.

49. Diller and Levy, "Child Labor," 690.

50. Stevenson, "Pursuing an End," 150–51.

51. Diller and Levy, "Child Labor," 691.

52. See http://www.nikebiz.com/nikeresponsibility/#workers-factories/main (accessed Oct. 17, 2008) and http://www.toy-icti.org/info/codeofbusinesspractices.html (accessed Oct. 17, 2008).

53. In 1951 the Treaty of Paris established the first mode of European cooperation in

the form of the European Coal and Steel Community. The six original members—Belgium, West Germany, Luxembourg, France, Italy, and The Netherlands—confederated for peace throughout the region through economic ties. The organization evolved into the European Economic Community in 1957 with the signing of the Treaty of Rome. The signatory countries agreed to reduce trade barriers and form a common market. In 1992 the Treaty of Maastricht established what we now know today as the European Union.

54. Emilie Hafner-Burton, Kiyoteru Tsutsui and John Meyer, "International Human Rights Law and the Politics of Legitimacy: Repressive States and Human Rights Treaties," *International Sociology* 23 (1) (2008): 115–41.

55. Nicola Smith, "EU Warns Balkan States as Entry Is Delayed," *Telegraph* (May 17, 2006), http://www.telegraph.co.uk/news/main.jhtml?xml=/news/2006/05/17/weu17 .xml&sSheet=/news/2006/05/17/ixnews.html; no longer accessible as of Oct. 13, 2008.

56. Emile Hafner-Burton, Kiyoteru Tsutsui, and John W. Meyer, "International Human Rights Law and the Politics of Legitimation: Repressive States and Human Rights Treaties," paper presented at the Harvard Human Rights Colloquium, 2007 (on file with author).

57. Anne-Marie Slaughter and William Burke-White, "Judicial Globalization," *Va. J. Int'l L.* 40 (2000): 1103, 1115, citing *Nanus Asia Co. v. Standard Charter Bank*, 1988 H.K.C. LEXIS 410, at 1, 8 (High Ct. Sept. 22, 1988).

58. Anne-Marie Slaughter and William Burke-White, "Judicial Globalization," 1112, citing *Hartford Fire Ins. Co. v. California*, 509 U.S. 764, 817 (1993) (Scalia, J., dissenting); Anne-Marie Slaughter, "Agora: Breard: Court to Court," *Am. J. Int'l L.* 92 (1998): 708; Anne-Marie Slaughter and William Burke-White, "An International Constitutional Moment," *Harv. Int'l L. J.* 43 (2002): 1.

59. Harold Hongju Koh, "The Globalization of Freedom," *Yale J. Int'l L. J.* 26 (2001): 305. Koh uses the phrase "age of globalization" to indicate the present time period, following the post–Cold War era. Harold Hongju Koh, "A United States Human Rights Policy for the 21st Century," *St. Louis L. J.* 46 (2002): 293, 303–4.

60. Donald Kettl, "The Transformation of Governance: Globalization, Devolution, and the Role of Government," *Pub. Admin. Rev.* 60 (2000): 488.

61. Oona Hathaway, "Do Human Rights Treaties Make a Difference?," *Yale L. J.* 111 (2002): 1935. Of countries identified by Amnesty International as the world's most extreme abusers during the period from 1976 to 2002, 77 percent ratified the ICESCR, 61 percent ratified the ICCPR, 56 percent ratified the CEDAW, and 51 percent ratified the CRC, while only 27 percent ratified the Convention Against Torture (CAT).

62. Ryan Goodman and Derek Jinks, "International Law and State Socialization: Conceptual, Empirical, and Normative Challenges," *Duke L. J.* 54 (2005): 983.

63. Ibid., 983.

64. Ibid., 984.

65. Ibid., 995.

66. Ibid.

67. Ibid., 996.

68. Goodman and Jinks stress the importance of an integrated, mechanism-based theory of law's influence in developing a richer, more useful, and empirical understanding of international law. They differentiate between their theory from variable-based theorizing because they see factors affecting the presence or strength of any particular mechanism as a secondary consideration. A mechanism-based theory helps to overcome the limitations of variable-based, correlational analysis. It also facilitates integration of diverse correlational findings by identifying why and how factors are related.

69. Allen Buchanan and Robert O. Keohane, "The Legitimacy of Global Governance Institutions," *Ethics & Int'l Aff.* 20 (2006): 405–37.

70. Martha Morgan, "Taking Machismo to Court: The Gender Jurisprudence of the Colombian Constitutional Court," *U. Miami Inter-Am. L. Rev.* 30 (1999): 253, 258.

71. CEDAW was ratified by Colombia in 1981. Article 40 of the 1991 constitution provides that "the authorities will guarantee the adequate and effective participation of women in the decision-making levels of Public Administration." Article 42 states that "family relations are based in the equality of rights and duties of couples and in reciprocal respect among all its members" and also provides that "any form of violence within the family is considered destructive of its harmony and unity, and will be punished according to the law." Article 43 declares that "women and men have equal rights and opportunities. Women cannot be subject to any type of discrimination." Article 53 includes equality of opportunity and special protection for women, maternity, and minors among the fundamental principles to be considered by Congress in enacting a labor law.

72. Colombia's *tutela* resembles but is much broader than the writ of habeas corpus. The court has interpreted the "fundamental rights" of the *tutela* broadly to include economic, social, and cultural rights. The court chooses to review *tutela* actions on the basis of their importance or the magnitude of the constitutional violation involved.

73. Sentencia No. C-481/98, (quoted in Morgan, "Taking Machismo to Court," 287); Eduardo Cifuentes Muñoz, "Mujer e igualdad," presented at conference in Guayaquil, Ecuador (Sept. 27, 1996) (on file with author).

74. In 1994 the court selected for review a *tutela* filed by a young man who had been refused admission to military school because of his homosexuality. In the face of strong Colombian moral and religious sentiments against homosexuality, a panel of the court ruled that he must be admitted. The court found that exclusion from military schools based on homosexuality violated the petitioner's rights to due process, to his good name, and to education. The court also relied on Article 16's guarantee of the right to free development of personality and Article 15's guarantee to the right to intimacy and one's good name. The ruling distinguished between the status of homosexuality and homosexual conduct, which like other sexual conduct, could be prohibited within the military. In this and other cases concerning discrimination against homosexuals the court acknowledged its role in resolving the controversial issue of whether homosexuality is a choice or biologically determined. The court expressed the opinion that if sexual orientation is biologically determined then discrimination on these grounds constituted sexual discrimination; however if sexual orientation is a matter of personal choice, the discriminatory laws infringe on the right to free development

of one's personality. The first gay marriage having legal effects was formalized before a notary in Bogotá in 1998.

75. While women's rights activists María Isabel Plata and María Cristina Calderón, respectively executive director and director of legal services for PROFAMILIA, gave high marks to the court's gender decisions, other feminists like Socorro Ramírez argue that the court has not gone far enough in addressing the *institutional* subordination of women as opposed to the *individualistic* aspects of discrimination. Morgan, "Taking Machismo to Court," 314–18.

76. Morgan, "Taking Machismo to Court," 255.

77. For example, see Justice Antonin Scalia's dissenting opinion in *U.S. v. Virginia (VMI)*, where he decries the court's disregard of tradition and claims that the democratic system is destroyed "if the smug assurances of each age are removed from the democratic process and written into the Constitution." 518 U.S. 515, 567 (1996) (Scalia, J., dissenting).

78. Interview with Eduardo Cifuentes Muñoz, quoted in Morgan, "Taking Machismo to Court," 334.

79. *D. K. Basu v. State of West Bengal*, AIR 1997 SC 610.

80. *D. K. Basu v. State of West Bengal*, para. 42A.

81. *Vishaka v. State of Rajasthan*, AIR 1997 SC 3011.

82. *Vishaka v. State of Rajasthan*, para. 14. In support of its argument the court cited a decision of the Australian high court that used a similar methodology: "The High Court of Australia in *Minister for Immigration and Ethnic Affairs v. Teoh*, 128 ALR 353, has recognized the concept of legitimate expectation of its observance in the absence of a contrary legislative provision, even in the absence of a Bill of Rights in the Constitution of Australia." Ibid.

83. *People's Union for Civil Liberties v. Union of India*, AIR 1997 SC 568.

84. Section 5 (2) of the Telegraph Act, 1885 (the Act).

85. *Pratap Singh v. State of Jharkhand,* AIR 2005 SC 2731.

86. Heterogeneity, rather than homogeneity, most likely reflects empirical reality. The contemporary expectation of cultural homogeneity increased with the nationalist ideals of the nineteenth and particularly the twentieth centuries. It is more myth than reality, however; the empirical occurrence of historical change and cross-cultural diversity has been with us far longer than the modern idea of nationalism.

87. Karl Popper, *The Logic of Scientific Discovery* (New York: Routledge, 1977).

88. Ronald Dworkin, "Is There Really No Right Answer in Hard Cases?," in R. Dworkin, *A Matter of Principle* (Cambridge, Mass.: Harvard University Press, 1985), 119–45.

89. Antony Anghie and B.S. Chimni, "Third World Approach to International Law," *Chinese J. Int'l L.* 2 (2003): 77, 99.

90. Michael Ignatieff, *Human Rights as Politics and Idolatry* (Princeton: Princeton University Press, 2001), 109.

91. Amy Gutmann and Dennis Thompson, *Democracy and Disagreement* (Cambridge, Mass.: Belknap Press, 1998), 4.

92. Jürgen Habermas, *Between Facts and Norms: Contributions to a Discourse Theory of Law and Democracy*, trans. William Rehg (Cambridge, Mass.: MIT Press, 1996).

93. Jürgen Habermas, *Theory of Communicative Action*, trans. Thomas McCarthy (Boston: Beacon Press, 1984).

94. Habermas, *Theory of Communicative Action*, 460.

95. Ibid., 218.

96. Article 15 of ECHR states: "(1) In time of war or other public emergency threatening the life of the nation any High Contracting Party may take measures derogating from its obligations under this Convention to the extent strictly required by the exigencies of the situation, provided that such measures are not inconsistent with its other obligations under international law. (2) No derogation from Article 2, except in respect of deaths resulting from lawful acts of war, or from Articles 3, 4 (paragraph 1) and 7 shall be made under this provision. (3) Any High Contracting Party availing itself of this right of derogation shall keep the Secretary-General of the Council of Europe fully informed of the measures which it has taken and the reasons therefore. It shall also inform the Secretary-General of the Council of Europe when such measures have ceased to operate and the provisions of the Convention are again being fully executed." Jeffrey A. Brauch, "The Margin of Appreciation and the Jurisprudence of the European Court of Human Rights: Threat to the Rule of Law," *Colum. J. Eur. L.* 11 (2005): 115.

97. Thomas O'Donnell, "The Margin of Appreciation Doctrine: Standards in the Jurisprudence of the European Court of Human Rights," *Hum. Rts. Q.* 4(1982): 474, 478; Howard C. Yourow, "The Margin of Appreciation Doctrine in the Dynamics of European Human Rights Jurisprudence," *Conn. J. Int'l L.* 3 (1987): 111, 118; Steven Greer, "The Margin of Appreciation: Interpretation and Discretion Under the European Convention on Human Rights" (Council of Europe, Human Rights Files No.17, 2000): 5.

98. Yutaka Arai-Takahashi, *The Margin of Appreciation Doctrine and the Principle of Proportionality in the Jurisprudence of the ECHR* (Ardsley, N.Y.: Transnational Publishers, 2002), 3.

99. Greer, "Margin of Appreciation," 5.

100. In Belgium and France, Islamic headscarves have been banned in primary and secondary state schools, but not in universities. In Germany, The Netherlands, Switzerland, and the United Kingdom, the headscarf is allowed in all public educational institutions. In Germany the debate focused on the right of teachers to wear the headscarf. In Chapter 5 I will discuss the headscarf issue in greater detail. Natan Lerner, "International Law and Religion: How Wide the Margin of Appreciation? The Turkish Headscarf Case, the Strasburg Court, and Secularist Tolerance," *Willamette J. Int'l L. & Disp. Resol.* 13 (2005): 65.

101. *De Wilde, Ooms & Versyp v. Belgium* (Vagrancy Case) (1979–80) 1 E.H.R.R. 373.

102. *Chrysostomos, Papachrysostomou & Loizidou v. Turkey*, App. Nos. 15299/89, 15300/89 & 15318/89, 68 Eur. Comm'n H.R. Dec. & Rep. 216, 242 (1991).

103. George Letsas, "Two Concepts of the Margin of Appreciation," *Oxford J. Legal Stud.* (2006): 706. Letsas goes further and says that there is no coherence in the current scholarly understandings of the doctrine.

104. *Rees v. United Kingdom*, App. No. 9532/81, (1987) 9 E.H.R.R. 56; *Cossey v. United Kingdom*, App. No. 10843/84, (1991) 13 E.H.R.R. 622; *Sheffield & Horsham v. United Kingdom*, App. Nos. 22885/93 & 23390/94, (1999) 27 E.H.R.R. 163.

105. *I. v. United Kingdom*, App. No. 25680/94, (2003) 36 E.H.R.R. 53; *Goodwin v. United Kingdom*, App. No. 28957/95, (2002) 35 E.H.R.R. 18.

106. *Goodwin*, 35 Eur. H.R. Rep., para. 74.

107. When the U.K. government confiscated a book containing information on sexual matters for adolescents the question was whether this amounted to a violation of freedom of expression under Article 10 of the ECHR. In a unanimous decision the judges held that "By reason of their direct and continuous contact with the vital forces of their countries, State authorities are in principle in a better position than the international judge to give an opinion on the exact content of these requirements as well as on the 'necessity' of a 'restriction' or 'penalty' intended to meet them." *Handyside v. United Kingdom* (1979–80) 1 E.H.R.R. 737, para. 48; *Otto Preminger Institute v. Austria*, App. No. 13470/87 (1995) 19 E.H.R.R. 34; *Muller and others v. Switzerland*, App. No. 10737/84 (1991) 13 E.H.R.R. 212 (1991).

108. *Frette v. France*, App. No. 36515/97 (2004) 38 E.H.R.R. 21.

109. *Frette v. France*, para. 41.

110. R. St. J. Macdonald, "The Margin of Appreciation," in R. St.J. Macdonald, F. Matscher, and H. Petzold, eds., *The European System for the Protection of Human Rights* (Boston: M. Nijhoff, 1993), 712. Rabinder Singh, who noted sloppy use of the margin of appreciation in the European context: "The margin of appreciation is a conclusory label which only serves to obscure the true basis on which a reviewing court decides whether or not intervention in a particular case is justifiable. As such it tends to preclude courts from articulating the justification for and limits of their role as guardians of human rights in a democracy." Rabinder Singh, "Is There a Role for the 'Margin of Appreciation,'" in *National Law after the Human Rights Act?* (E.H.R.L.R., 1999), 1, 15–22.

111. Yuval Shany, "Towards a General Margin of Appreciation Doctrine in International Law," *Eur. J. Int'l L.* 16 (2005): 907 (citing Henkin, "That 'S' Word: Sovereignty, and Globalization, and Human Rights, et cetera," *Fordham L. Rev.* 7 (1999): 68).

Chapter 5

1. Press Release, "Human Rights Watch, Sharia Stoning for Nigerian Woman" (Aug. 20, 2002).

2. Press Release, "Human Rights Watch," 6.

3. Interview with Hawa Ibrahim in Atlanta, Ga. (Aug. 2004). In past years northern Nigerian states have increasingly applied sharia law to criminal cases and handed down sentences of amputation for theft and death by stoning for adultery. Moreover in 2002 a twenty-nine-year-old man became the first person in southern Nigeria to be punished under Islamic law when he was given 100 lashes for engaging in premarital sex. He was flogged before a crowd of hundreds in front of the main mosque in Ibadan, Oyo state.

4. Self-described republicans such as Michael Sandel place special emphasis upon the national political community and argue for measures that increase civic engagement

and public-spiritedness. Michael Sandel, *Democracy's Discontent: America In Search of a Public Policy* (Cambridge, Mass.: Belkap Press of Harvard University, 1996). There is increased recognition of the multinational nature of contemporary states, however. These political measures have been widely discussed in the recent literature on nationalism, citizenship, and multiculturalism. Will Kymlicka, *Muliculural Citizenship: Liberal Theory of Minority Rights* (New York: Clarendon Press, 1995); Stephen Macedo, *Diversity and Distrust: Civic Education in Multicultural Diversity* (Cambridge, Mass.: Harvard University Press, 2000); Yael Tamir, *Liberal Nationalism* (Princeton: Princeton University Press, 1993).

5. A. Glenn Mower, Jr., *Regional Human Rights: A Comparative Study of the West European and Inter-American Systems* (Westport, Conn.: Greenwood Press, 1991), 45–46, cited in Cecilia Naddeo, "Co-Adjudicating Human Rights Conflicts: The Supreme Court of Argentina and the Inter-American System of Human Rights" (Apr. 2007): 18; unpublished J.S.M. thesis, Stanford University (on file with author).

6. The court was established in 1998, and its charter allows individuals to take cases directly to it. European Court of Human Rights (ECHR), *Convention for the Protection of Human Rights and Fundamental Freedoms* as amended by Protocol 11 (Nov. 1, 1998), ETS No. 155, available at http://www.echr.coe.int/NR/rdonlyres/D5CC24A7–DC13–4318–B457–5C9014916D7A/0/EnglishAnglais.pdf. It replaced the European Commission of Human Rights, which was created in 1954, and a limited Court of Human Rights that was promulgated in 1959 to enforce the convention. *European Court of Human Rights, Historical Background,* http://www.echr.coe.int/ECHR/EN/Header/The+Court/The+Court/History+of+the+Court/; accessed Nov. 2, 2007.

7. The six original members signed the 1957 Treaty of Rome that created the European Economic Community (EEC) or "common market."

8. The jurisprudence of the European Court of Human Rights is also influencing the European Court of Justice (the latter adjudicates only cases between the twenty-seven member states of the EU) and has led to a lively debate on the inconsistencies between their judgments. Because of the growing importance of these issues for the EU, the European Union in 2007 established a new agency, the European Union Agency for Fundamental Rights. Its seat is in Vienna.

9. The Organization of American States has its own foundational charters and specialized human rights documents that are administered by the Inter-American Human Rights Commission and the Inter-American Human Rights Court. The commission has been hearing human rights disputes since 1965. It is staffed by seven commissioners drawn from all over the region, including the U.S. and Canada. In 2007, for example, the commissioners came from the U.S., Paraguay, Brazil, El Salvador, Antigua and Barbuda, Venezuela, and Argentina. The commission refers unresolved disputes to the court, and the docket of the court reflects an increasing number of cases over the past ten years.

10. Argentina, Barbados, Bolivia, Brazil, Chile, Colombia, Costa Rica, Dominican Republic, Ecuador, El Salvador, Guatemala, Haiti, Honduras, Mexico, Nicaragua, Panama, Paraguay, Peru, Suriname, Uruguay, and Venezuela.

11. Antigua and Barbuda, Bahamas, Belize, Canada, Cuba, Guyana, Saint Lucia,

Saint Kitts and Nevis, Saint Vincent and the Grenadines, Trinidad and Tobago, and the United States.

12. Dominica, Grenada, and Jamaica. Jamaica does accept the competence of the Inter-American Court on Human Rights to receive and examine communications in which a *state party* alleges that *another state* party has violated the human rights set forth in the convention. *American Convention on Human Rights*, art. 61 §1, Nov. 22, 1969, 1144 U.N.T.S. 123 (entered into force July 18, 1978).

13. The entire body of primary law of the inter-American system of human rights comprises the American Convention on Human Rights, its Protocol to Abolish the Death Penalty, and its Additional Protocol in the Area of Economic, Social and Cultural Rights (Protocol of San Salvador), as well as the Inter-American Convention to Prevent and Punish Torture, the Inter-American Convention on Forced Disappearance of Persons, the Inter-American Convention on the Prevention, Punishment and Eradication of Violence against Women (Convention of Belém do Pará), and the Inter-American Convention on the Elimination of All Forms of Discrimination against Persons with Disabilities.

14. "[*Ubuntu*] is a culture which places some emphasis on communality and on the interdependence of the members of a community. It recognizes a person's status as a human being, entitled to unconditional respect, dignity, value and acceptance from the members of the community of which such a person happens to be part. It also entails the converse, however. The person has a corresponding duty to give the same respect, dignity, value and acceptance to each member of that community. More important, it regulates the exercise of rights by the emphasis it lays on sharing and co-responsibility and the mutual enjoyment of rights by all." Christopher Roederer, "The Transformation of South African Private Law After Ten Years of Democracy: The Role of Torts (Delict) in the Consolidation of Democracy," *Colum. Hum. Rts. L. Rev.* 37 (2006): 447, 500 (citing Justices Mahomed and Mokgoron in *S. v. Makwanyane*, 1995 [3] SA 391 [CC]).

15. Abortions were made illegal in Ireland in 1861 under the British Offences Against the Persons Act of that year. The law continued in effect even after Irish independence in 1937.

16. U.N. Comm. on the Elimination of Discrimination against Women, *Fourth & Fifth Periodic Report*, U.N. Doc. CEDAW/C/IRL/CO/4–5 (July 22, 2005), available at http://daccessdds.un.org/doc/UNDOC/GEN/N03/409/07/PDF/N0340907.pdf?OpenElement.

17. *Attorney General v. X*, 1 I.R. 1 (1992), available at http://www.bailii.org/ie/cases/IESC/1992/1.html. This case involved a fourteen-year-old rape victim who had become pregnant and had sought, with the help of her parents, to travel to England to obtain an abortion. After one of her parents contacted the police to inquire whether some fetal tissue should be preserved as DNA evidence for the ongoing rape investigation, the attorney general responded by obtaining an injunction preventing the girl from traveling outside the country for a period of nine months. The family countered by presenting the girl's risk of suicide, which was evident to several witnesses who had heard suicidal remarks made by the girl. The Supreme Court held that abortion is permitted *within* Ire-

land when "it is established as a matter of probability that there is a real and substantial risk to the life, as distinct from the health, of the mother which can only be avoided by the termination of her pregnancy." *Attorney General v. X*, 37. It then follows that because the abortion was permissible in Ireland, it was also permissible for the girl to travel abroad to obtain one.

18. *Attorney General v. X*, 65.

19. *A. v. E. Health Bd.*, 1 I.L.R.M. 460 (1998) (H. Ct., Nov. 28, 1997) (Ir.). The High Court held that "the District Court may authorize travel for an abortion in circumstances where the proposed abortion would be permissible under Irish law, namely because continuation of pregnancy posed a real and substantial risk to the girl's life." It upheld a district court's ruling that the girl's psychiatric condition entitled her to an abortion *in* Ireland under Irish law and thus she was also entitled to travel abroad to obtain one: "the amended Constitution does not now confer a right to abortion outside of Ireland. It merely prevents injunctions against traveling for that purpose." *A. v. E. Health Bd.*, 15.

20. Other cases in the ECHR backlog challenge the Irish laws more directly. The court also refused to hear similar cases because they have not exhausted their legal avenues in Ireland. *D. v. Ireland*, App. No. 26499/02 (unpublished), http://www.reproductiverights.org/pdf/D.inadmissibility.pdf; accessed Sept. 29, 2007.

21. See *The Irish Times* Web site for the survey, http://scripts.ireland.com/polls/head2head/index.cfm?fuseaction=yesnopoll&pollid=7873&subsiteid=352; accessed Sept. 29, 2007.

22. The official figure is 45,000 since 1967, and in the 1990s it is alleged that between 1,500 and 10,000 women who stated in British hospital records that they were "Irish" sought abortions annually.

23. In *D. v. Ireland*, the ECHR found that a case filed by a woman who wished to travel to the U.K. to obtain an abortion of twins, one of which stopped developing at the age of eight weeks and the other suffering from severe chromosomal abnormality, could not be heard since the plaintiff did not exhaust her local remedies. The court found that the plaintiff should have obtained legal advice on those substantive and procedural uncertainties, and it issued a plenary summons allowing her to apply for an urgent, preliminary hearing in chambers to obtain the High Court's response to her timing and publicity concerns. It is true that it is assumed by the above that the applicant would continue during those steps an already advanced pregnancy.

24. *Tysiąc v. Poland*, App. No. 5410/03, para. 113 (unpublished), http://cmiskp.echr.coe.int/tkp197/viewhbkm.asp?action=open&table=F69A27FD8FB86142BF01C1166DEA398649&key=61401&sessionId=961717&skin=hudoc-en&attachment=true; accessed Sept. 29, 2007.

25. An Islamic religious group had sued the Bavarian state, claiming that the law is unconstitutional under the state constitution because it eliminated Muslim symbols from the classroom yet still allowed display of Christian and Jewish images. It sought to have the Bavarian Constitutional Court uphold a 2003 decision of the German Constitutional Court that had ruled that, under the laws at the time, a Muslim teacher had

the right to wear a headscarf in class. The German court had also ruled, however, that new laws banning the practice could be passed in German states in order to ensure an acceptable balance in law between religious freedom and neutrality in schools.

26. *Leyla Şahin v. Turkey*, ELR 198 (2004); *Leyla Şahin v. Turkey*, App. No. 44774/98 2005–XI Eur. Ct. H.R. 55.

27. *Kavakçı v. Turkey*, App. No. 71907/01 (2007), available at http://www.echr.coe .int/ECHR/EN/Header/Case-Law/HUDOC/HUDOC+database/ (in French).

28. Kavakçı is a dual citizen of Turkey and the U.S. "World: Middle East Citizenship Twist in Headscarf Row," BBC News, May 12, 1999, http://news.bbc.co.uk/2/hi/middle_east/342070.stm; accessed Oct. 13, 2008.

29. Naddeo, "Co-Adjudicating Human Rights Conflicts."

30. Naddeo, ibid., 16, notes, "A paramount example of a recalcitrant state [within the OAS] is . . . the United States. The . . . United States [position can be] summarized: 'With regard to each implication or direct assertion in the Commission's report that the American Declaration of the Rights and Duties of Man itself accords rights or imposes duties, some of which the United States has supposedly violated, the United States reminds the Commission that the Declaration is no more than a recommendation to the American States. Accordingly, the Declaration does *not* create legally-binding obligations and therefore *cannot* be "violated." ' " Response of the Government of the United States of America to the Inter-American Commission on Human Rights, Report 85/00 concerning Mariel Cubans (Case 9903), Summary of Response, at 2 (Oct. 23, 2000), available at http://www.cidh.org/Respuestas/USA.9903.htm.

31. *Villagran Morales v. Guatemala*, Inter-Am. C.H.R. (ser. C) No. 63 (Nov. 19, 1999).

32. Inter-American Court of Human Rights, http://www.corteidh.or.cr/docs/supervisiones/villagran_14_06_051.doc; accessed Feb. 12, 2008.

33. *Juridical Condition and Human Rights of the Child*, Inter-Am. Ct. H.R. (ser. 17.) Advisory Opinion OC-17/2002 (Aug. 28, 2002), available at http://www.corteidh.or.cr/docs/opiniones/seriea_17_ing.doc.

34. *Claude Reyes v. Chile*, Judgment of Sept. 19, 2006, Inter-Am. Ct. H.R. (ser. C) No. 151.

35. *Joint Statement Regarding the Chilean Access to Government-Held Information Bill*, Aug. 8, 2007, available at http://www.article19.org/pdfs/press/chile-foi-statement.pdf.

36. This case has been submitted to a "friendly settlement" under Article 41 of the Commission's Rules of Procedure. If a settlement is reached its terms will be published by the commission; conversely if a settlement is not reached, the commission will proceed to consider the admissibility of the petition in accordance with the American Convention.

37. Communication with a legal officer of the Supreme Court of the City of Buenos Aires on September 17, 2007 (on file with author).

38. *Ximenes Lopes v. Brazil*, Judgment of July 4, 2006, Inter-Am. Ct. H.R. (ser. C) No. 149.

39. See source description, http://www.inverso.org.br/index.php/content/view/ 15215.htm; accessed Nov. 4, 2007 (in Portuguese).

40. *Winston Caesar v. Trinidad and Tobago*, Inter-Am. Ct. H.R. (ser. C) No. 123, para. 73 (March 11, 2005).

41. *The Prosecutor v. Zejnil Delalic, Zdravko Mucic (aka "Pavo"), Hazim Delic, and Esad Landzo (aka "Zenga")* ("Celebici case"), Case Number IT-96-21-T, judgment of Nov. 16, 1998.

42. Inter-American Commission, *2006 Annual Report*, ¶718 (Mar. 3, 2007), available at http://www.cidh.oas.org/annualrep/2006eng/Chap.3w.htm.

43. *Case of Hilaire v. Trinidad and Tobago*, Preliminary Objections, Judgment of Sept. 1, 2001, Inter-Am. Ct. H.R. (ser. C) No. 80; *Case of Constantine et al. v. Trinidad and Tobago*, Preliminary Objections, Judgment of Sept. 1, 2001, Inter-Am. Ct. H.R. (ser. C) No. 82. *Case of Benjamin et al. v. Trinidad and Tobago*, Preliminary Objections, Judgment of Sept. 1, 2001, Inter-Am. Ct. H.R. (ser. C) No. 81. In these latter cases the Inter-American Court decided "if the current situation persists, to report on it to the General Assembly of the OAS, pursuant to Article 65 of the American Convention and Article 30 of the Statute of the Inter-American Court of Human Rights." *Hilaire, Constantine and Benjamin et al. v. Trinidad and Tobago* Case, Order on Compliance with Judgment, Order of Nov. 27, 2003, Inter-Am. Ct. H.R, available at http://www.corteidh.or.cr/docs/ supervisiones/hilaire_27_11_03_ing.doc.

44. Naddeo, "Co-Adjudicating Human Rights Conflicts," 6, cites Janet Koven Levit, "The Constitutionalization of Human Rights in Argentina: Problem or Promise?," *Colum. J. Transnat'l L.* 37 (1999): 288–92, and Thomas M. Franck and Arun K. Thiruvengadam, "International Law and Constitution-Making," *Chinese J. Int'l L.* 2 (2003): 467, 512–14. Moreover the impact of international and regional human rights law on Argentine domestic courts in the 1990s has been thoroughly covered in Martin Abregu and Christian Courtis, eds., *La aplicación de los tratados sobre derechos humanos por los tribunales locales* [The Adjudication of Human Rights Treaties by Domestic Courts] (Buenos Aires: CELS, Centro de Estudios Legales y Sociales, 1997); Victor Abramovich, Alberto Bovino, and Christian Courtis, eds., *La aplicación de los tratados de derechos humanos en el ámbito local. La experiencia de una decada (1994–2005)* [The Adjudication of Human Rights Treaties by Domestic Courts: The Experience of a Decade (1994–2005)] (Buenos Aires: CELS, Centro de Estudios Legales y Sociales, 2007).

45. Corte Suprema de Justicia de la Nación [CSJN], 7/7/1992, "Ekmekdjian, Miguel Angel c/ Sofovich, Gerardo y otros," Fallos 1992-315-1492. See, among other commentators, Holly Dawn Jarmul, "The Effects of Decisions of Regional Human Rights Tribunals on National Courts," *N.Y.U. J. Int'l. L. & Pol.* 28 (1996): 311, 327–28, and Thomas Buergenthal, "International Tribunals and National Courts: The Internalization of Domestic Adjudication," in *Recht zwischen Umbruch und Bewahrung: Völkerrecht, Europarecht, Staatsrecht: Festschrift für Rudolf Bernhardt* (Berlin and New York: Springer-Verlag, 1995), 688. These sources are cited in Naddeo, "Co-Adjudicating Human Rights Conflicts," 5.

46. Article 75, Section 22, of the Constitution of Argentina now states: "Congress

is empowered . . . to approve or reject treaties concluded with other nations and international organizations, and concordats with the Holy See. Treaties and concordats have a higher hierarchy than laws. The American Declaration on the Rights and Duties of Man; the Universal Declaration of Human Rights; the American Convention on Human Rights; the International Pact of Economic, Social and Cultural Rights; the International Pact on Civil and Political Rights and its empowering Protocol; the Convention on the Prevention of Genocide; the International Convention on the Elimination of all Forms of Racial Discrimination; the Convention on the Elimination of all Forms of Discrimination against Woman; the Convention against Torture and other Cruel, Inhuman or Degrading Treatments and Punishments; the Convention on the Rights of the Child; *in the full force of their provisions, they have constitutional hierarchy* [i.e. status], *do not repeal any section of the First Part of this Constitution and are to be understood as complementing the rights and guarantees recognized herein.* They shall only be denounced, in such event, by the National Executive Power after the approval of two-thirds of all the Members of each House." Const. Arg., Art. 75, §22 (translated by Cecilia Naddeo; emphasis added).

47. *The Prosecutor v. Hernán Javier Bramajo*, Supreme Court of Argentina, Case number 44.891, judgment of Sept. 12, 1996 (Fallos 1996-319-1840).

48. Corte Suprema de Justicia de la Nación [CSJN], 9/12/1996, "Bramajo, Hernán Javier s/ incidente de excarcelacion—causa numero 44.891—," Fallos 1996-319-1840.

49. *The Prosecutor v. Horacio David Giroldi*, Supreme Court of Argentina, Case number 32/93, judgment of July 4, 1995, *Fallos* 1995-318-514.

50. Corte Suprema de Justicia de la Nación [CSJN], 4/7/1995, "Giroldi, Horacio David y otros/recurso de causación—causa No. 32/93—," Fallos 1995-318-514.

51. Naddeo notes "the reduced number of cases in which the Inter-American Commission's jurisprudence was quoted as a guide to construe regional provisions seems to suggest that their arguably non-binding nature for the state concerned hinders its possible conception as a precedent *vis-à-vis* the jurisprudence of the Supreme Court of Argentina. Furthermore, while the Commission's published reports are the final decision on a case adjudicated at the regional level, its content remains subject to be challenged before the Inter-American Court in a subsequent similar case." Naddeo, "Co-Adjudicating Human Rights Conflicts," 85.

52. This tendency resembles the relatively recent increased number of contentious cases resolved by the Inter-American Court as compared to the number of advisory opinions rendered by the same judicial monitoring body.

53. Corte Suprema de Justicia de la Nación [CSJN], 9/20/2005, "Casal, Matías Eugenio y otros/robo simple—causa No. 1681—," Fallos 2005-328.

54. "Casal, Matías Eugenio y otros/robo simple," cited in Naddeo, "Co-Adjudicating Human Rights Conflicts," 72.

55. In this case Claudia Beatriz Acosta and twelve others received sentences of life in prison. These convictions were appealed by means of a special procedure before a criminal chamber. Once the initial appeals were rejected, the defendants' lawyer filed a second appeal directly to the Supreme Court of Argentina, which dismissed it on March

17, 1992. With domestic judicial remedies exhausted, the convicts petitioned the Inter-American Commission requesting, among other things, that Argentina be found responsible for breaching the American Convention by failing to guarantee them their right as criminal defendants to appeal their conviction to a higher court. In a first confidential report the Inter-American Commission agreed with the petitioners. In a second, public report the commission prompted Argentina "to take the most appropriate measures to repair the harm suffered by the persons" sentenced to prison pursuant to the state's obligation under Article 2 of the American Convention. Accordingly the successful petitioners initiated a habeas corpus procedure before a domestic court claiming that the regional monitoring body's report entitled them to immediate release from prison. The case again reached the Supreme Court of Argentina. The Supreme Court began by emphasizing the fact that Argentina has committed itself to comply only with the judgments issued by the Inter-American Court. The justices recalled that case law of the regional court may serve as a guide to ascertain the responsibilities undertaken by the state vis-à-vis the recommendations issued by the Inter-American Commission against Argentina. The justices read those comments as recognition of the nonbinding force of Inter-American Commission recommendations. Corte Suprema de Justicia de la Nación [CSJN], 12/22/1998, "Acosta, Claudia Beatriz y otros s/ habeas corpus," Fallos 1998-321-3555, ¶13, cited in Naddeo, "Co-Adjudicating Human Rights Conflicts," 7.

56. Clarence Dias, "Regional Human Rights Bodies," in *Human Rights Law Resources* (2001), available at http://www.austlii.edu.au/au/other/HRLRes/2001/15/.

57. ASEAN collectively denounced the Vietnamese invasion of Cambodia. Li-Ann Thio, "Implementing Human Rights in ASEAN Countries: Promises to Keep and Miles to Go Before I Sleep," *Yale Hum. Rts. & Dev. L.J.* 2 (1999): 1, 9.

58. Association of Southeast Asian Nations, *Overview: Association of Southeast Asian Nations*, http://www.aseansec.org/64.htm; accessed Oct. 29, 2007.

59. The ASEAN Security Community aims to ensure that countries in the region live at peace with one another and with the world in a just, democratic, and harmonious environment. Recognizing the interdependence of countries, the ASEAN Regional Forum (ARF) was established in 1994 to achieve this goal. The ARF agenda calls for the organization to evolve in three broad stages: the promotion of confidence-building, the development of preventive diplomacy, and the elaboration of approaches to conflicts. Current participants in the ARF include Australia, Bangladesh, Brunei Darussalam, Cambodia, Canada, China, European Union, India, Indonesia, Japan, Democratic People's Republic of Korea, Republic of Korea, Laos, Malaysia, Mongolia, Myanmar, New Zealand, Pakistan, Papua New Guinea, Philippines, Russian Federation, Singapore, Thailand, Timor Leste, United States, and Vietnam.

60. The ASEAN Economic Community aims at achieving economic integration; creating a stable, prosperous, and highly competitive ASEAN economic region in which there is a free flow of goods, services, investment, and a freer flow of capital; fostering equitable economic development; and reducing poverty and socioeconomic disparities by the year 2020. In this spirit the ASEAN Free Trade Area was launched in 1992, aiming to promote the region's competitive advantage as a single production unit.

61. The ASEAN Socio-Cultural Community, in consonance with the goal set by ASEAN Vision 2020, envisages a Southeast Asia bonded in partnership as a community of caring societies and founded on a common regional identity: "The Community shall foster cooperation in social development aimed at raising the standard of living of disadvantaged groups and the rural population, and shall seek the active involvement of all sectors of society, in particular women, youth, and local communities." In order to achieve these goals, ASEAN plans to adopt Work Programs on Social Welfare, Family, and Population; on HIV/AIDS; on Community-Based Care for the Elderly; and on Preparing ASEAN Youth for Sustainable Employment and Other Challenges of Globalization. ASEAN also plans to promote collaboration among seventeen member universities through the ASEAN university network, exchange programs, the annual ASEAN Culture Week, the ASEAN Youth Camp, and other measures.

62. Thio speculates that this was attributable to Myanmar being seen as less of a threat to regional stability. Thio, "Implementing Human Rights," 43.

63. Ibid., 45.

64. Ibid., 51.

65. Ibid., 51.

66. Eva Brems, *Human Rights: Universality and Diversity* (The Hague: Martinus Nijhoff Publishers, 2001), 80.

67. "The European Union believes trade with the countries in South East Asia has a promising future. Human rights questions, however, are throwing a wrench in attempts to improve political and economic relations." Martin Schrader, *Tackling Sour EU-ASEAN Relations* (Deutsche Welle, Oct. 3, 2005), http://www.dw-world.de/dw/article/0,1433,1514270,00.html; accessed Oct. 13, 2008.

68. Cited in Helen Stacy, "Western Triumphalism: The Crisis of Human Rights in the Global Era," *Macquarie U. L. Rev.* 2 (2002): 193.

69. Background information on AHRC can be found at http://www.alrc.net/doc/mainfile.php/background/2/; accessed June 15, 2007.

70. AHRC's regional scope covers Cambodia, India, Myanmar, South Korea, Indonesia, Malaysia, Australia, Bangladesh, Bhutan, Hong Kong, and Thailand. Daniel D. Bradlow, "Recent Development: Foreword: Hong Kong: Preserving Human Rights and the Rule of Law," *Am. U. J. Int'l L. & Pol'y* 12 (1997): 361, 421.

71. Seth R. Harris, "Recent Development: Asian Human Rights: Forming a Regional Covenant," *Asian-Pac. L. & Pol'y J.* 1 (2000): 17, 7.

72. The forum is composed of those independent national human rights organizations that are established in accordance with the Paris Principles. The Paris Principles require that an institution be guaranteed independence by statute or constitution; be pluralistic in membership; and possess autonomy from the government, broad membership based on universal human rights standards, adequate powers of investigation, and sufficient resources. For more information about the forum, see their Web site at http://www.asiapacificforum.net/about; accessed Nov. 4, 2007.

73. The Indonesian Human Rights Commission comprises three subcommissions that carry out five mandates. The Sub-Commission for Education and Public Aware-

ness is charged with informing the national and international communities about the "national and international concept of human rights"; in so doing, annual reports are made available to both the Indonesian president and the Indonesian people. The Sub-Commission for Monitoring the International Conventions on Human Rights makes recommendations on ratification of various human rights treaties. The Sub-Commission for Monitoring the Implementation of Human Rights critiques the performance of government agencies, provides a forum for the airing of individual grievances, and initiates investigations in its own right.

74. Thio, "Implementing Human Rights," 71.

75. Ibid., 67–68.

76. Ibid., 65–68.

77. OHCHR Regional Office for South-East Asia in Bangkok, *Work Plan 2006–2007*, available at http://www.un.or.th/ohchr/about/workplan.doc. Objectives and priorities have been set and a detailed list of activities has been defined. These activities include organizing workshops and meetings for relevant groups, establishing information collection systems, building channels of communication, developing national systems, creating working groups, providing and delivering training programs, and revising existing programming to include human rights issues. For an example of the content of human rights training conducted by the UN, see "Human Rights Training for the Police, Security & Army Personnel, U.N.," *Regional Seminar on Security Sector Reform in the National and Regional Contexts*, Phuket, Thailand (Sept. 1–2, 2006), available at http://www.parliament .go.th/ipuseminar/asset/PPT010.pdf?PHPSESSID=741664b621c16ed2400889df2abcca66.

78. "Working with governments, citizen groups, and local and international non-governmental organizations, the Asia Foundation promotes increased understanding and protection of human rights. The Foundation's approach is built on the premise that effective protection of human rights ultimately depends on accountable government, the rule of law, an informed and active public, and the increased opportunities that accompany economic growth." Asia Foundation, *Human Rights*, available at http://www .asiafoundation.org/Governance/humanrights.html; accessed Nov. 4, 2007.

79. The working group is a coalition of national working groups from ASEAN states, which are composed of representatives of government institutions, parliamentary human rights committees, academia, and NGOs. The working group follows a step-by-step, constructive, and consultative approach when it engages governments and other key players in the region. It strongly recommends the establishment of an inter-governmental human rights commission, and it submitted a Draft Agreement for the Establishment of the ASEAN Human Rights Commission to ASEAN officials in 2002. For more on the organization, see the Working Group Web site at http://aseanhrmech. org/aboutus.html; accessed June 15, 2007. For more on the Draft Agreement on the Establishment of the ASEAN Human Rights Commission, see http://aseanhrmech.org/ downloads/draft-agreement.pdf; accessed June 15, 2007.

80. *Working Group Statement on the ASEAN Foreign Ministers Consensus for a Human Rights Commission in the ASEAN Charter*, available at http://aseanhrmech.org/ news/statement-on-asean-foreign-ministers.html; accessed Oct. 29, 2007.

81. Thio, "Implementing Human Rights ia ASEAN Countries," 53.

82. Ibid., 56.

83. J. Oloka-Onyango, "Human Rights and Sustainable Development in Contemporary Africa: A New Dawn, or Retreating Horizons?," *Buff. Hum. Rts. L. Rev.* 6 (2000): 39, 44.

84. Ibid., 51.

85. Dinah Shelton, "Protecting Human Rights in a Globalized World," *B.C. Int'l & Comp. L. Rev.* 25 (2002): 273, 396, (citing "4 Nations Shedding Curbs on Executions," *Chicago Sun-Times*, July 5, 1998, 45). Shelton explains that the countries had planned to have Trinidad and Tobago as the seat of the new Caribbean court. "Trinidad and Tobago to be Centre for Caribbean Court," *Lawyer*, (Aug. 4, 1998): 36.

Chapter 6

1. Both the ICTR and ICTY presidents have been briefing the UN Security Council on their respective "completion strategies." The latest reports (S/2008/322 of May 13, 2008, and S/2008/326 of May 14, 2008, respectively) convey a more or less confident approach toward complying with the demands of UN Security Council Resolutions 1503 and 1534 but they anticipate delays of at least one year in both first and second (appeal) instances.

2. Since its creation the ICTR tried thirty-five people, and cases with regard to another twenty-seven suspects are ongoing in 2008. In the same year the ICTY still had another twenty-six individuals at trial, nine cases on appeal, and eleven individuals awaiting trial. Furthermore, three main suspects—Ratko Mladić, Goran Hadžić, and Stojan Župljanin—are still at large.

3. Kingsley Chiedu Moghalu, *Global Justice: The Politics of War Crimes Trials* (Stanford: Stanford University Press, 2008).

4. Alison Renteln argues for the "human right to culture" as a fundamental principle that inheres in such constitutional guarantees as equal protection, freedom of association and religion, the right to counsel, and the right to a fair trial. She supports the establishment of an official cultural defense in criminal law that would allow accused persons to introduce evidence concerning their culture and its relevance to their case. Renteln's principle is restricted to practices resulting in "irreparable harm" to others. Alison Dundes Renteln, *The Cultural Defense* (New York: Oxford University Press, 2004).

5. The Archbishop of Canterbury, Dr. Rowan Williams, James Callaghan Memorial lecture, "Religious Hatred and Religious Offence" (Jan. 29, 2008), delivered in the House of Lords.

6. Tariq Ramadan, *Western Muslims and the Future of Islam* (New York: Oxford University Press, 2004), 31.

7. Maleiha Malik, "Faith and the State of Jurisprudence," in Peter Oliver, Sionaidh Douglas-Scott, and Victor Tadros, eds., *Faith in Law. Essays in Legal Theory* (Oxford: Hart Publishing, 2000), 31.

Bibliography

Books and Articles

Álvarez, José E. "Crimes of States/Crimes of Hate: Lessons from Rwanda." *Yale J. Int'l L.* 24 (1999): 365.

———. "Do Liberal States Behave Better? A Critique of Slaughter's Liberal Theory." *Eur. J. Int'l L.* 12 (2001): 183.

———. "Seeking Legal Remedies for War Crimes: International versus National Trials." *J. Int'l Inst.* 6 (1998): 1.

———. "Who's Afraid of the 'New World Order'?" *Law Quad. Notes* 39 (1996): 40.

Anghie, Antony. *Imperialism, Sovereignty and the Making of International Law.* Cambridge: Cambridge University Press, 2005.

Anghie, Antony, and B. S. Chimni. "Third World Approach to International Law." *Chinese J. Int'l L.* 2 (2003): 77.

Arai-Takahashi, Yutaka. *The Margin of Appreciation Doctrine and the Principle of Proportionality in the Jurisprudence of the ECHR.* Ardsley, N.Y.: Transnational Publishers, 2002.

Bagwati, Jagdish. *In Defense of Globalization.* New York: Oxford University Press, 2004.

Bell, Daniel. *East Meets West: Human Rights and Democracy in East Asia.* Princeton: Princeton University Press, 2000.

Benhabib, Seylia, *The Claims of Culture: Equality and Diversity in the Global Era.* Princeton: Princeton University Press, 2002.

Bentham, Jeremy. *Nonsense upon Stilts* (1843). Reprinted in *The Collected Works of Jeremy Bentham: Rights, Representation, and Reform,* edited by Philip Schofield et al. Charlottesville, Va.: InteLex Corporation, 2000.

Betts, Wendy S., Scott N. Carlson, and Gregory Gisvold. "The Post-Conflict Transitional Administration of Kosovo and the Lessons-Learned in Efforts to Establish a Judiciary and Rule of Law." *Mich. J. Int'l L.* 22 (2001): 371.

Bodin, Jean. *The Six Bookes of a Common-weale.* Edited by Kenneth Douglas McRae. Translated by Richard Knolles. London: Adam Islip, 1606.

Brauch, Jeffrey A. "The Margin of Appreciation and the Jurisprudence of the European Court of Human Rights: Threat to the Rule of Law." *Colum. J. Eur. L.* 11 (2005): 115.

Brems, Eva. "Reconciling Universality and Diversity in International Human Rights Law." In *Human Rights with Modesty: The Problem of Universalism*, edited by András Sajó. Leiden and Boston: Martinus Nijhoff Publishers, 2004.

———. "Conflicting Human Rights: An Exploration in the Context of the Right to a Fair Trial in the European Convention for the Protection of Human Rights and Fundamental Freedoms." *Hum. Rts. Q.* 25 (2005): 294.

———. "Indirect Protection of Social Rights by the European Court of Human Rights." In *Exploring Social Rights: Between Theory and Practice*, edited by Daphne Barak-Erez and Acyal M. Gross. Oxford: Hart Publishing, 2007.

———. *Human Rights: Universality and Diversity.* The Hague: Martinus Nijhoff Publishers, 2001.

Brownlie, Ian. *International Law and the Use of Force by States.* Oxford: Clarendon Press, 1963.

Buchanan, Allen. *Justice, Legitimacy and Self Determination.* Oxford: Oxford University Press, 2003.

Buchanan, Allen, and Robert O. Keohane. "The Legitimacy of Global Governance Institutions." *Ethics & Int'l Aff.* (2006): 405.

Buchanan, Allen, and Margaret Moore, eds. *State, Nations, and Borders.* Cambridge: Cambridge University Press, 2003.

———. "International Human Rights Law and the Politics of Legitimacy: Repressive States and Human Rights Treaties." *International Sociology* 23 (1) (2008): 115.

Carter, Barry E., Phillip R. Trimble, and Allen S. Weiner. *International Law.* 5th ed. New York: Aspen Publishers, 2007.

Chayes, Abraham, and Antonia Handler Chayes. "On Compliance." *Int'l Org.* 47 (1993): 175.

Cole, Wade M. "Sovereignty Relinquished? Explaining Commitment to the International Human Rights 1966–1999." *Am. Soc. Rev.* 70 (2005): 472.

Cottier, Thomas, Joost Pauwelyn, and Elisabeth Bürgi. "Linking Trade Regulation and Human Rights in International Law: An Overview." In *Human Rights and International Trade*, edited by Thomas Cottier, Joost Pauwelyn, and Elisabeth Bürgi. New York: Oxford University Press, 2005.

Damrosch, Lori F. "Commentary on Collective Military Intervention to Enforce Human Rights." In *Law and Force in the New International Order*, edited by Lori F. Damrosch and David J. Scheffler. Boulder, Colo.: Westview Press, 1991.

———. *Enforcing International Law Through Non-Forcible Measures.* Collected Courses of The Hague Academy of International Law (1997): 269.

———. *Enforcing Restraint: Collective Intervention in Internal Conflicts.* New York: Council on Foreign Relations Press, 1993.

Delanty, Gerard. *Inventing Europe: Idea, Identity, Reality.* Basingstoke, UK: Macmillan, 1995.

Dezalay, Yves, and Bryant G. Garth, eds. *Global Prescriptions: The Production, Exportation, and Importation of a New Legal Orthodoxy.* Ann Arbor: University of Michigan Press, 2002.

Dicey, Albert Venn. *Introduction to the Study of the Law of the Constitution.* London: Macmillan and Co., 1908.

———. "Note and Comment: The Promise of Hybrid Courts." *Am. J. Int'l L.* 97 (2003): 295.

Dickinson, Laura. "The Relationship Between Hybrid Courts and International Courts: The Case of Kosovo." *New Eng. L. Rev.* 37 (2003): 1059.

Diller, Janelle M., and David A. Levy. "Child Labor, Trade and Investment: Toward the Harmonization of International Law." *Am. J. Int'l L.* 91 (1997): 663.

Donnelly, Jack. "Human Rights, Democracy, and Development." *Hum. Rts. Q.* 21 (1999): 608.

———. *International Human Rights.* 3rd ed. Boulder, Colo.: Westview Press, 2006.

Drexler, Elizabeth F. *Aceh, Indonesia: Securing the Insecure State.* Philadelphia: University of Pennsylvania Press, 2008.

D'Souza, Dinesh. *The End of Racism.* New York: Free Press, 1995.

Dworkin, Ronald. *A Matter of Principle.* Cambridge, Mass.: Harvard University Press, 1985.

Ehrenberg, Daniel S. "The Labor Link: Applying the International Trading System to Enforce Violations of Forced and Child Labor." *Yale J. Int'l L.* 20 (1995): 361.

Eizenstat, Stuart E., John Edward Porter, and Jeremy M. Weinstein. "Rebuilding Weak States." *Foreign Aff.* (Jan.–Feb. 2005): 135.

Evans, Tony. *The Politics of Human Rights: A Global Perspective.* London: Pluto Press, 2001.

Falk, Richard. *Human Rights Horizons: The Pursuit of Justice in a Globalizing World.* New York: Routledge, 2000.

Finnemore, Martha. *The Purpose of Intervention: Changing Beliefs About the Use of Force.* New York: Cornell University Press, 2003.

———. "Institutional Organizations as Teachers of Norms: The United Nations Educational, Scientific, and Cultural Organization and Science Policy." *Int'l Org.* 47 (1993): 565.

———. *National Interests in International Society.* New York: Cornell University Press, 1996.

Finnemore, Martha, and Michael N. Barnett. *Rules for the World: International Organizations in Global Politics.* Ithaca, N.Y.: Cornell University Press, 2004.

Fox, Gregory H. "Comment on Sovereign Equality." In *United States Hegemony and the Foundations of International Law*, edited by Michael Byers and Georg Nolte. Cambridge: Cambridge University Press, 2003.

———. "Strengthening the State." *Indian Journal of Global Legal Studies* 7(1999): 35.

———. "The ICJ's Decision in *Bosnia and Herzegovina v. Serbia and Montenegro.*" *Am. Soc. Int'l L. Newsl.* (Am. Soc. Int'l L., Washington, D.C.), spring 2007.

Fox, Gregory H., and Brad R. Roth, eds. *Democratic Governance and International Law.* Cambridge: Cambridge University Press, 2000.

———. "Democracy and International Law." *Review of International Studies* 27 (2001): 327.

Franck, Thomas M. "The Emerging Right to Democratic Governance." *Am. J. Int'l L.* 86 (1992).

———. *Fairness in International Law and Institutions.* New York: Oxford University Press, 1995.

Gentili, Alberico. *De Iure Belli Libri Tres: On Defending the Subjects of Another Against Their Sovereign.* Translated by John C. Rolfe. Oxford: Clarendon Press, 1933.

Glendon, Mary Ann. *A World Made New: Eleanor Roosevelt and the Universal Declaration of Human Rights.* New York: Random House, 2001.

Goldsmith, Jack L., and Eric A. Posner. *The Limits of International Law.* New York: Oxford University Press, 2005.

Goodman, Ryan. "The Difference Law Makes: Research Design, Institutional Design, and Human Rights." *Am. Soc. Int'l L. Proc.* 98 (2004): 198.

Goodman, Ryan, and Derek Jinks. "How to Influence States: Socialization and International Human Rights Law." *Duke L. J.* 54 (2004): 621.

———. "International Institutions and the Mechanisms of War." *Am. J. Int'l L.* 99 (2005): 507.

———. "International Law and State Socialization: Conceptual, Empirical and Normative Challenge." *Duke L. J.* 54(2005): 983.

———. "Measuring the Effects of Human Rights Treaties." *Eur. J. Int'l Law.* 13 (2003): 171.

Gross, Leo. "The Peace of Westphalia 1648–1948." *Am. J. Int'l L.* 42 (1948): 20.

Gourevitch, Victor, ed. and trans. *Rousseau: "The Discourses" and Other Political Writings.* Cambridge: Cambridge University Press, 1997.

Gutmann, Amy, and Dennis Thompson. *Democracy and Disagreement.* Cambridge: Belknap Press, 1998.

Habermas, Jürgen. *The Theory of Communicative Action.* Translated by Thomas McCarthy. Boston: Beacon Press, 1984.

———. *Between Facts and Norms: Contributions to a Discourse Theory of Law and Democracy.* Translated by William Rehg. Cambridge, Mass.: MIT Press, 1996.

———. "Interpreting the Fall of a Monument." *German L. J.* 4 (2003): 701.

Hafner-Burton, Emilie, Kiyoteru Tsutsui, and John Meyer, "International Human Rights Law and the Policy of Legitimacy: Repressive States and Human Rights Treaties." *International Sociology* 23:1 (2008): 115–41.

Hamilton, Alexander, James Madison, and John Jay. *The Federalist: With Letters of "Brutus."* Edited by Terence Ball. Cambridge: Cambridge University Press, 2003.

Hardin, Russel. "Group Boundaries, Individual Barriers." In *Boundaries, Ownership, and Autonomy: Diverse Ethical Perspectives,* edited by Terry Nardin and David Miller. Princeton: Princeton University Press, 2000.

Hardt, Michael, and Antonio Negri. *Empire.* Cambridge, Mass.: Harvard University Press, 2001.

Hathaway, Oona. "Do Human Rights Treaties Make a Difference?" *Yale L. J.* 111 (2002): 1935.

Hathaway, Oona, and A. Lavinbuk. "Rationalism and Revisionism in International Law." *Harv. L. Rev.* 119 (2006): 1404.

———. "Making Human Rights Treaties Work: Global Legal Information & Human Rights in the 21st Century." *Int'l J. Legal Info.* 31(2003): 312.

———. "Between Power and Principle: A Political Theory of International Law." *U. Chi. L. Rev.* 72(2005): 469.

———. "The Cost of Commitment." *Stan. L. Rev.* 55(2003): 1821.

Helfer, Laurence R., and Anne-Marie Slaughter. "Toward a Theory of Effective Supranational Adjudication." *Yale L. J.* 107 (1997): 273.

———. *The Age of Rights.* New York: Columbia University Press, 1990.

———. "Human Rights and State 'Sovereignty.'" *Ga. J. Int'l & Comp. L.* 25 (1995): 31.

———. "That 'S' Word: Sovereignty, and Globalization, and Human Rights, et cetera." *Fordham L. Rev.* 7 (1999): 68.

Hobbes, Thomas. *Leviathan.* 1651. Reprint, Indianapolis: Bobbs-Merrill, 1958.

Honig, Bonnie. "My Culture Made Me Do It." In *Is Multiculturalism Bad for Women?*, edited by Joshua Cohen, Matthew Howard, and Martha C. Nussbaum. Princeton: Princeton University Press, 1999.

Ignatieff, Michael. *Human Rights as Politics and Idolatry.* Princeton: Princeton University Press, 2001.

Ishay, Micheline R. *The History of Human Rights: From Ancient Times to the Globalization Era.* Berkeley: University of California Press, 2004.

Jackson, John H. "Sovereignty-Modern: A New Approach to an Outdated Concept." *Am. J. Int'l L.* 97 (2003): 781.

———. *The World Trade Organization: Constitution and Jurisprudence.* Chatham House Papers. London: Royal Institute for International Affairs, 1998.

Jackson, Robert. *The Global Covenant: Human Conduct in a World of States.* Oxford: Oxford University Press, 2000.

Kant, Immanuel. "Critique of Judgment." In *Toward Perpetual Peace and Other Political Writings on Politics, Peace, and History*, edited by Pauline Kleingeld. Translated by David L. Colclasure. New Haven: Yale University Press, 2006.

———. "Idea for a Universal History with a Cosmopolitan Purpose." In *Kant's Political Writings*, edited by Hans Reiss. Translated by H. B. Nisbet. Cambridge: Cambridge University Press, 1970.

———. "Perpetual Peace." In *Kant's Political Writings*, edited by Hans Reiss. Translated by H. B. Nisbet. Cambridge: Cambridge University Press, 1970.

———. *Perpetual Peace.* Filiquarian Publishing, 2007.

———. *Metaphysical Elements of Justice: Part One of the Metaphysics of Morals.* 2d ed. Translated by John Ladd. Indianapolis: Hackett Publishing Co., 1999.

Khagram, Sanjeev, James V. Riker, and Kathryn Sikkink, eds. *Restructuring World Politics— Transnational Social Movements, Networks, and Norms.* Minneapolis: University of Minnesota Press, 2002.

Koh, Harold Hongju. "A United States Human Rights Policy for the 21st Century." *St. Louis L. J.* 46 (2002): 293.

———. "The Globalization of Freedom." *Yale J. Int'l L.* 26 (2001): 305.

Koskenniemi, Marti. *The Gentle Civilizer of Nations: The Rise and Fall of International Law, 1870–1960.* Cambridge: Cambridge University Press, 2004.

———. *From Apology to Utopia: The Structure of International Legal Argument.* Cambridge: Cambridge University Press, 2005.

Krasner, Steven D. *Sovereignty: Organized Hypocrisy.* Princeton: Princeton University Press, 1999.

Kukathas, Chandran. "Are There Any Cultural Rights?" *Pol. Theory* 20 (1992): 105.

Kymlicka, Will. *Multiculural Citizenship: Liberal Theory of Minority Rights.* New York: Clarendon Press, 1995.

Lauterpacht, Hersch. *International Law and Human Rights.* New York: Frederick Praeger, 1950.

———. "States as Subjects of International Law." In *International Law: Being the Collected Papers of Hersch Lauterpacht*, edited by Elihu Lauterpacht. Cambridge: University Press, 1977.

———. "The League of Nations." In *International Law: Being the Collected Papers of Hersch Lauterpacht*, edited by Elihu Lauterpacht. Cambridge: Cambridge University Press, 1977.

Lerner, Natan. "International Law and Religion: How Wide the Margin of Appreciation? The Turkish Headscarf Case, the Strasburg Court, and Secularist Tolerance." *Willamette J. Int'l L. & Disp. Resol.* 13 (2005): 65.

Letsas, George. "Two Concepts of the Margin of Appreciation." *Oxford J. Legal Stud.* 26 (2006): 706.

Levit, Janet Koven. "The Constitutionalization of Human Rights in Argentina: Problem or Promise?" *Colum. J. Transnat'l L.* 37 (1999): 288.

Locke, John. "The Social Contract." In *Special Contract: Essays by Locke, Hume and Rousseau*, edited by E. Barker, J. Locke, D. Hume, and J. Rousseau. London: Oxford University Press, 1948.

MacCormick, Neil. *Questioning Sovereignty.* Oxford: Oxford University Press, 2001.

Meyer, John W. "World Models, National Curricula, and the Centrality of the Individual." In *School Knowledge in Comparative and Historical Perspective*, edited by Aaron Benovat and Cecilia Braslavsky. Hong Kong: Springer, 2006.

Meyer, John, and Gili S. Drori. "Scientization: Making a World Sage for Organizing." In *Transnational Governance: Institutional Dynamics of Regulation*, edited by Marie-Laure Djelic and Kerstin Sahlin-Andersson. Cambridge: Cambridge University Press, 2006.

Meyer, John, Gili S. Drori, and Hokyu Hwang. *Globalization and Organization.* Oxford: Oxford University Press, 2006.

Minow, Martha. *Breaking The Cycles of Hatred.* Princeton: Princeton University Press, 2002.

Montesquieu, Charles de. *The Spirit of the Laws*. 1748, published anonymously. Reprint, Kitchener, Ont.: Batoche, 2001.

Morgan, Lewis H. *Ancient Society*. New York: Henry Holt and Company, 1907.

Morgan, Martha. "Taking Machismo to Court: The Gender Jurisprudence of the Colombian Constitutional Court." *U. Miami Inter-Am. L. Rev.* 30 (1999): 253.

Mouffe, Chantal, ed. *The Challenge of Carl Schmitt*. New York: Verso, 1999.

Mower, A. Glenn. *Regional Human Rights: A Comparative Study of the West European and Inter-American Systems*. New York: Greenwood Press, 1991.

Mutua, Makau. "Savages, Victims and Saviors: The Metaphor of Human Rights." *Harv. Int'l L. J.* 42 (2001): 201.

Naddeo, Cecilia. "Co-Adjudicating Human Rights Conflicts: The Supreme Court of Argentina and the Inter-American System of Human Rights." J.S.M. thesis, Stanford University, 2007.

Oloka-Onyango, J. "Human Rights and Sustainable Development in Contemporary Africa: A New Dawn, or Retreating Horizons?" *Buff. Hum. Rts. L. Rev.* 6 (2000): 39.

Philpott, Daniel. *Revolutions in Sovereignty*. Princeton: Princeton University Press, 2001.

Popper, Karl. *The Logic of Scientific Discovery*. New York: Routledge 1977.

Proudhon, Pierre. *Recherches sur la constitution du droit des gens*. New York: Garland Publishers, 1972.

Pufendorf, Samuel. *De Jure Naturae et Gentium Libri Octo*. Oxford: Clarendon Press, 1934.

Rawls, John. *The Law of Peoples*. Cambridge: Harvard University Press, 1999.

Reisman, Michael. "Why Regime Change Is (Almost Always) a Bad Idea." *Am. J. Int'l L.* 98 (2004): 516.

———. "Sovereignty and Human Rights in Contemporary International Law." *Am. J. Int'l L.* 84 (1990): 866.

Reiss, Hans, ed. *Kant's Political Writings*. Translated by H. B. Nisbet. Cambridge: Cambridge University Press, 1970.

Renteln, Alison Dundes. *The Cultural Defense*. New York: Oxford University Press, 2004.

Rousseau, Jean-Jacques. *Rousseau: "The Discourses" and Other Early Political Writings*. Edited and translated by Victor Gourevitch. Cambridge: Cambridge University Press, 1997.

Said, Edward. *Culture and Imperialism*. New York: Knopf, 1993.

Sandel, Michael. *Democracy's Discontent: America in Search of a Public Policy*. Cambridge, Mass.: Belknap Press of Harvard University, 1996.

———. *Public Philosophy: Essays on Morality in Politics*. Cambridge, Mass.: Harvard University Press, 2005.

Sassen, Saskia. *A Sociology of Globalization*. 1st ed. New York: W.W. Corton, 2007.

———. *Losing Control? Sovereignty in an Age of Globalization*. New York: Columbia University Press, 1996.

————. *Territory, Authority, Rights: From Medieval to Global Assemblages*. Princeton: Princeton University Press, 2006.

Sen, Amartya. *Development as Freedom*. New York: Anchor Books, 1999.

Shany, Yuval. "Towards a General Margin of Appreciation Doctrine in International Law." *Eur. J. Int'l L.* 16 (2005): 907.

Sharkh, Miriam Abu. "History and Results of Labor Standard Initiatives, An Event History and Panel Analysis of the Ratification Patterns, and Effects, of the International Labor Organization's First Child Labor Convention." Ph.D. dissertation, Freie Universität Berlin, 2002.

————. "Time Bound Programmes: A Review of Experiences and Lessons Learned." IPEC, ILO, 2006.

Shelton, Dinah. "International Human Rights Law: Principled, Double, or Absent Standards?" Symposium on Law and Inequality: The Next 25 Years. *Law & Inequality* 25 (2007) 467.

————. "Protecting Human Rights in a Globalized World." *B.C. Int'l & Comp. L. Rev.* 25 (2002): 273.

————. *Regional Protection of Human Rights*. Oxford: Oxford University Press, 2008.

Shelton, Dinah, Richard B. Lillich, Hurst Hannum, and S. James Anaya. *International Human Rights: Problems of Law, Policy and Practice*. 4th ed. New York: Aspen, 2006.

Simmons, Beth A. "International Law and State Behavior: Commitment and Compliance in International Monetary Affairs." *Am. Pol. Sci. Rev.* 94 (2000): 819.

Simmons, Beth A., and Lisa L. Martin. "International Organizations and Institutions." In *Handbook of International Relations*, edited by Walter Carlsnaes, Thomas Risse, and Beth A. Simmons. London: Sage Publications, 2002.

Slaughter, Anne-Marie. "Agora: Breard: Court to Court." *Am. J. Int'l L.* 92 (1998): 708.

————. "Judicial Globalization." *Va. J. Int'l L.* 40 (2000): 1103.

————. *A New World Order*. Princeton: Princeton University Press, 2004.

Slaughter, Anne-Marie, and William Burke-White. "An International Constitutional Moment." *Harv. Int'l L. J.* 43 (2002): 1.

————. "Judicial Globalization." *Va. J. Int'l L.* 40 (2000): 1103.

Smith, Adam. "Theory of Moral Sentiments." In *Adam Smith: Selected Philosophical Writings*, edited by James R. Otteson. Exeter: Imprint Academic, 2004.

Smolin, D.M. "Conflict and Ideology in the International Campaign Against Child Labor." *Hofstra Lab. & Emp. L. J.* 16 (1999): 383.

Spivak, Gayatri. *The Postcolonial Critic: Interviews, Strategies, Dialogues*, edited by Sarah Harasym. New York: Routledge, 1990.

Stanley, Stephen Macedo. *Diversity and Distrust: Civic Education in Multicultural Diversity*. Cambridge, Mass.: Harvard University Press, 2000.

Stevenson, Benjamin James. "Pursuing an End to Foreign Child Labor Through U.S. Trade Law: WTO Challenges and Doctrinal Solutions." *UCLA J. Int'l l. & For. Aff.* 7 (2002): 129.

Stiglitz, Joseph E., *Globalization and Its Discontents*. New York: W.W. Norton & Company, 2002.

Strayer, Joseph Reese. *On the Medieval Origins of the Modern State*. Princeton: Princeton University Press, 1970.

Tamir, Yael. *Liberal Nationalism*. Princeton: Princeton University Press, 1993.

Taylor, Charles. "Conditions of an Unforced Consensus on Human Rights." In *The East Asian Challenge for Human Rights*, edited by J. R. Bauer and D. Bell. Cambridge: Cambridge University Press, 1999.

Teitel, Ruti G. "Transitional Justice Genealogy." *Harv. Hum. Rts. J.* 16 (2003): 69.

Teson, Fernando, and Guido Pincione. *Rational Choice and Democratic Deliberation: A Theory of Discourse Failure*. Cambridge: Cambridge University Press, 2006.

Tesón, Fernando R. *A Philosophy of International Law*. Boulder, Colo.: Westview Press, 1998.

———. *Humanitarian Intervention: An Inquiry into Law and Morality*. Irvington-on-Hudson, N.Y.: Transnational Publishers, 1997.

Thio, Li-Ann. "Implementing Human Rights in ASEAN Countries: Promises to Keep and Miles to Go Before I Sleep." *Yale Hum. Rts. & Dev. L. J.* (1999): 2.

Vattel, Emmerich de. *The Law of Nations*. Translated by Charles G. Fenwick. Washington, D.C.: Carnegie Institution of Washington, 1916.

Vitoria, Francisco de. *De Indis et De ivre belli relectiones*. Washington, D.C.: Carnegie Institution of Washington, 1917.

Wagner, Margaret, and Paul Finkelman. *The Library of Congress Civil War Desk Reference*. New York: Simon & Schuster, 2002.

Weinstein, Jeremy. "Autonomous Recovery and International Intervention in Comparative Perspective." Working Paper 57. Washington, D.C.: Centre for Global Development, 2005.

———. *Inside Rebellion: The Politics of Insurgent Violence*. Cambridge: Cambridge University Press, 2007.

Wolff, Christian Von. *The Law of Nations Treated According to a Scientific Method*. Translated by Joseph H. Drake. New York: Oceana, 1964.

Yourow, Howard C. "The Margin of Appreciation Doctrine in the Dynamics of European Human Rights Jurisprudence." *Conn. J. Int'l L.* 3 (1987): 111.

Zakaria, Fareed. "Culture Is Destiny: A Conversation with Lee Kuan Yew." *Foreign Aff.* 73 (1994): 109–26.

Žižek, Slavoj. "Critical Responses—A Symptom—Of What?" *Critical Inquiry* 29 (2003): 499.

Cases and Treaties

Advisory Proceedings on the Legal Consequences for States of the Continued Presence of South Africa in Namibia (South West Africa) Notwithstanding Security Council Resolution 276 (1970), 1970 I.C.J. Pleadings 639–40, 644, 672, 678–97 (Aug. 5).

Agreement Establishing the World Trade Organization, April 15, 1994, 33 I.L.M. 1144 (entered into force Jan. 1, 1995).

American Convention on Human Rights, Nov. 22, 1969, 1144 U.N.T.S. 123 (entered into force July 18, 1978).

Arrest Warrant of 11 April 2000 (*Democratic Republic of the Congo v. Belgium*), judgment of Feb. 14, 2002.

Avena and Other Mexican Nationals (*Mex. v. U.S.*), 43 I.L.M. 581 (2004).

Chrysostomos, Papachrysostomou & Loizidou v. Turkey, App. Nos. 15299/89, 15300/89 & 15318/89, 68 Eur. Comm'n H.R. Dec. & Rep. 216, 242 (1991).

Code Napoleon; or, The French Civil Code. Literally Translated from the Original and Official Edition, Published at Paris, in 1804. By a Barrister of the Inner Temple. Translated by George Spence. London: William Benning, Law Bookseller, 1827.

Commonwealth of Australia. *Report of the National Inquiry into the Separation of Aboriginal and Torres Straight Islander Children from Their Families.* 1997.

Continental Shelf (Libyan Arab Jamahiriya/Malta), Application for Permission to Intervene by Italy, 1984 I.C.J. 3 (Judgment of June 3).

Continental Shelf (Tunisia/Libyan Arab Jamahiriya), Application for Permission to Intervene by Malta, 1981 I.C.J. 3 (Judgment of April 14).

Convention for the Protection of Human Rights and Fundamental Freedoms, as amended by Protocol 11 (Nov. 1, 1998), ETS No. 155.

Convention Revising the General Act of Berlin, Feb. 26, 1885, and the *General Act and Declaration of Brussels*, July 2, 1890.

Cossey v. United Kingdom, App. No. 10843/84, (1991) 13 E.H.R.R. 622.

D. K. Basu v. State of West Bengal, AIR 1997 SC 610.

De Wilde, Ooms & Versyp v. Belgium (Vagrancy Case) (1979–80) 1 E.H.R.R. 373.

Filártiga v. Peña-Irala, 630 F.2d 876, 884 (2d Cir. 1980).

Frette v. France, App. No. 36515/97, (2004) 38 E.H.R.R. 21.

General Agreement on Tariffs and Trade, Oct. 30, 1947, 61 Stat. A-11, 55 U.N.T.S. 194.

Geneva Convention for the Amelioration of the Condition of the Wounded and Sick in Armed Forces in the Field, Aug. 12, 1949, 6 U.S.T. 3114, 75 U.N.T.S. 31.

Geneva Convention for the Amelioration of the Condition of the Wounded, Sick and Shipwrecked Members of Armed Forces at Sea, Aug. 12, 1949, 6 U.S.T. 3217, 75 U.N.T.S. 85.

Geneva Convention Relative to the Protection of Civilian Persons in Time of War, Aug. 12, 1949, 6 U.S.T. 3516, 75 U.N.T.S. 287.

Geneva Convention Relative to the Treatment of Prisoners of War, Aug. 12, 1949, 6 U.S.T. 3316, 75 U.N.T.S. 135;

Goodwin v. United Kingdom, App. No. 28957/95, (2002) 35 E.H.R.R. 18.

Handyside v. United Kingdom, (1979–80) 1 E.H.R.R. 737.

Hartford Fire Ins. Co. v. California, 509 U.S. 764, 817 (1993) (Scalia, J., dissenting).

Human Rights Watch. "Justice in Motion: The Trial Phase of the Special Court for Sierra Leone" (2005), available at http://www.hrw.org/reports/2005/sierraleone1105/.

Human Rights Watch. "Protectors or Pretenders? Government Human Rights Commissions in Africa." Benin, 2001.

I v. United Kingdom, App. No. 25680/94, (2003) 36 E.H.R.R. 53.

I/A Court H.R., Case of Benjamin et al. v. Trinidad and Tobago. Preliminary Objections. Judgment of Sept. 1, 2001, Series C No. 81.

I/A Court H.R., Case of Caesar v. Trinidad and Tobago. Merits, Reparations and Costs. Judgment of March 11, 2005. Series C No. 123.

I/A Court H.R., Case of Claude Reyes v. Chile. Merits, Reparations and Costs. Judgment of Sept. 19, 2006. Series C No. 151.

I/A Court H.R., Case of Constantine et al. v. Trinidad and Tobago. Preliminary Objections. Judgment of Sept. 1, 2001. Series C No. 82.

I/A Court H.R., Case of Hilaire, Constantine and Benjamin et al. v. Trinidad and Tobago. Monitoring Compliance with Judgment. Order of the Inter-American Court of Human Rights of Nov. 27, 2003.

I/A Court H.R., Case of Hilaire v. Trinidad and Tobago. Preliminary Objections. Judgment of Sept. 1, 2001. Series C No. 80.

I/A Court H.R., Case of the "Street Children" (Villagrán-Morales et al.) v. Guatemala. Merits. Judgment of Nov. 19, 1999. Series C No. 63.

I/A Court H.R., Case of Ximenes Lopes v. Brazil. Merits, Reparations and Costs. Judgment of July 4, 2006. Series C No. 149.

Independent International Commission on Kosovo. *The Kosovo Report: Conflict, International Response, Lessons Learned.* 2000.

International Covenant on Civil and Political Rights, G.A. res. 2200A (XXI), 21 U.N. GAOR Supp. (No. 16) at 52, U.N. Doc. A/6316 (1966), 999 U.N.T.S. 171 (entered into force March 23, 1976).

International Covenant on Economic, Social and Cultural Rights, G.A. res. 2200A (XXI), 21 U.N. GAOR Supp. (No. 16) at 49, U.N. Doc. A/6316 (1966), 993 U.N.T.S. 3 (entered into force Jan. 3, 1976).

International Status of South West Africa, Advisory Opinion, 1950 I.C.J. Pleadings 324 (July 11).

Juridical Condition and Human Rights of the Child, Inter-Am. Ct. H.R. (ser. 17.) Advisory Opinion OC-17/2002 (Aug. 28, 2002).

Karen Noelia Llantoy Huamán v. Perú. Communication No. 1153/2003, U.N. Doc. CCPR/C/85/2003 (2005).

Kavakçı v. Turkey, App. No. 71907/01, (2007).

Land and Maritime Boundary between Cameroon and Nigeria (*Cameroon v. Nig.*), 1999 I.C.J. 275 (Order of Oct. 21).

Land and Maritime Boundary between Cameroon and Nigeria (*Cameroon v. Nig.*), 1999 I.C.J. 101 (March 25).

Land, Island and Maritime Frontier Dispute (*El Sal. v. Hond.*), Application for Permission to Intervene, 1990 I.C.J. 3 (Order of Feb. 28).

Lawrence v. Texas, 539 U.S. 558 (2003).

Legality of the Use by a State on Nuclear Weapons in Armed Conflict, Advisory Opinion, 1996 I.C.J. 226 (July 8).

Leyla Şahin v. Turkey, App. No. 44774/98, European Court of Human Rights, judgment of June 29, 2004.

Liberia. *Report to the U.N. Committee to the Convention on the Rights of the Child.* 2002.

Mabo v. State of Queensland (1992), 107 ALR 1.

Miguel Ángel Ekmekdjian v. Gerardo Sofovich et al., Supreme Court of Argentina, judgment of July 7, 1992 (Fallos 1992–315–1492).

Military and Paramilitary Activities in and Against Nicaragua (*Nicar. v. U.S.*), (request by El Salvador) Declaration of Intervention, 1984 I.C.J. 215 (Order of Oct. 4); Haya de la Torre (*Colom. v. Peru*), (request by Cuba), 1951 I.C.J. 71 (Judgment of June 13).

Minister for Immigration and Ethnic Affairs v. Teoh (1995), 128 ALR 353.

Muller and others v. Switzerland, App. No. 10737/84, (1991) 13 E.H.R.R. 212.

Nanus Asia Co. v. Standard Charter Bank, S. Ct. of Hong Kong, judgment of Sept. 22, 1988.

Nuclear Tests (*Austl. v. Fr.*), Application for Permission to Intervene by Fiji, 1973 I.C.J. 320 (Order of July 12).

Nuclear Tests (*N.Z. v. Fr.*) Application for Permission to Intervene by Fiji, 1973 I.C.J. 324 (Order of July 12).

Otto Preminger Institute v. Austria, App. No. 13470/87, (1995) 19 E.H.R.R. 34.

People v. Chen, No. 87–7774 (N.Y. Sup. Ct., Mar. 21, 1989).

People's Union for Civil Liberties v. Union of India, AIR 1997 SC 568.

Pratap Singh v. State of Jharkhand, AIR 2005 SC 2731.

Protocol to the American Convention on Human Rights to Abolish the Death Penalty, adopted at Asunción, Paraguay, on June 3, 1990, at the Twentieth Regular Session of the General Assembly, and Additional Protocol to the American Convention on Human Rights in the Area of Economic, Social and Cultural Rights "Protocol of San Salvador," adopted at San Salvador, El Salvador, on Nov. 17, 1988, at the Eighteenth Regular Session of the General Assembly.

Rees v. United Kingdom, App. No. 9532/81, (1987) 9 E.H.R.R. 56.

Roper v. Simmons, 543 U.S. 551 (2005).

Royal Commission on Aboriginal Deaths in Custody. *Report,* 1991.

Sheffield & Horsham v. United Kingdom, App. Nos. 22885/93 & 23390/94 (1999) 27 E.H.R.R. 163.

The Prosecutor v. Horacio David Giroldi, Supreme Court of Argentina, Case number 32/93, judgment of July 4, 1995 (Fallos 1995–318–514).

The Prosecutor v. Hernán Javier Bramajo, Supreme Court of Argentina, Case number 44.891, judgment of Sept. 12, 1996 (Fallos 1996–319–1840).

The Prosecutor v. Matías Eugenio Casal, Supreme Court of Argentina, Case number 1681, judgment of Sept. 20, 2005 (Fallos 2005–328).

Trade Act of 1974 (codified as amended at 19 U.S.C. §2411 (2000) E.H.R.R.).

Tysiąc v. Poland (Application No. 5410/03), European Court of Human Rights, judgment of March 20, 2007.

United Nations. Convention on the Elimination of All Forms of Discrimination against Women. G.A. Res. 51/68, §6, U.N. GAOR, 51st Sess., Supp No. 49, U.N. Doc. A/Res/51/68 (Dec. 12, 1996) (extending two annual CEDAW committee sessions of three weeks each).

United Nations. Committee on the Elimination of Discrimination against Women. *CEDAW Report of the Secretariat, Twenty Ninth Session*, 17–18, U.N. Doc. CEDAW/C/2003/II/4 (May 14, 2003).

United Nations. Committee on the Elimination of Discrimination against Women. *Fourth & Fifth Periodic Report*. U.N. Doc. CEDAW/C/IRL/CO/4–5, July 22, 2005.

United Nations. Committee on the Elimination of Racial Discrimination. Consideration of Reports Submitted by States Parties under Article 9 of the Convention (2007). U.N. Doc. CERD/C/CZE/CO/7.

United Nations Secretary-General Kofi Annan. Speech to Open the General Assembly, Sept. 20, 1999.

United Nations Security Council. S.C. Res. 794, U.N. Doc. S/RES/794, Dec. 3, 1992.

United Nations Security Council. S.C. Res. 929, U.N. Doc. S/RES/929, June 2, 1994.

United Nations Security Council. S.C. Res. 940, U.N. Doc. S/INF/50, Dec. 15, 1994.

United Nations Security Council. S.C. Res. 770, U.N. Doc. S/RES/770, Aug. 13, 1992, and S.C. Res. 816, U.N. Doc. S/RES/816, March 31, 1993.

United Nations Universal Declaration of Human Rights. G.A. Res. 217A (III), 71, U.N. GAOR, 3d Sess., U.N. Doc. A1810 (Dec. 10, 1948).

Vishaka v. State of Rajasthan, AIR 1997 SC 3011.

Index

Abdi Noor, Sophia, 214n3
abortion, 151–53, 224nn15,17, 225nn19,20,22,23
Abregu, Martin, 227n44
Acosta, Claudia Beatriz, 228n55
Adams, John Quincy, 19
Adem, Khalid, 109, 125–26
Afghanistan, 174
Africa, 33, 42, 77; and abolition of slave trade, 19–20; African Charter on Human and Peoples' Rights, 149; African Commission on Human and People's Rights, 149; and Berlin Conference, 23; civil wars in, 76; colonialism in, 23, 26, 48, 79, 84–85, 146, 149, 187n61; families in, 168; female genital cutting in, 7, 109–10, 111–12, 132, 168–69, 176–77; human rights commissions in, 44, 193n24; *ubuntu* in, 149, 166, 224n14. *See also* Democratic Republic of Congo; Liberia; Rwanda; Sierra Leone; South Africa; Sudan, The
African Union, 108, 149; African Court on Human and Peoples' Rights, 144, 145, 146, 147, 149–50, 167, 168–69, 176–77; and South Africa, 167–68; and The Sudan, 172
Albania, 47
American Convention on Human Rights, 148, 155–59, 168, 224n13, 227n43, 228n46, 229n55
American Declaration of the Rights and

Duties of Man, 148, 157–58, 226n30, 228n46
Amnesty International, 54, 218n61
Anghie, Antony, 185n25
Annan, Kofi, 48, 94, 195n44
Antigua, 54
Arab honor killings, 7, 47–48, 195nn42,43
Arafat, Yasser, 66
Argentina: *Bramajo* case, 158; Constitution, 157–58, 227n46; *Giroldi* case, 158; human rights abuses in, 43, 63; inter-American human rights law in, 157–59, 227n44; repeal of amnesty laws in, 43; Supreme Court, 157–59, 228n55
Aristide, Jean-Baptiste, 94
ASEAN. *See* Association of Southeast Asian Nations
Asia, 33, 48, 84, 196n52; Asian values debate, 12–13, 79, 161, 162–64, 167–68; civil wars in, 76; colonialism in, 84, 162; economic crisis of 1998, 161; NGOs in, 163. *See also* Association of Southeast Asian Nations (ASEAN)
Asia Foundation, 164, 231n78
Asian Human Rights Commission (AHRC), 163
Asian Legal Resource Centre (ALRC), 163
Asian values debate, 12–13, 79, 161, 162–64, 167–68
Asia Pacific Forum of National Human Rights Institutions, 163, 165, 230n72

Milošević, Slobodan, 39, 60, 93, 201n91
Mladić, Ratko, 57, 61, 202n93, 232n2
Montenegro, 57, 200nn80,81
Montesquieu, Charles de, 14; *L'esprit des lois*, 18; and Pufendorf, 185n33; on savage vs. barbarian peoples, 24–25; on slavery, 18
Moreno-Ocampo, Luis, 63, 64, 202n103
Morgan, Lewis Henry, 29; *Ancient Society*, 11–12
Mouzas, Jenny, 188n69
Moyle, Helen, 188n69
Moynier, Gustave, 23
Mugabe, Robert, 46, 168
Mukabutera, Julienne, 55
Mukangango, Consolata, 66
multiculturalism: Asian values debate, 12–13, 79, 161, 162–64, 167–68; critique of international human rights system based on, 8, 11–13, 29–30, 32, 35, 36, 47–50, 75, 138–39, 143, 170. *See also* cultural diversity
Musharraf, Pervez, 1–2, 3, 183n1
Mutua, Makau, 4
Myanmar: and ASEAN, 161; Buddhist monks in, 12–13, 79, 165; human rights abuses in, 12–13, 76, 79, 165; Aung San Suu Kyi, 13

Naddeo, Cecilia, 228n51
Namibia, 58, 201n84
naming and shaming, 45–46, 47, 194n34
Napoleon Bonaparte, 18
national interest, 89, 172, 194n35; and margin of appreciation, 135–36; relationship to international law, 8, 9, 11, 183n4
nationalism, 4, 24, 188n6363, 220n85
National Patriotic Front of Liberia (NPFL), 37–38
NATO, 145; intervention in Bosnia, 91; intervention in Kosovo, 58, 89, 93, 94–95, 96, 99, 101, 103
natural law (jus naturale), 8–9, 17
Nauru, 198n70
Nelson, Paul, 117
Nepal: human rights abuses in, 76
Netherlands, The, 16–17, 20, 137, 193n28,

221n100; and European Coal and Steel Community, 51, 147
New Zealand, 160; and East Timor, 97; indigenous people of, 25
Nicaragua, 97
Niger, 44, 215n24
Nigeria, 38, 39, 191n8, 215n24; sharia law in, 141–43, 144, 222n3
nongovernmental organizations (NGOs): as advocates for human rights, 8, 10, 13, 27, 28, 29, 33, 45, 57, 75, 111–14, 117–18, 120–21, 138, 143, 163, 172, 176; and female genital cutting, 111–12; and globalization, 114, 117–18, 120–21; and International Court of Justice (ICJ), 57–58; and International Criminal Court (ICC), 57; and Paris Principles, 230n72
norm penetration and hybrid courts, 73, 204n119
North American Free Trade Agreement (NAFTA), 120, 145
North Korea, 80, 213n82
Norway, 33, 110, 153
Ntezimana, Vincent, 66
nuclear weapons: threat or use of, 201n86
Nuremberg trials, 5, 14, 40, 55, 58, 61, 73

Oda, Shigeru, 203n107
Organization of American States, 51; and disappeared children in Guatemala, 155; Inter-American Commission on Human Rights, 144, 145, 146, 147, 148–49, 154–55, 156, 157, 158, 159, 165, 223nn9–11, 226nn30,36, 228n51, 229n55; Inter-American Court of Human Rights, 43, 144, 145, 146, 147, 148, 154–59, 168, 223nn9–11, 224n12, 227n43, 228nn51,52, 229n55; and United States, 148, 155, 160, 223n9, 226n30
Ottawa Process, 194n34
Ottoman Empire, 82, 90

Pakistan: Benazir Bhutto, 1, 2; and British colonialism, 3; Chaudhry, 1, 2–3, 183n1; Islamist movement in, 3; judiciary in, 1–3, 127, 183n1; Musharraf, 1–2, 3, 183n1; Pakistan People's Party, 1

Stanford Studies in Human Rights

Mark Goodale, editor

Editorial Board

Abdullahi A. An-Na'im
Upendra Baxi
Sally Engle Merry
James Nickel
Fernando Tesón
Richard A. Wilson

Stanford Studies in Human Rights brings together established and emerging voices from the interdisciplinary field of human rights studies. The series publishes work from a range of perspectives, including ethnographic studies of human rights in practice, critical reflections on the idea of human rights, new proposals for a more effective international human rights system, and historical accounts of the rise of human rights as a globalized moral discourse.